PLAY THE BEST COURSES

PLAY THE BEST COURSES

Great Golf in the British Isles

Peter Allen

STANLEY PAUL

London Melbourne Auckland Johannesburg

Stanley Paul & Co. Ltd

An imprint of Century Hutchinson Ltd
Brookmount House, 62–65 Chandos Place,
Covent Garden, London WC2N 4NW

Century Hutchinson Australia (Pty) Ltd
PO Box 496, 16–22 Church Street, Hawthorn,
Melbourne, Victoria 3122

Century Hutchinson New Zealand Limited
PO Box 40–086, Glenfield, Auckland 10

Century Hutchinson South Africa (Pty) Ltd
PO Box 337, Bergvlei 2012, South Africa

First published 1973
Revised edition 1987

© Sir Peter Allen 1973, 1987
Drawings © Stanley Paul & Co. Ltd 1987

Set in Linotron Palatino by Wyvern Typesetting Ltd, Bristol
Printed and bound in Great Britain by R. J. Acford Ltd., Chichester

British Library Cataloguing in Publication Data

Allen, *Sir* Peter, *1905–*
Play the best courses: great golf in
the British Isles.
1. Golf courses——Great Britain
796.352'06'841   GV984
ISBN 0–09–172806–1

For Consuelo Allen and Alan Booth
whose hard work and happy co-operation
made this book possible

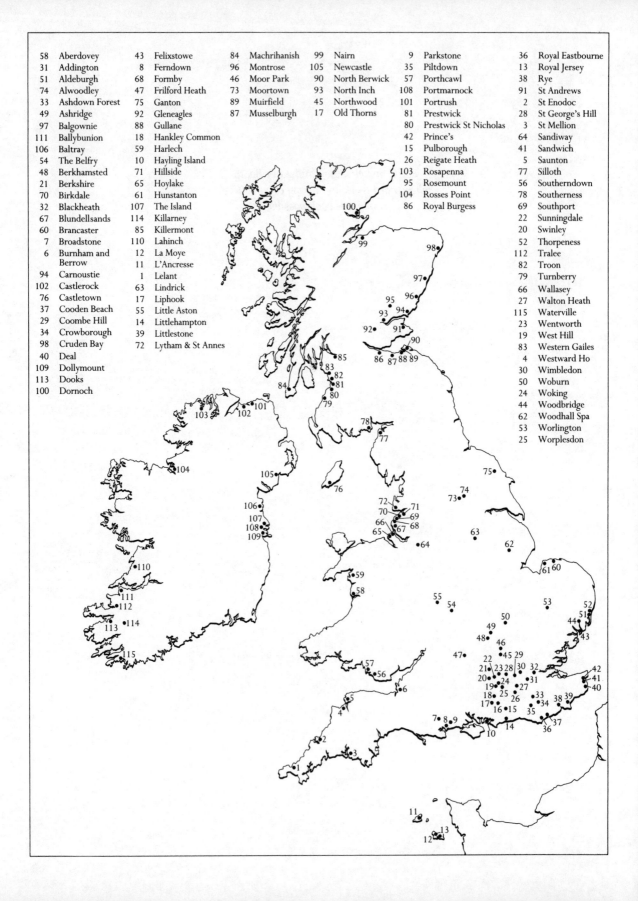

CONTENTS

Chapter 1

INTRODUCTION

This is the up-to-date version of a book of the same name which was published in 1973.

The plan of this book is to give a fair survey of golf courses in the British Isles. I have, therefore, selected some hundred odd courses in Great Britain and Ireland – 116 in all – to discuss and describe; 23 of these are in Scotland, 15 in Ireland, 4 in Wales, 3 in the Channel Islands, one in the Isle of Man and the rest (70) in England.

I most certainly do not claim that the courses described in this book are the hundred best in the British Isles. To do so would be to provoke an outcry that this or that course should certainly be included among the elect. What I do claim is that all the courses included are good ones, that space prevented a much wider survey and that the limitations of my own knowledge were also becoming apparent. There are, I believe, over 2000 golf clubs in the British Isles, several with more than one course, so that any process of selection is bound to leave out some, indeed many, good courses. The magazine *Golf World* selected the 50 best courses in the British Isles in its issue of November 1986. I'm glad to say that 48 of these are in my choice, and the other two would probably have been included if I had known them. This, therefore, is a personal choice.

In this book we range widely from the windy seaside links to the sandy heather and pine country, to golf on hard downland, on low-lying estuarine turf, on flinty common land and on the rich meadow grass of ancestral parks. This exhibits at once the great charm of golf, its infinite variety, for all these courses have this in common, that while they are different, they are all enjoyable to play, exacting in their demands for skill and memorable for their special features.

It is one of the greatest pleasures of this great game that none of the courses on which we play it are the same – sometimes similar, no doubt, but never the same; then, the game varies from day to day with the strength and direction of the wind and the dryness or otherwise of the turf. By comparison, cricket, football, lawn tennis and all the court games are sadly confined, and confined by a deadly sameness of terrain. Add to that exactly the right degree of difficulty, and you have a pastime in golf unexcelled by any other. Moreover, its pleasures and pains last a lifetime, for as you get older you sometimes get wilier and what you lose in length you may recover in accuracy and in avoiding the stupid stroke. No pastime is better able to separate, as Gene Sarazen puts it, 'the cream from the milk' and no pastime demands more character and concentration. As Herbert Warren Wind, the most perceptive of golf writers, says, 'Perhaps it is nothing more than the best game man has devised.'

My qualifications for writing about golf are unchanged: fifty years, before my legs failed me, of striving at it with fierce enjoyment and never with more than modest success. I write, therefore, from the standpoint of the single-figure handicap player, shall we say six, rather than for the scratch man and even less for the professional, though let it be said that the percentage of all scores in Open Championships which beat par is modest indeed, so that many of the pros that survive to the end have probably played to one or two handicap. Nevertheless, it is fair to admit that tournament golf is a different affair from club golf and it is from this latter standpoint that I try to write. My standard is that in still air a decent drive goes 225–230 yards, a No. 4 iron shot about 165 yards and a No. 9 iron shot 110 yards. In my descriptions we play from the ordinary men's tees or the ordinary medal tees at most and never off the full championship length, as this for players of my standard and degree of decrepitude makes for too much hard labour in the round.

In an earlier book I was able to write only about courses that I knew at first hand; here, with a much wider selection, this was not so easy. To give a balanced picture I wished to include a number of fine courses that just demanded to go in whether I knew them or not. My shortcomings were most conspicuous in Scotland and here I had the great good fortune to be able to call on a good friend Sam McKinlay, the former Walker Cup player and Editor of the *Glasgow Evening Times*, who has most generously closed five important gaps for me. Apart from these there are fewer than half a dozen courses included that I have not actually played on, walked round or been driven round by a friendly secretary.

That the descriptions are ill-balanced and lack uniformity I must admit, but golf course descriptions tend to be tedious if too stereotyped. Patric Dickinson reminds us that 'The late A. C. M. Croome wisely wrote "no

number of written words can convey an impression accurate in every detail of any course to the mind of a person who has never seen it" and he goes on to add, "nor will a photograph really tell more than a menu".' So the descriptions vary in length and no doubt in depth of perception, but I have included after each one a card of the course according to the latest available information. I considered the suggestion that details might be added of locations, telephone numbers, names of secretaries and professionals, green fees and conditions of play for visitors, but I rejected this because these things change and this book is intended to be something of a work of reference. What does not change, namely the locations of these courses, can be found on the map.

As for conditions of play for visitors, few courses these days will not welcome the properly introduced stranger on a week-day. Comparatively few will be as welcoming to the visitor at the week-end unless he plays with a member; if he is allowed to play without a member the week-end green fees are liable to be steep. The best advice to give on this subject is to suggest carrying a letter of introduction from the secretary of one's own club and if possible a letter from a member of the club one visits. Then, few if any doors will be closed. Beware of St Andrews, however; starting times on the Old Course are balloted for on the day before during July, August and September.

As this is a new version of an earlier work I have not thought it reasonable to rewrite for the sake of rewriting, so some, indeed many, passages may appear again here, but brought up to date, edited and perhaps slightly or significantly changed. There is ample precedent for this in the works of the Master, for long and frequent passages in Bernard Darwin's *Golf Courses of the British Isles* reappear in *Golf Courses of Great Britain*. I have followed, too, the plan of the earlier book and arranged the courses in a geographical pattern which seems to me the best for a guide like this, starting in Scotland, as we should, then moving down to London; after this swinging around the rest of the UK and ending in Ireland, where perhaps the best golf of all is to be found.

There have, of course, been many changes since the first edition in 1973, but fewer than expected in the courses themselves. Nearly every course has been re-measured and a maddening number of small changes has resulted. However, we hope to have checked and rechecked 2268 holes and if we have made any errors, forgive us. There has been a tendency for courses to grow longer and remodelling has usually meant tighter golf. Some fine new courses have been built, but in spite of this, clubs seem to be full up and almost bursting at the seams.

The number of courses used for the Open Championship is unaltered with the welcome return of Sandwich to the rota of courses played. The Amateur Championship, which makes less exacting demands, has confirmed Ganton as the only inland course used and brought in two new links, Hillside in Lancashire, and to everyone's joy Royal Dornoch.

Since 1972, the players and the style of play have, of course, changed. Immense sums of depreciated money are now available for golfing entertainers; thus the Australian Greg Norman won more dollars on that part of the US circuit he played in 1986 than Ben Hogan won in his whole career. There is perhaps a danger here that complaints from money professionals may be heard that, for example, the fairways at Sandwich are too uneven or the rough at Muirfield too tough. To reduce or ease natural features in order to provide target golf or stadium golf, is to miss the point; the task of the tournament players is to show how best to combat the natural features of the course and the wind and weather that confront them. In this demand, the game of golf is unique. The demand for 'fairness' is best answered I think by the great Jack Nicklaus: 'who ever expected golf to be fair?'

Changes have come, of course, in the period since the first edition in the names on the tournament leader board. Jack Nicklaus has confirmed his greatness with one more win at St Andrews and by winning the Masters at Augusta at the age of 46, but the greatest American performances here have come from Tom Watson who has won our Open five times in nine years. That apart, the signs that American ascendancy is no longer total are plain to see. Equally fine golfers have arisen in Japan, in Australia and in Europe, even in the British Isles, which in Sandy Lyle have at last produced an Open Champion. Spain has been conspicuous in producing a fine crop of first-class tournament players to follow the Miguel brothers, with Ballesteros their fine leader, while Australia has brought on Greg Norman to follow Peter Thomson. Western Germany has a world-class player now in Langer and it will be interesting to see which of these giants will go ahead to a succession of victories or, like some, fade away after a success or two.

Amateur golf has changed considerably. The many good players all seem to be young and just waiting to turn pro and reap the golden harvest. Our own championship shows a swing from British or American successes. Among our winners we have had a Frenchman and a brilliant young Spaniard and among the British a man from Wales and, after a long interval, one from Northern Ireland.

Many people have contributed to this book and I have quoted freely from other works. The hard work and support given by my helper and colleague Alan Booth has been absolutely invaluable. My wife Consuelo has cast a most useful lay woman's eye on the general readability of the book and has put in interminable hours in typing the manuscript, without which this book would never have been written. I am most grateful to her. For typing effort my thanks, too, to Mrs R. M. Harris.

I have had very helpful advice over the years from Herbert Warren Wind, and most notably the invaluable contribution from Sam McKinlay. Golf secretaries all over the British Isles have responded without fail to requests for cards and those invaluable little booklets which many clubs produce.

Conspicuous among these helpers have been: Cdr. Ashton at Liphook, Mr D. G. Lee at Hankley Common, Mr Eric Svensson at Hayling Island and Mr Webb, the head green keeper at Old Thorns. David Cameron Smail from Prestwick provided much good material and so, too, did Charles Cruikshank from Royal Wimbledon, also Mr Leishman from Prestwick St Nicholas. Wg.-Comd. McCrea was most helpful at Walton Heath and Capt. Hitchen at Sandwich. So also was Cdr. Bradley at Rye. Mr Hart came over to Prince's especially to help, while Mr Milton of Royal Eastbourne was good enough to write a special note for me. So did Mr Griffiths at Aberdovey. Thanks, too, to Mr Beveridge at St Andrews, Mr W. T. Train at Southerness and Mr Geddes at Saunton for special papers and to Mr Guy in Jersey for a most useful contribution.

In the West of Ireland on our visit there we were most kindly and hospitably received by Mr Courtney at Waterville, Capt. O'Connell at Killarney, Mr Walsh at Ballybunion, Mr O'Sullivan at Dooks and Mr Duncan Gray, the links superintendent at Lahinch. And my word, what superb golf is on offer there!

Chapter 2

THE CHAMPIONSHIP LINKS
OF SCOTLAND

Golf has been played in Scotland for a long time. For instance, it is reported that it was a popular game in 1411 when St Andrews University was founded. By 1457 it was so well established, whatever its form, that it had to be 'utterly cryed down and not to be used', and it was again prohibited by statute in 1491 lest it interfere with archery practice and the defence of the Realm. Then after peace with England in 1502 the restrictions came off and golf got going again. From then on members of the Scottish Royal House, who were great lovers of golf, could indulge their pleasure. The earliest reference to golf in England comes from Catherine of Aragon, the first wife of Henry VIII, who is quoted as writing to Cardinal Wolsey, in 1513: 'And all his subjects be very glad, Master Almoner, I thank God, to be busy with golf, for they take it for pastime, my heart is very glad to it.'

The first Royal Golfer of note was King James IV, who died fighting the English at Flodden Field in 1513; his son, James V, was a well-known player, and his daughter Mary, Queen of Scots, was also; indeed she was criticised for playing so soon after her husband Darnley was murdered. When the thrones were united in 1603 under James VI of Scotland as James I of England, golf came south with the Scots. It is believed that a golf club was organised near the palace in London at Blackheath in 1608, though there is no firm evidence for this, which is not to say that golf wasn't played there.

No doubt, golf on Blackheath led to the first international match, for it is said a dispute arose about the origins of the game between two of the English gentry, who in their ignorance claimed it for South Britain, and King Charles II's brother, James, Duke of York, who in 1681 and 1682 was Commissioner from his brother to the Scottish Parliament. To settle this argument a match was fixed on Leith links between the two English fops and the Duke and his Scottish partner, the cobbler John Patersone with whom the Duke sensibly chose to play. According to Robert Clark in *Golf* in 1893: 'not only was Patersone the best golfer of his day but one whose ancestors had been equally celebrated from time immemorial'. The Duke and his partner won handsomely. The shoemaker got his share of the stake, or all of it, some versions say, and with it built himself a house in the Canongate in Edinburgh called the 'Golfer's Land', which, alas, has been pulled down, notwithstanding the escutcheon fixed on it by the grateful Duke, bearing the newly-organised arms of the Patersone family with the crest of a hand grasping a golf club and the motto 'Far and Sure'.

In these early days of golf in Scotland, where

was it played and on what sort of ground? I imagine the game began with an impromptu set-up, hitting to holes in the ground or even a post or a tree rather to exercise or display virtuosity than make a match. Then in the late eighteenth and early nineteenth centuries came a prescribed course, but with widely different ideas as to how many holes there should be and what they should be like. In these days, when to match American orthodoxy you must have two nines of roughly equal length, each ending at the clubhouse, with two par threes and two par fives in each nine, the golf course of 200 years ago seems wildly anarchic. Eighteen holes was certainly not standard and can be attributed to the layout of St Andrews and the influence of the Royal and Ancient Club, but it in turn started its life with twenty-two holes. Leith links, its origins lost in the mists of time, had only five holes in its heyday, varying between 414 and 496 yards in length, and, my word, what effort the Duke and John Patersone must have applied to do even one of them in five! While Leith had only five holes, subsequently enlarged to seven, and St Andrews had a round of twenty-two, though using only twelve actual holes in the turf, Montrose had no fewer than twenty-five.

Well, Leith has gone as a golf course, though

I hit two surreptitious shots there some years ago just to say I'd done it, but with the ground surrounded by houses, street lamps and hard roads, with tennis courts and rugby posts at one end, it needs a long stretch of the imagination to picture the Duke and John Patersone playing their big money game there. Brunstfield links in the centre of Edinburgh is also historic turf, but it is equally confined and you can't easily picture James IV and Mary Queen of Scots playing on this rather flaccid grass, but they did. But at least golf, even if of the dismallest pitch and putt sort, is still played here, and here for old times sake I, too, have played; but today it is not really a golf course. The glory has departed from old Musselburgh but as a former home of the Championship it will rate a short description in this chapter. However, St Andrews, the Championship links par excellence, has triumphantly survived these early rough games on common land and Prestwick, too, in its own way.

Also in the category of a surviving golf course in the true sense from medieval times is the course at Perth on the North Inch, where golf has been played certainly for 400 years and very probably for more than 500, and this too will be described in due course.

Prestwick

To start our tour of the Championship courses of Scotland we must begin at Prestwick on the Ayrshire coast where the first Open Championship was held in 1860 and each year afterwards until 1870 when young Tom Morris, the greatest player of his generation, won the Championship Belt outright. Three rounds of twelve holes of Prestwick were played for the Championship and it was all over in one day. Young Tom's Belt now resides with other famous trophies in the Royal and Ancient Clubhouse at St Andrews. Prestwick commissioned two exact replicas of the Belt in 1985 to com-

memorate 125 years of the Championship, one of which was appropriately won, and won outright, by a Scot, Sandy Lyle, at Sandwich.

In the circumstances of the 1870s, rough unkempt fairways and greens mown with a scythe, and with the stony gutta balls and uncouth implements of the day, young Tommy's score of 149 for thirty-six holes at Prestwick in 1870 is surely one of the greatest day's golf in the entire history of the game. Prestwick has changed much since then, but the area inside the former perimeter retains a lot of the charm of the old original links. This ground is an excellent illustration of what constitutes true links land, that sandy sparse turf by the sea, once, in times long past, submerged by the waters and now the nursery ground for sharp keen seaside grass on fairways and greens and formidable coarse rough amid the dunes.

Prestwick has had its day they say, no longer suitable for the Open Championship, impossible for crowd control, too short for the big guns – though playing it not long ago in half a gale of bitter wind from the north-west after a soaking March you'd hardly think so. Well, I suppose it's true, and certain it is that the Open hasn't been here since that disastrous afternoon in 1925 when Macdonald Smith, five strokes ahead of the field with one round to go, was destroyed by the mob who crowded in to see him win. The Amateur has not been here since 1952, when there was an all-American final, but it was a delight to welcome it back in 1987.

And yet and yet . . . It is to me much more than a museum of what golf was like seventy-five years ago: I find it still a wonderfully subtle and exacting links. True, there are a lot of old-fashioned features, like wooden sleepers in the faces of some of the bunkers, blind shots and tiny greens with protecting humps and hillocks which may kick your ball away, often unfairly which can't appeal to the lordly professionals of today, many of whom don't like this sort of golf.

You start with a tough hole, a short par four, which is unusual, but the shot up the narrowing fairway with an out-of-bounds wall on your right is exceedingly tight with a wind across your line off the sea. This is a fairly recent hole dating from the 1870s. Bernard Darwin recalls seeing a friend who was feeling a little brittle hit his first shot on to the railway from which it kicked back on the fairway; he then hit his second on to the line also and this time it kicked back onto the green and ran into the hole. The second is an ordinary short hole of no great terrors and then comes 'the Cardinal', a 482-yard par five with a minute green – which par

fives should have – amid the humps by the Pow Burn; on the way the vast sleepered Cardinal bunker lying right across the fairway has to be carried by the second shot.

The fourth is a wonderfully good par four 382 yards, with a narrow drive between the Pow Burn on the right and bunkers on the left; the green is, as it were, in the crook of the arm of the burn so that catastrophe is never far off, as J. H. Taylor found in his disastrous last round with Harry Vardon in the Open Championship in 1914, Vardon's sixth Open, and the end of an era in more ways than one.

The fifth is – or are – the 'Himalayas', a big blind thump of over 200 yards over a huge sandhill, very old fashioned, of course, but not easy, with the green heavily bunkered and none too big.

Four holes follow to the turn, good tough, exacting holes, but somehow they don't seem part of the old links – and indeed they are not – being out in the fields by the railway; nevertheless if we can leave these fields with two fives and two fours we can be reasonably satisfied; I'd settle for that, anyway.

The tenth is 454 yards and so rated at par 4, but as it goes straight out into the prevailing wind, five is much more like it. The hole is not much of a favourite of mine, but the green is on an upper level and has to be 'fetched' by a proper shot, usually my third. Eleven is a fine short hole, comparatively new, with a bunker short of the left-hand edge of the green which gathers any ill-hit stroke. Twelve takes two big plain hits down a plain flat fairway and then a nice pitch to a small green set among humps and mounds; it was once protected in front by a stone wall, long since departed, where in the Open of 1908 James Braid lashed his brassie home to get a three as Bernard Darwin tells us in *My first Open*.

The thirteenth, 'Sea Headrig' at 460 yards is reachable in two but no longer by me, alas; the short approach shot to the green is beset by heavily folded humpy ground, and the green, on a little plateau, must be one of the smallest on any first-class course, but what a superb hole to do in four, at which to play a cunning run-up to scuttle across the folded ground up the final slope and lie close to the hole; to me this is a jewel of a hole.

At the fourteenth you drive across the 'Goosedubs', reedy marshy ground and a carry not to be despised off the back tee with any wind against you; then you pitch up over some bunkers to a generously big green in front of the clubhouse windows.

You finish with the 'Loop' and if you think that four holes of 347, 288, 391 and 284 yards with sixteen strokes to do them in are a piece of cake you can think again. The fifteenth has the narrowest fairway I know anywhere. I hit a good shot there a few years ago, about 230 yards I suppose, and at that point my ball lay in the middle of the fairway eight yards from the rough on the right and nine yards from the rough on the left – and the rough is rough. The green is small and tightly bunkered. The sixteenth, 'the Cardinal's Back', has a less exacting tee shot, but a tiny green which runs away from you perched above the end of the great Car-

dinal bunker. The seventeenth is the 'Alps', where if you hit a good drive you can hit a blind second shot over a great sandhill. You scramble to the top hoping you are on the small green, but instead find you are probably in the historic sleepered bunker in front of it from which Freddie Tait played his famous shot out of water in the final of the Amateur in 1899 and John Ball followed that with as good a shot off hard, wet sand. Perhaps not a good hole by today's standards, I suppose, but I hope they never change it.

Only at the last do you fancy your chances of a three, for it's not at all long and not at all difficult if you get your drive away. Well, that's the round; I think you'll find that somehow a good score has eluded you, but these small keen greens and the humps and the hollows round them don't help, and the rough, as I say, is rough. The bunkers, too, are deep and uncompromising and numerous. And there is the wind, the almost incessant wind.

Perhaps from among many championships results here one might select an odd one, the Amateur of 1928 which was won by a dis-

Prestwick Golf Club: Medal Card

NAME	YARDS	PAR	NAME	YARDS	PAR
1 Railway	346	4	10 Arran	454	4
2 Tunnel	167	3	11 Carrick	195	3
3 Cardinal	482	5	12 Wall	513	5
4 Bridge	382	4	13 Sea Headrig	460	4
5 Himalayas	206	3	14 Goosedubs	362	4
6 Elysian Fields	362	4	15 Narrows	347	4
7 Monkton Miln	430	4	16 Cardinal's Back	288	4
8 End	431	4	17 Alps	391	4
9 Eglinton	444	4	18 Clock	284	4
	3250	35		3294	36
				3250	35
				6544	71

tinguished and under-rated British player, Phil Perkins. Odd, because that same year he also got into the final of the US Amateur, losing to Bobby Jones; only thrice have British players reached this final, once when Harold Hilton won both Amateurs in 1911 and the other time in 1936 when Jack McLean lost at the 37th hole. Perkins stayed in America and turned pro and was joint runner-up to Sarazen in the US Open of 1932. We should add, too, Lawson Little's prodigious win over Jack Wallace in 1934. Round in 66 in the morning and nine up he

started after lunch 3 3 4 3 3 and won by 14 and 13. This, my helpful correspondent David Cameron Smail points out, is rather different from the start by the Ayrshire top pair in a county match who began 8 3 11 and were then one up.

So to the clubhouse, a splendid Victorian survival with modern overtones, and a charming old-fashioned atmosphere with a warm and friendly welcome from the members and good food and drink in generous measure.

My helpful correspondent has provided

Prestwick Golf Course 1851 Course

NAME	YARDS	BOGEY	TEE	GREEN
1 Back of Cardinal	578	6	'1860'	16th
2 Alps	391	4	17th	17th
3 Tunnel (Red)	167	3	2nd	2nd
4 Wall	482	5	3rd	3rd
5 Sea Headrig	460	5	13th	13th
6 Tunnel (White)	350	4	14th Blue	2nd
7 Green Hollow	165	3	3rd Forward	15th
8 Station	162	3	16th Blue	17th
9 Burn	298	4	18th	Cardinal
10 Lunch House	290	4	17th	15th
11 Short	97	3	16th	13th
12 Home	359	4	14th Medal	'1860'
	3799	48		

_____Marker

_____Player

_____

In the case of a STYMIE, this card is 6" deep

some information about the original 1851 links which seems to me relevant if it only reveals the almost incredible fact that young Tom on his famous day in 1870 did the 578-yard first hole in three strokes, a real Victorian 'albatross' and holed the twelve holes in a record 47, namely 3 5 3 5 6 3 3 3 4 3 4 5. The old twelve-hole links has been, as it were, newly laid out for play with all its crossings and inconveniences to be circumvented if one should try it. The recreated twelve-hole course only departs from the 1851 course insofar as the occasional tee or green is a few yards from its predecessor – the first five holes, however, are identical in all respects to the 1851 course.

The original twelve holes were first played competitively – by the members – in the Eglinton (Autumn) Medal in 1851. Robert Hay won with a two-round score of 133. Between then and 1869 the best two-round score recorded by a member was 116. Thereafter the medals became eighteen holes, made up of the twelve holes, with the first six repeated.

St Andrews

It is now time to move on to St Andrews, though Patric Dickinson says in his enjoyable book, 'There is nothing new to say about St Andrews, just as there is nothing new to say about Shakespeare.' Indeed, I had thought of writing the whole of this section in quotations.

After all, who could describe the first hole better than Bernard Darwin:

With this preliminary observation, we may tee up our ball in front of the Royal and Ancient Club-house for one of the least alarming tee-shots in existence. In front of us stretches a vast flat plain, and unless we slice the ball outrageously on to the sea beach, no harm can befall us. At the same time we had much better hit a good shot, because the Swilcan Burn guards the green, and we want to carry it and get a four. It is an inglorious little stream enough: we could easily jump over it were we not afraid of looking foolish if we fell in, and yet it catches an amazing number of balls. It is now part of golfing history that when Mr Leslie Balfour Melville won the Amateur Championship (in 1895) he beat successively at the nineteenth hole Mr W. Greig, Mr Laurence Auchterlonie and Mr John Ball (in the final), and all three of these redoubtable persons plumped the ball into this apparently paltry little streamlet with their approach shots.

What Bernard Darwin would have made of the traffic lights which once warned off the walkers on the path across the first and last fairways called Granny Clark's Wynd from the assaults of the golfers, I dread to think.

In the 99th Open Championship in 1970 there was an incident at the first hole which I would not have believed if I had not seen it. On the last day when a stiff wind was blowing up the course, one of the less well-known American players, Tom Shaw, had to take wood for his second and ended far up at the back of the green; from there he putted down the fast slope and his ball ran on and on and finally trickled into the burn. So there he was lifting out, still short and four strokes played. He did the only thing possible in the circumstances and holed his chip for a five.

Love at first sight is rare at St Andrews, and many famous players, especially from abroad, have taken a dim view of the links on first acquaintance and then have later come to love it. Perhaps the most famous of these is the late Bobby Jones, who wrote:

Beginning with the puzzled dislike I had felt for the Old Course when I first played in 1921, by 1930 I had come to love it. I thought that I appreciated its subtleties. I had taken great pains to learn the location of all the little pot bunkers and felt that I had a complete familiarity with all the devious little slopes and swales which could deflect well-intended shots in such exasperating ways. I may have been flattering myself, yet I felt very confident that I should encounter no opponent having an advantage over me on the score of local knowledge. Truly if I had had to select one course on which to play the match of my life, I should have selected the Old Course.

Sam Snead, on the other hand, although he won the 1946 Open here said that it looked 'the sort of real estate you couldn't give away'.

Robert Trent Jones, the great American golf architect, sums it up very well:

The first few rounds a golfer plays on the Old Course are not likely to alter his first estimate that it is vastly overrated. He will be puzzled to understand the rhapsodies that have been composed about the perfect strategic position of its trapping, the subtle undulations of its huge double greens, the endless tumbling of its fairways, which seldom give him a chance to play a shot from a level stance. Then, as he plays on, it begins to soak in through his pores that whenever he plays a fine shot, he is rewarded; whenever he doesn't play the right shot, he is penalised, in proportion; and whenever he thinks out his round hole by hole, he scores well. This is the essence of strategic architecture; to encourage initiative, reward a well-played, daring stroke more than a cautious stroke, and yet to insist that there must be planning and honest self-appraisal behind the daring.

All this must be true, because so many and such different people are agreed on it, but alas I am still at the stage short of idolatry. While I have played a good many rounds on the Old Course I have not played enough to know it really intimately, especially the different moods brought about by the wind. The effect of the wind was, however, forcibly brought home to all of us who watched the play in the Open Championship in 1970. On the first day which was played in a flat calm, until the evening thunderstorm which finished play for the day, the pros murdered the course with no fewer than twenty-three scores under 70; Neil Coles had a 65 and Horton a 66, while Tony Jacklin, defending his title, went out in 29 – holing a pitch at the ninth – and might well have done a 65 had he been able to finish that night. As Henry Cotton said, 'the Old Course is hardly a championship test on a still day with the fairways lying so perfect and the greens soft'.

Next day when there was a fair breeze from the west, a very different tale was told, but there were still five rounds that day under 70. On the third day the breeze was still firmer and the number of rounds under 70 fell to two. Finally, on the last day when there was a really stiff breeze, it might indeed be called a wind, there wasn't a single score in the 60s and indeed only one, a 71 by 53-year-old John Panton, below the par of 72. Incidentally, 80 was first beaten at St Andrews in 1859 by Allan Robertson, the best player of his day, with a 79 and Young Tommy reduced the record to 77 ten years later. Of course the reason why the Old course can play so much below its length of 6951 yards is that there are only two par threes; if there were four, there would be, say, 300–350 yards more to add to the two-shot holes and it would be a different story altogether.

As I say, I'm still in the state of ignorance which feels that the Old Course is rather too subtle and that there are too many unattractive holes, difficult though they may be, to offset the excellence of the others. While the eleventh, twelfth, thirteenth and fourteenth, for example, are as good as you can find, the eighth, ninth and tenth are poor stuff to my iconoclastic eye and I've not much time for the first and eighteenth, although I have visited both the Swilcan Burn at the first and the 'Valley of Sin' at the last, like many better players before me.

Having said that, I will be the first to admit that I enjoy and respect the Old Course in full measure, that it has some of the most delightful shots and holes you can find anywhere, that several of these qualify for what Henry Longhurst reminds us was the late Tom Simpson's test of greatness, that you start worrying about the hole before you get to it, while you know that almost to the last moment of any round you can meet disaster: as I once heard that renowned octogenarian handicap player, the late Admiral Benson, say on Medal

Day, 'I was going well until I had an eleven at the seventeenth', I would, however, allow myself to ask the impertinent question: cannot some of the blemishes in the Old Course be changed? After all, the course has been changed greatly in the last century, in spite of some transatlantic beliefs to the contrary; the course was widened in 1832, the whins and heather were cut back and double greens built. The nature of the fairways and greens has often been much softened. The first green built in 1870 is thus comparatively recent and the famous black sheds in the Station Master's garden at the seventeenth were also once new; while the surface of the sixth green is no longer composed of 'earth, heather and shells without a blade of grass'.

True, the Old Course, except for some back tees and few bunkers, has been altered little since 1913, but it would be a pity to believe that nothing must ever be altered again. I suppose there was an uproar when the 'Kruger' and 'Mrs Kruger' bunkers were put in at the ninth at the turn of the century, but I think there might be a case for a little moulding to be applied to that tennis court of a green or even an 'Eisenhower' bunker added: possibly there might even be a case for replacing Halket's bunker to catch a sliced drive at the first hole or even 'Tam's Coo' between the 'Principal's Nose' and the railway at the sixteenth.

However, let us return to the Old Course as it is, rather than as it was or might be. As so many have observed, the subtlety of the bunkering is a striking feature, though the irreverent might be tempted to think that at some holes where the bunkers are just where you want to go, the subtlety is rather like that of a battle-axe. To me the slopes and contours of the greens are the most delightful features; many of the greens are on small plateaux, like the second, twelfth, fourteenth and seventeenth, and some on quite high ones, the two 'High' holes and the long fifth, for example. Moreover, the size and alignment of the greens usually match the shot admirably. Thus the twelfth hole, which needs only a short approach, offers you a narrow green on a little plateau set across the line which would be unfair for a longer shot; the green at the par five fourteenth is also small and difficult, as it should be, as is that at the seventeenth.

A distinctive feature of the Old Course is what I might call the 'Protective Ridge', such as that which protects the entrance to the beautifully-moulded plateau green at the second; similarly at the third, a small ridge covers the run into the green. At the long fifth it is very pronounced – ridge, swale, plateau green; the sixth has it too very conspicuously, also the tenth and the short eighth.

Another feature, as Bernard Darwin points out, is the fierce proximity of the bunkers to the greens, which often deters you from playing to the pin, so leaving yourself with a long and difficult putt. A wild shot indeed can sometimes give you a world-record putt; I believe that one of 110 yards is possible. The whole links is surprisingly flat and thereby easy on the feet, flat, that is, not level, for the fairways are full of small humps and hollows, undulations and waves. Then as Laurence Auchterlonie, the honorary professional of the Royal and Ancient Club pointed out, the lie of the land draws a misdirected shot inexorably into certain bunkers even from a great distance away.

Now, assuming that we have crossed the burn successfully at the first and got a four, we must address ourselves to a stiff run out to the north-west which will take us in a straight line, more or less, to the seventh green and the shores of the River Eden. These holes are immensely affected by the wind; with a breeze from the east they can seem surprisingly short, but with a 'Guardbridge wind' from the north-west they can seem brutally long. The second hole, the 'Dyke', shows this admirably, for your second shot can require an eight-iron or a spoon to cover its 411 yards; if you have a long shot the temptation to hit away to the right, away from the tightly bunkered left hand side, is great, but then you may have a really difficult run-in to the holeside. This is a superb hole.

The third hole, the 'Cartgate Out', which shares a double green with the fifteenth, is dominated all the way from the tee by the deep Cartgate bunker which eats right into the left side of the green; again the 'protective ridge' keeps a clear view of the bottom of the pin from you. Next the 'Ginger Beer' hole of 430 yards demands a very tough drive over or to either side of a big bluff and is again protected by a large hillock in the centre of the fairway in front of the green. At this point if we have four fours on the book or three fours and a five if the wind is adverse, we've done very well, for at the fifth the 'Hole o' Cross Out' at 514 yards we will assuredly need three to get up even if we avoid the sporadic crop of bunkers about 220 yards from the tee; we can then hit with fair confidence with our second and end with a pitch to the huge double green of about an acre which is shared with the thirteenth, the 'Hole o' Cross In'.

The 374-yard sixth, the 'Heathery Hole Out', has heather and whins to the right, as its name says, and once more a pronounced protective ridge in front of the green; I have a fond memory of this not very memorable hole, for it yielded me a birdie in my first Medal when I badly needed some support from evil things past and for bad things to come.

The 'High Hole Out' shares a green with the short eleventh and the lines of play cross here; although the hole is only 364 yards long it has very tight drive with again a rough bluff in the centre of things and the high plateau green has some desperate slopes if you have a long putt. Next comes the short flat eighth hole over a ridge and small bunker to a huge green; I don't think highly of it. Nor do I care for the 307-yard ninth; the hole is totally flat and the green a flat continuation of the fairway. None the less drama occurred here in the first round of the Open in 1921, a championship charged with drama all the way. Jock Hutchison, the eventual winner (who as a spry octogenarian graced

the play in the Masters' Tournament at Augusta for years with Fred McLeod – who was then nearing 91) holed the eighth in one stroke. At the ninth his drive, racing up the baked fairway, looked headed for the hole; a spectator rushed out of the crowd and pulled out the flag, whereupon the ball hit the hole and just stayed out; by that intemperate interference the rare achievement of two successive holes in one, and an unheard-of-feat in a championship, might have been recorded. As it was, Hutchison was pretty well served by fate, for not only did two other iron shots hit the pin but by an unlucky and, let it be said, stupid accident, Roger Wethered backed and trod on to his ball at the fourteenth hole in the third round and lost a penalty stroke; in spite of this he had a 72 and was drawing up to the leaders. Here again I must quote Bernard Darwin, who says:

It is always assumed as an incontestable and logical proposition that if he had not incurred this penalty stroke he would have beaten Hutchison by one stroke. This seems to me an unjustifiable assumption. If he had not incurred the penalty Mr Wethered might have beaten Hutchison by one stroke or by more than one stroke or he might not have tied with him. To assume otherwise is to neglect one obvious fact, that every happening in a round of golf has some effect on the player's mind and the state of his mind has some effect on his stroke. It is such an assumption as we all make about our own rounds but it is founded on unsound premises. All we can say about this penalty stroke is that Mr Wethered did very unluckily lose a shot at a particular hole. What would have happened if he had not, no human being can tell.

What did happen, however, was that in a splendid last round of 71 Wethered pitched short at the eighteenth into the 'Valley of Sin' and took five, whereas if he had got his four he would have won outright; 'Bernardo's' verdict was 'one can only grieve because a five at that last hole is not merely the loss of a stroke, it is a waste of a stroke'. As it was, Jock Hutchison had the formidable task of needing a 70 to tie and he got it, a splendid tough finish.

After this long digression let us resume our round, with, I hope, a score of under 40 on the card after nine holes. The tenth, a 318-yarder, ought not to harm us, and just as well, for now we get down to brass tacks with the 172-yard eleventh, the 'High Hole In'. This hole has been described so often that I will not try to do it again at any length. It is dominated by the steep slope of the plateau green towards the tee, the evil little pot-bunker 'Strath' under the right-hand wing of the green, and a hideous pit, the 'Hill' bunker, about ten feet deep under the left-hand wing. You mustn't go over or you'll never stop the return shot out of the rough grass of the shore of the Eden, so you are often short from the tee or go into Scylla or Charybdis. Many famous cards have gone to the winds here. Bobby Jones, Arnaud Massy and your humble author have all come to grief in the Hill bunker. It is fair to say that with the softer condition of the course this is not as terrifying a hole as it used to be.

After this the twelfth, the 316-yard 'Heathery Hole In', must seem to come as a relief, especially as you can see from the tee nothing, nothing at all, to impede your straight run to the green. Well, that's too bad, for there are at least six bunkers strewn across the fairway, all hidden on the reverse slopes of undulations. It seems inconceivable that anyone could have designed such deliberately malicious bunkering as this and indeed they did not, for what we are playing is the fairway of the original 'High Hole Out' the wrong way round. When played in the opposite direction this fairway has no hidden bunkers and is perfectly fair and reasonable; the tee to the twelfth hole was then far over to the left of the present twelfth tee. However, the hidden bunkers are there now and you have to play either a tight tee shot down the extreme right edge of the fairway or away far to the left. The former gives you the easier pitch to the narrow plateau green, and very narrow it is with the slope of the green running away from you.

The thirteenth at 401 yards is a beautiful two-shotter; according to Henry Longhurst, Tom Simpson, the great golf architect and connoisseur of life in general, has stated that this is the best single hole in golf. He describes it as

the hole that perhaps above all others embraces every classic feature of design. The area that receives the second shot under normal conditions is not visible, is ragged and unkempt and may well kick the ball all over the place even into the Lion's mouth . . . or the Hole O'Cross bunker. Only part of the flag-stick can be seen for the second shot. No part of the green is in view. Finally when the ball does climb on to the green it is met with a diabolical tilt or slope away from the player which makes it difficult to hold the ball on the green which as usual is a low plateau closely guarded. If an architect were to lay out such a hole as this today, he would be considered certifiable.

On a straight line you mustn't drive too far or like my powerful friend Rush you run out of fairway where a ridge comes across; the long hitter has to go away over some bunkers far to the left. For me there is a fairly substantial second shot over the broken humpy ground up to the big double green with two bunkers on the right eating into its very edge: a three there one evening with the aid of my five-wood in the closing stages of my golfing life was sweet indeed.

Fourteen is the 'Long Hole In', 523 yards off the Medal tee and 560 for the Championship. You can slice over the wall out-of-bounds easily enough or pull your tee shot into the 'Beardies', a nest of odious pot bunkers; then as 'Hell' bunker is 410 yards from our tee you have an important decision. If you've hit a good drive you can go out and carry 'Hell', but if you are in doubt then play safe and go over to the left beyond the Elysian Fields, for 'Hell' is no place to enjoy yourself. In any case, you need a delicate third to get on, because the green is on a steep plateau of no great size which runs away from you. This hole is a rare thing, a first-rate par five of not excessive length.

To get the best shot to the fifteenth, 401 yards, you must drive over to the left, for a protective ridge comes in on the right of the fairway to hinder the approach if you are too far over on that side; but, of course, a drive to the left is beset by bunkers, including the large Cottage bunker.

The 351-yard sixteenth, the 'Corner of the Dyke', is a splendid hole. You have the choice of driving between the 'Principal's Nose' and the track of the old railway, a bare thirty-yard gap which gives a comparatively simple shot into the green, or away to the left and safety, but needing a longer and tougher shot to the green because then the 'Wig' bunker comes into the picture. Those who feel they can carry the 'Principal's Nose' have to watch or they'll be carrying it and finding themselves in 'Deacon Sime' just beyond.

Next comes the famous 'Road Hole', 461 yards long, with its narrow green right up against the hard gravelly path and then the metalled road itself. The play of the hole is ruled by the small 'Road' bunker which eats into the left flank of the green. The mouldings of the plateau are such that any shot at all weakly hit to the green inevitably runs into the 'Road' bunker. Once in it you have to dunch the ball out on to the narrowest part of the green with the road beyond, an alarming shot. Before all this you have to drive over an out-of-bounds intrusion which was once occupied by the black sheds of the 'Station Master's Garden' if you wanted to get the best line. For a time with the new hotel nearby you drove over a wire mesh erection said to be equal in size and shape to the sheds. This I am glad to say has now been taken down and suitable solid buildings to match the old sheds have been installed.

To get home here with two big hits gives supreme satisfaction, but your mind is never free from all the tales of disaster you have heard about it. In any competition the players can never relax until this hole is behind them. In the 1960 Centenary Championship Arnold Palmer never tamed this hole and so failed to beat Nagle. Here Tom Watson in his great duel with Ballesteros in 1984 came to grief.

Watson will long remember the misjudgement at 17 which cost him the chance of equalling Harry Vardon's total of six Open titles, to achieve which at St Andrews had been his great ambition. Ironically, it was the two-iron club which had so splendidly made sure of his victory the previous year at Royal Birkdale that this time brought disaster. In the match ahead, Ballesteros – who had dropped a shot at the seventeenth on the previous three days – hit his drive into the left rough, then powered a six-iron to the front of the green, taking two putts for his par. Watson, taking the bold line, hit over the sheds, far along the fairway, but was undecided on his choice of a three or two-iron approach – knowing he had dropped three shots at this hole on the first two days from the left rough and parred it on the third day with a two-iron from the fairway. This, no doubt, decided his final selection of a two-iron, which he intended to draw; instead he pushed it and it bounded on and over the green on to the road and clattered against the wall. He was just able to punch a seven iron superbly on to the green, but as he lined up his putt from 30 ft. a roar from the eighteenth told him all he needed to know – that Ballesteros had birdied the hole. If he holed his putt for par Watson too would have needed a birdie to tie – but he took two putts, and the eagle two to force a play-off was a miracle he could not produce. So Ballesteros had the joy of winning at St Andrews his second Open.

The 'Road' Hole also played a significant part in Bobby Jones's winning of the 'Grand Slam' in 1930. In this first championship he won that year, the British Amateur, he had a desperate match with Cyril Tolley; Jones's second had gone past the 'Road' bunker and hit a spectator, but lay well, near the green; Tolley was close to the bunker and hit a beautiful little chip over it to lie dead. Bob had to bottle an eight-foot putt to get a half, which he did, and then won at the nineteenth with the help of a stymie. In the 1970 Championship there were some fine fours here especially from Nicklaus and Sanders, the runner-up, and Dr Marsh's three-iron shot to the heart of the green to clinch the Walker Cup of 1971 for our side will long be remembered. The dreadful fate which befell the fine Japanese player Tommy Nakajima in the 1978 Open is also typical of this hole. On the green in two he putted into the bunker, took five to escape and finally holed out in nine.

After the seventeenth, the last hole is a let-down and a relief, the counterpart of the first across the plain. The Swilcan Burn is no danger and the green is very large for a 354-yard hole; there are no bunkers and there is only the 'Valley of Sin', a depression in front of the left side of the green which catches a weakly-hit shot and from which you almost invariably take three more to get down. The green has often been driven, notably by Nicklaus in the last round of the 1970 Open and in the play-off next day. The 'Valley of Sin' I think cost Doug Sanders the 1970 title for 'he had only', as they say, to get down in three more from 75 yards to win. But just like you and me playing for the monthly medal at 'Little Mudheap', Sam McKinlay's famous course, Sanders determined not to be short and pitched a poor thin shot right over the 'Valley of Sin' up to the back of the green, leaving himself a difficult long downhill putt. He left it three and a half feet short and as all the world knows he missed the putt and lost the trophy. It was not his fourth shot which cost him the championship but his second.

I like a story told about Guy Ellis, a man of some eccentricity, at the eighteenth. He came in at the very end of the field one medal day and some friends came out of the clubhouse to find out how he had done. His ball lay at the back of the green, a difficult downhill putt. After some figuring his friends said, 'Guy, if you hole that you'll tie for second place.' After a prolonged study of the putt from both sides he said, 'I can't hole it', and picked his ball up and walked into the clubhouse.

The stories of St Andrews are innumerable, but best of all I enjoy this one from J. B. Salmond's *Story of the R. and A.*:

Captain, later Admiral, Maitland Dougall is remembered particularly in the annals of our Club because of his famous feat at the Autumn Meeting in 1860. An extraordinary tempest was raging on the Medal Day, and the rain was lashing down. A vessel was in distress in the bay, the lifeboat was launched at the mouth of the Swilcan, but there was difficulty in manning it. Maitland Dougall, who was to play in the Medal, took the stroke-oar. The lifeboat was five hours at sea. When it returned, Maitland Dougall went on to the tee to play his round, which he completed, and succeeded in winning the Club Gold Medal by returning 112 strokes. He had bored a hole in his ball and put in some buck-shot so that the ball would keep low in the heavy wind.

The Admiral went on to more successes, as he won no fewer than fifteen Medals in his time. Two portraits of him hang in the clubhouse of the neighbouring Scotscraig Club, a virile handsome figure with a bold jutting nose, an eagle eye and majestic whiskers like a more splendid Mr Gladstone. The first hole at Scotscraig links, where he was captain, is still called the 'Admiral' to this day. Maitland Dougall has another claim to fame, as he was the only witness, from his home nearby, of the Tay Bridge disaster when in thick and wicked weather in December 1879 the bridge and a train on it were blown down in a raging gale with the loss of all on board.

I had heard that a Japanese group was intending to construct a replica of the Old Course on a site in Japan, with detailed measurements exactly followed. If this were so I fear they would be wasting their money but later reports say that this course will only have St Andrews features. Without the soil, the climate, the surroundings and the atmosphere there is no hope of making even a colourable imitation. Many attempts have been made to copy St Andrews' holes and all I think are failures.

The atmosphere at the headquarters of golf can be magnificent, such as the wonderful occasion of Bobby Jones being admitted as a Freeman of the Burgh. The club, too, on suitable

St Andrews, Old Course: Medal and Championship Cards

NAME	M	C	PAR	NAME	M	C	PAR
1 Burn	370	374	4	10 Bobby Jones	318	338	4
2 Dyke	411	411	4	11 High	172	170	3
3 Cartgate	352	405	4	12 Heathery	316	312	4
4 Ginger Beer	419	470	4	13 Hole o' Cross	398	427	4
5 Hole o' Cross	514	567	5	14 Long	523	560	5
6 Heathery	374	414	4	15 Cartgate	401	413	4
7 High	359	364	4	16 Corner of the Dyke	351	380	4
8 Short	166	163	3	17 Road	461	466	4
9 End	307	359	4	18 Tom Morris	354	358	4
	3272	3527	36		3294	3424	36

Total 6566 or 6951 yards: par 72

occasions such as the Autumn dinner, has on view its superb trophies, setting off the high style of the captains at the top table in their red coats. When I was young there used to be a Golf Club Ball at St Andrews at the time of the Autumn meeting and I remember the glamour of the occasion with the scarlet tail coats of the captains, the plaid sashes of the ladies and kilts swinging in the reels; 'Oh, the great days in the distance enchanted'.

Musselburgh

The Open Championship was played at Musselburgh six times between 1874 and 1889, and in those days no fewer than four famous clubs used the public links, Royal Musselburgh, the Honourable Company of Edinburgh Golfers, the Edinburgh Burgesses and the members of Edinburgh Bruntsfield. But then the glory departed, the clubs taking themselves off to new courses and links like Muirfield; the Championship went with them leaving the nine holes of Musselburgh links to decay away to its present minor status.

The surroundings are bleak, a bit of scruffy common hemmed in by an undistinguished racecourse and a gasworks, some terrace houses, and a pub. When I visited it in 1966 the clubhouse was a locked shed on which was painted, in an amateur hand, 'Golf Charges, Adults 1s., Juveniles 6d.' The boys from Loretto School nearby played here sometimes. The course was then a travesty, the bunkers were grown over, there were no flags or even flag-sticks and no tee boxes or any pilferable material; the coarse thick turf and the rails of the racecourse made nonsense of the third and fourth holes, aided by iron fences running across the line of play. There were narrow fairways, appalling rough, tiny coarse greens with the holes gouged out of the earth by an uncouth crew of small urchins.

And yet even then you somehow could just see a glimmer of the old glories, the second hole – originally the first – called the 'Graves', with the green in its dell, the next 'Linkfield', a tough two-shot hole spoiled by the racecourse, then the long fourth, 'Mrs Forman's', up to the end of the course to the pub which is still Forman's Inn. After that there was a long one-shot hole across the end of the links, the 'Sea Hole', followed by the present sixth over a once big bunker, 'Pandy' (Pandemonium), now hidden under grass but still with the steeply-banked step green; Willie Park of Musselburgh, who laid out so many courses in the 'nineties, copied it a number of times, for example at the thirteenth (now the third) at Huntercombe. I must say that the copies, or imitations which I have seen much improve on the original, though with the Musselburgh green reduced in size and the hole when I was there cut for some reason on the very steepest part of the bank, one got no real idea of the hole as it used to be played by golfers.

The round ends with a two-shot hole out towards the beach and then two drive and run-up holes back to the pavilion, the 'Hole Across' and suitably enough the 'Gas'. In its palmy days the round ended with the one-shot hole with which it now begins, a good clout on to a plateau green, a very tricky shot to gauge to a hole with no flagstick. However, I am delighted to learn that since reaching its low point twenty years ago there has been a decided upward turn in the condition of old Musselburgh with fairly good greens, decently mown fairways, bearable rough, flags and flagsticks and tee boxes. Only the vandals at 'Mrs Forman's' defy correction but otherwise a fair, decent layout of a former era has been reinstated – excellent. There was, however, a threat of an enlargement of the racecourse which would probably have put paid to the old links. We have just heard that this development has cut short the fourth hole.

Musselburgh is famous for the Park family, who have been associated with the town for 400 years. Old Willie Park won the Open Championship four times, his brother Mungo won it once and his son Willie Junior twice in 1887 and 1889. Young Willie Park's daughter has been Scottish Ladies' Champion and played for Great Britain in recent times. In the words of the *Golfer's Handbook*:

For twenty years old Willie Park had a standing challenge in 'Bell's Life', London, to play any man in the world for £100 a side, and he was always ready to defend his challenge. Old Willie Park played numerous matches against Old Tom [Morris]; no two professionals ever played so many big matches for stakes over different greens. The big matches took place in 1856, 1858, 1862, 1871 and 1882. The last match came to an abrupt finish at Musselburgh when Willie stood two up and six to play. Bob Chambers [the head of the Edinburgh house of publishers], the referee, stopped play because spectators were interfering with the balls. Chambers and Morris went into Forman's public house and Park, after waiting some time, sent a message that if Morris did not come out and finish the match, he would play the remaining holes alone and claim the stakes. This he did.

The spectators at Musselburgh – 'they damned miners', Andrew Kirkaldy called them – were notorious for protecting the interests of their own favourites and judicious kicks to the balls were frequent. J. H. Taylor suffered so badly from these attentions in his challenge match with young Willie Park in 1895 that Vardon in his great challenge match in 1899,

Musselburgh Golf Course – Card		
NAME	YARDS	PAR
1 The Short Hole	130	3
2 The Graves	350	4
3 Linkfield	450	4
4 Formans	350	4
5 The Sea Hole	130	3
6 Pandy	360	4
7 The Bathing Coach	420	4
8 The High Hole	220	3
9 The Gas Works	300	4
	2710	33

Total 2710 yards: par 33

also with young Willie, refused to play the Scottish half at Musselburgh and they played at North Berwick instead.

The Championship here in 1883 produced a dramatic finish, which robbed the local champion, Bob Ferguson, of four straight wins which would have matched the record of young Tom Morris of ten years before. Willie Fernie, in spite of a ten at one hole, scored 159 for the thirty-six holes, but the redoubtable champion forced a tie by finishing with three threes. In the play-off Ferguson was a stroke ahead and got his four, the regulation figure at the last. But

Fernie, in the words of Robert Browning, 'not only drove the green but holed a long "steal" for a two and the Championship.'

All along the coast south and east of Edinburgh is a great and famous chain of golf links, as extensive and magnificent as a similar chain along the west coast of Scotland. Longniddry, New Luffness, Gullane, with three courses, Muirfield and North Berwick, renowned names these and renowned golf too. The turf along this length of coast is of particularly fine quality and the greens made from it are exceptional.

Muirfield

Of these links, Muirfield is the most famous, though perhaps not the best known, for it is the private club of the Honourable Company of Edinburgh Golfers, a society founded in 1744, ten years before the Royal and Ancient and unlike the public links of St Andrews or Carnoustie has not been thrown open to all and sundry. Be that as it may, the club knows how to be host to a modern championship, as those of us who saw the 1966, 1972 and 1980 Opens can assert, and the upkeep and grooming of the links are impeccable. The bunkers – all of them – are famous with their walls of turf sods as neatly put together as an expertly made dry-wall. As Jack Nicklaus said, 'The most fastidiously-built bunkers I have ever seen, the high front walls faced with bricks of turf fitted together so precisely you would have thought a master mason had been called in.'

Muirfield, which has had its ups and downs in public esteem, began later than nearly all the other famous Scottish links, being opened in 1891. It was first used for the Open Championship in 1892 when it came in for a lot of criticism. Confined inside a stone wall then, it gave, not wholly unreasonably, the impression of being an inland course. As Bernard Darwin puts it: 'Andrew Kirkaldy had many years ago called Muirfield "an auld watermeadie" and there

was just enough truth in the aphorism to make it unforgettable. Now the wall has been thrown down and some of the sandhills have become part of the course with a great gain in picturesqueness and probably of golfing quality also.'

Continuing with Bernard Darwin for a moment – for who can put it better:

Muirfield still retains and always will retain a certain inland character. This proceeds from the fact that we are always or nearly always playing our shots between two lines of rough. I regard St Andrews and Rye as the most entirely seaside golf courses. There we are either on the course or we are in a bunker or a hazard. There is no fairway and no rough. [I must say I take leave to disagree with this statement as too sweeping.] Muirfield is the exact converse: there is a very distinct fairway and very distinct rough. Sometimes the rough is more and sometimes less severe.

Well, at the Open of 1966 the rough was, I should say, at its most severe and that knee-length grass bending before a stiff breeze on the last day was a terrifying sight; it certainly destroyed a number of cards, notably Arnold Palmer's and Phil Rodgers's on that afternoon. In 1972 the rough was less fierce and there was very little wind throughout this championship and so also in 1980.

The progression of scoring in the Open Championship recently is interesting, reflecting more the difficulties of wind and weather rather than improvements in skill. In 1966 Nicklaus scored 282 and only three men beat the par 284; in 1972 Trevino scored 278 and five players beat par. In 1980 when play was at its easiest here Watson scored 271 and eleven beat par; scores in the 60s were plentiful and there was even a 63 by Aoki of Japan.

Muirfield differs from the other great links in other ways. For instance, it lacks the obscurities and subtlety of St Andrews with its hidden bunkers and protective slopes, or the ancient complexities of Prestwick. It is not a straight-out-and-home links – for which much thanks indeed. It follows the almost required pattern of American courses of today, two loops of nine holes – the second loop being inside the first – and two par threes and two par fives in the first nine and two par threes and a par five in the second. Moreover, for all the proud traditions of the Honourable Company, the course has never been a sacred cow to be preserved unmolested; major changes have been made – thus the course has been substantially altered twice – and minor changes in bunkering and other hazards frequently introduced, such as the planting of trees on the right of the eighth hole to prevent any further use of Walter Hagen's bold short-cut to the green which served him so well in 1929 with two birdies on the last day's play. For the 1987 championship the ninth, already a difficult hole, is lengthened to 510 yards.

None the less, some admirable traditions are prized by the Honourable Company. After all, they drew up the first set of rules of golf, in 1744 – ten years before those of the R. & A – when they were housed at Leith Links, and their first winner of the Silver Club, which made him 'Captain of the Golf', surgeon John Rattray got involved in 'the 45'. He was called out in the early hours of the morning to attend the wounded of Prince Charles Edward's army after the Battle of Prestonpans; he followed the

White Cockade to Derby and retreated with it, too, being taken at the stricken field of Culloden, though he was later released. And the pictures in the clubhouse are a notable collection, including Raeburn's full-length portrait of his fellow member Alexander Keith, and the portrait, which adorned the cover of the 1966 Open Championship programme, of William St Clair of Roslin, four times captain of the club, who was the last descendant of an ancestor who came over with William the Norman in 1066 and may well have spent the night before the Battle of Hastings with the rest of the invading army in my garden on Telham Hill.

So to the golf. The first thing to note about the play at Muirfield is that it's all above board; you can see what is demanded of you, the bunkers are all on view and like it or not the play is laid out before your eyes. Let us see this through the eyes of Herbert Warren Wind, that perceptive golf writer from the United States:

Muirfield's great quality is its frankness – its honesty. There are no hidden bunkers, no recondite burns, no misleading and capricious terrain. Every hazard is clearly visible. Chiefly for this reason, the course has always been extremely popular with foreign golfers and especially Americans; it has a sort of 'inland' flavour that makes visitors feel much more at home on it than on any other British championship course. Moreover, Muirfield is perhaps the most beautifully-conditioned course in Britain.

So much taken by Muirfield was Jack Nicklaus that he has created his own course in its honour in the United States called Muirfield Village.

Sam McKinlay, the international golfer, says this:

When I was younger and still enjoyed a modest competence in golf, I used to think that if I had to play a match for my life on a course of my choice I would plump for Muirfield. It is the best and fairest of courses – not, perhaps, the course where I would choose to play all my golf if my activities had to be restricted to one links, for it is a little too fierce, too long, too exposed to the winds that sweep down Gullane Hill or in from the North Sea. But a man who has command of his game and of himself will fare better at Muirfield than almost any other course I know. It rewards the good shot, penalises the bad one, and is so constructed that it is a complete examination of the player.

Muirfield, I suppose, would meet Tom Simpson's test of what constitutes a great course – 'a course that provides entertainment for every class of golfer, a searching difficult test for the good player and quite another, less exacting one, for the medium player and long handicap man'.

Well, what's the snag? There must be one, or this would be the one great perfect course in all the world. So let's say it in a little quiet voice – it somehow lacks charm. There are no identifiable weaknesses. It is a fair, just examination as Hoylake is. You respect it, you respect it tremendously, but somehow don't quite get to love it.

You start out with three par fours, the first a stiff one which proved to be the toughest hole of all in the '66 Open. The second and third are of no great length, and here the great players are hoping for birdies, then a well-bunkered par three, followed by a 558-yard hole where in 1966 Nicklaus got up with a drive and an eight-iron downwind and several eagles were scored in 1972 and 1980 in spite of there being more bunkers on this hole than at any other. The sixth is a tough dog-leg with bunkers on the left and the seventh a difficult par three back into the prevailing wind. The eighth is a famous hole, 444 yards now for the championship with a great cluster of bunkers on the right of the fairway where the drive reaches, and a cross bunker in front of the green. Hagen used to take his own line far away to the right here, but this has now been bottled up with a growth of buckthorn. Along the left side of the fairway is Archerfield Wood, dark and sinister, which plays a part as Graden Sea Wood in Robert Louis Stevenson's story *The Pavilion on the Links*.

The ninth, now lengthened, is a really tough par five hole with a narrow target area for the drive and then a very tight shot indeed up to the green with bunkers on the right and a wall and out-of-bounds on the left.

The second nine is rather easier than the first and some very low scores have been done on it. The tenth, 475 yards, with a west wind sweeping across at right angles, can give a lot of

	C	M	PAR		C	M	PAR
1	450	444	4	10	475	471	4
2	351	345	4	11	385	350	4
3	379	374	4	12	381	376	4
4	180	174	3	13	152	146	3
5	559	506	5	14	449	442	4
6	460	436	4	15	417	391	4
7	185	151	3	16	188	181	3
8	444	439	4	17	550	501	5
9	504	460	5	18	448	414	4
	3521	3329	36		3445	3272	35

Muirfield Links: Championship and Medal Cards

Total 6966 and 6601 yards: par 71

trouble, and indeed the rough here put paid to Arnold Palmer's chances in 1966; it is written in the 1972 Open Programme that 'the left rough at the tenth still throbs to this day from the thrashings of the great man's death throes'. The last two holes, however, have been the most notable for separating the men from the boys. The seventeenth at 542 yards, although Roberto de Vicenzo did it in two in the 1948 championship, eluded all the contestants on the last day of the 1966 Open except Jack Nicklaus, although it was played with the help of a brisk breeze. In 1972 the hole was notorious for Lee

Trevino's holed chip from over the green in the last round which broke Tony Jacklin's heart. The last hole, a really tough 447-yarder, with three bunkers on the left and one on the right waiting to grab your drive, bunkers in front of the green and on either side of it, produced its dramas in 1972 including Trevino's holed chip from the rough for a three and his fifth successive birdie in the third round. In all he holed three chips in this championship, one an outrageous piece of luck at the short sixteenth where he hit the pin first bounce from a terrible bunker shot and fell into the hole for a two.

Royal Troon

This famous club which was founded in 1878 now bears the proud name of Royal Troon, achieving the honour in the year of the club's centenary.

Troon is next door to Prestwick on the Ayrshire coast and came into the championship rota in 1923 when Arthur Havers won a welcome victory for Britain after two years of American success. Although it is so close to Prestwick – there is even a party-fence I believe – Troon is considerably different, less humpy, bumpy and hillocky, but with bigger bolder sandhills, a more straightforward layout, less charming, longer and I suppose for the modern ball, tougher. Troon also surpasses Prestwick in its coastal scenery, over to the hills of Arran and beyond and down to Ailsa Craig.

The course has been lengthened a number of times, notably in 1962 for the championship which Arnold Palmer so spectacularly won, and can now be stretched to over 7000 yards. Some changes were also made for 1973 and for 1982. This I suppose is necessary – though I would prefer some limitation of the ball – and I suppose that if Arnold Palmer, Nicklaus and Co. went to work on 6500-yard Prestwick they might score in the very low sixties; I'd love to see them try.

Palmer has described his championship here

in his excellent book *My Game and Yours*, but unfortunately his management organisation refused to allow a quotation to be made. I had liked particularly Palmer's resolve not to get 'locked into a life-and-death struggle with the course' and all that followed. That year, Palmer gave everybody a lesson on how to play a fast, dry links as Troon was, winning from Nagle by six shots and scoring three out of the six rounds in the entire tournament under 70, one of them a spreadeagling 67. In contrast, Gary Player couldn't cope at all and failed to survive 'the cut' while Jack Nicklaus, not yet at his majestic peak, wallowed along twenty-nine shots behind Palmer in the aggregate. It might be said that almost single-handed by his example and encouragement, Arnold Palmer put our Open Championship back on the map. He was therefore deservedly honoured in 1982 with Honorary Life Membership of Royal Troon where he had won so spectacularly. At the ceremony he was much moved and also, be it said, much loved.

Another famous victory here was that of Charlie Yates – a close friend of mine in his later years – from Atlanta, Georgia, who took our Amateur Championship the first time it was played at Troon in 1938, beating the Irishman Cecil Ewing in the final. This was the famous year in Walker Cup history when Britain won its only victory up to that time, after we had been whitewashed at Pine Valley in 1936 and this description of Charlie and his friends by Henry Longhurst caught my fancy:

Four of their side hailed from the south, and wickedly good players they were too: Ed White, from Texas, slim and dark with humorous film-star eyes; Walter Emery, of Oklahoma City, a big, happy-go-lucky fellow of infinite zest; Reynolds Smith from Dallas, stocky, dark and determined; and Charlie Yates, a wise-cracking, happy-go-lucky young protegé of Bobby Jones down in Atlanta. So infectious, incidentally, were Yates's high spirits that two years later he accomplished the unprecedented feat of standing on the steps of the Royal and Ancient clubhouse at St Andrews after the Walker Cup match and inducing the crowd to accompany him in 'A wee doch an' doris'.

The voices of this quartet intrigued their British visitors, who had not heard the like except in the movies and hardly believed it then. Their average age was twenty-three, which in golfing maturity is equivalent perhaps to thirty over here. They chewed stubs of black cigars and let forth a barrage of wise-cracking good humour. Emery had a broad-brimmed hat and needed only a lasso hanging from his golf bag to complete the picture.

Another famous win at Troon in the Amateur was that of John Beharrell, who took the Championship of 1956 a few weeks after his eighteenth birthday, the youngest winner up to that time.

Weiskopf's win in the '73 Open was a good one in spite of the fact that he is said to have disliked the course. His win was notable in that in 72 holes he never once took three putts. The other event we all remember of that year was 70-year-old Gene Sarazen's hole in one at the eighth. In 1982 Tom Watson won his fourth Open title, Peter Oosterhuis finishing one stroke behind.

Well, we had better go out and have a look at the links, which is one of the out-and-home variety. The first six holes run south along the shore, three fairly undemanding par fours of under 400 yards as a start, of gradually increasing difficulty, and we had better take not more than thirteen shots over them, for we get into the long-hitting area from then on, the 522–556-yard fourth with a long one-shotter next and then the 577-yard sixth (544 yards off my tee) with a new narrow green no longer on a plateau, a big hole in every sense of the word.

We then turn away from the coast with a

	NAME	M	C	PAR		NAME	M	C	PAR
1	Seal	357	362	4	10	Sandhills	385	437	4
2	Black Rock	381	391	4	11	The Railway	421	481	4/5
3	Gyaws	371	381	4	12	The Fox	427	432	4
4	Dunure	522	556	5	13	Burmah	411	468	4
5	Greenan	194	210	3	14	Alton	175	180	3
6	Turnberry	544	577	5	15	Crosbie	445	457	4
7	Tel-el-Kebir	381	389	4	16	Well	533	542	5
8	Postage Stamp	123	126	3	17	Rabbit	210	233	3
9	The Monk	387	419	4	18	Craigend	374	425	4
		3260	3411	36			3381	3645	35/36

Troon Golf Club, Old Course: Medal and Championship Cards

Total 6641 or 7056 yards: par 71/72

most attractive hole, a mild dog-leg, among the sandhills with many traps for the drive and a plateau green on a saddle between hills. After this we have the shortest hole in British championship golf, the 126-yard 'Postage Stamp', originally 'Ailsa', named for the hump behind the green which resembles the island of Ailsa Craig in shape. Awful disasters have happened here, for the green is proportionately small and the protecting bunkers deep and grasping. In 1950 in the Open a German amateur scored fifteen here, having visited all three of the protecting bunkers and enjoying five strokes in one of them; he did well to complete the round in 92.

Leaving 'the Stamp' with a three, we hope, we turn into the sandhills with three difficult and testing holes, with a notably big carry off the tee at the tenth now somewhat eased to give a better view, as we turn for home and a recently lengthened and most difficult eleventh hole, which might be named for Arnold Palmer, up to the railway, before the 'Fox', the twelfth, takes us back towards the sea to a two-tier green. So a straight run-in via a big sixteenth to the difficult tight seventeenth one-shotter, a 210-yard stroke to a plateau green and then a tightly bunkered 374-yard hole finishes the round.

Carnoustie

As I have said, one of the pleasures of golf as opposed to, say, cricket or lawn tennis, is that no two courses are alike, nor are they expected to be. While Bramall Lane may differ from the Worcester County Ground in its surroundings, the playing surfaces can only vary to a minor degree, but at golf no part of any course need resemble any part of any other. Carnoustie is quite different from St Andrews, Prestwick, Muirfield or Troon, better in some respects, less good in others, but a splendid testing, difficult links in its own right. Near Dundee, on the east coast of Angus, it is a public course and a number of clubs' members play on it. This style of things is common in Scotland, as at St Andrews, at Musselburgh in the old days, at North Berwick and at Montrose. The amenities, which have been improved, used to suggest that it was less trouble to change your shoes in the car park than to make more elaborate arrangements. However you may get organized, you are without doubt in for a first-class exacting round of golf.

The feature of Carnoustie is the water hazards which, in the shape of two burns, the Barry Burn and Jockie's Burn, wind all over the place, usually where you would least like to

encounter them. The links is flat, the fairways, while carrying a fair share of small undulations, are much less humpy than many; attractive dark sea-woods of fir break up the monotony; while you are not distracted by any view of the sea, there is, as on so many good golf courses, the railway along one flank. The scenery, it must be acknowledged, lacks the charm of Troon or Turnberry.

You start out with a generous hole of 401 yards with a nice gathering green in a hollow to help you on your way. You then play a similar but rather longer and tighter hole in the same direction avoiding 'Braid's bunker' about 230 yards out in mid-fairway. The third is a beautiful drive-and-pitch back towards town to a small green with Jockie's Burn to carry with the pitch. So far, so good. The fourth, out again along the other side of the sea-wood you skirted on the third, is a longer par four, but still not very long; yet somehow more fives get on the card here than should.

The fifth is a beauty, dog-legged to a plateau green but still not too long for the ordinary player. Here Ben Hogan holed a chip from a sandy lie in his last round in the '53 Championship to make his victory almost certain, remarking afterwards, 'No one does anything unless the Lord's with him.' The sixth, a par five, gives a lot of trouble to the pros who are looking for a four, while for us there are mid-fairway bunkers about 210 yards from the tee, and then Jockie's Burn edging into the fairway about 200 yards further on. You follow with a par four along the out of bounds to the left, then an undistinguished short hole and then a big two-shotter to the railway, just a bit longer and softer to the run of the ball than it looks.

The tenth hole is 'South America', a two-shot hole of 406 yards for us but 455 for 'them' with the Barry Burn to be carried with the second shot rather too close to the front apron of the green for comfort. This hole caused more trouble in the 1968 Open than many, largely because the wind was consistently against. The name of this hole is attributed to a farewell party for a citizen of the town, David Nicoll, who was off to seek his fortune; in the morning after the party he woke up there – and never went any farther. After this the eleventh back parallel is not too tough, nor is the twelfth, in spite of its protective ridge in front of the green, provided, and only provided, that we play it as a par five.

Thirteen is a short hole but tightly bunkered, so fours are common enough. After that come the 'Spectacles', a fine slashing hole of 476 yards with its green backing on to that of the fourth. The hole gets its name from the two big bunkers in the face of the ridge across the fairway nearly 400 yards from the tee which blinds the view to the hole and traps the timid shot or the shot played after an indifferent drive. Fifteen is an absolute beauty, a two-shot hole of 424 yards or 463 yards to a green in a shallow dell, a wonderfully satisfying hole at which to get a four. The sixteenth is a terribly tough par three, of 235 yards or 248 yards off the tournament tee to a small plateau green which rises towards the back. In consequence, it would not meet Tom Simpson's requirement that the back of a green must never be higher than the front; 'that gives the golfer confidence

and that the architect must never give him'. All the same, in the '68 Championship against the wind, it looked and was an extremely hard hole.

At the seventeenth we have to cross the snake path of the Barry Burn thrice, so there are three chances of getting into it, and then we have to hit a firm shot home to a small gathering green, quite hard to find at 432 yards. The eighteenth is 440 yards back to the clubhouse and here you may have to cross the Burn twice, unimportantly from the tee and bitterly importantly with a long second or a short pitch, for it runs right across, bang in front of the green. For the tournament player this hole can demand a terrible decision: to go for it and fail or play short and miss a four. In the Open of 1968 when the hole was lengthened to 525 yards very few players were on it in two and many fives were recorded. It is now back to par four.

To my taste this is one of the great links: without a wind, not too harsh and not too rough on the man content with an 80. But if you want a 72 then you've got to play golf.

Although golf has been played here for centuries Carnoustie came late into the championship rota – in 1931 – and I suppose its greatest moments came in 1937 when Henry Cotton beat the best of the world's players and in 1953 when Hogan came over to try to win the British Open to add to his US title. His views of the links differ somewhat from ours, but they are interesting and refreshing. His summing up is perhaps allowable. 'I play to win and I think the Lord has let me win for a purpose. I hope that purpose is to give courage to those people who are sick or injured and broken in body' – well said.

Gary Player won a fine victory here in 1968, his slashing wood against the wind to within a foot of the hole at the 'Spectacles' in the last round clinching the championship. In 1975, the last time the Open was here, there was a tie, Newton of Australia losing the play-off to an 'unknown' American Tom Watson. The Amateur has been here three times.

Carnoustie Links: Medal and Championship Cards

NAME	M	C	PAR	NAME	M	C	PAR
1 Cup	401	406	4	10 South America	406	455	4
2 Gulley	418	464	4	11 Dyke	367	370	4
3 Jockie's Burn	321	345	4	12 Southward Ho	476	482	5
4 Hillocks	375	381	4	13 Whins	145	167	3
5 Brae	377	391	4	14 Spectacles	487	482	5
6 Long	521	575	5	15 Luckyslap	424	463	4
7 Plantation	376	395	4	16 Barry Burn	235	248	3
8 Short	149	172	3	17 Island	438	432	4
9 Railway	427	475	4	18 Home	453	440	4
	3365	3604	36		3431	3539	36

Total 6796 or 7143 yards: par 72

Carnoustie has given many fine golfers to the world such as the Smith brothers and Stewart Maiden, who was the mentor of the great Bobby Jones.

Turnberry

Turnberry on the southern Ayrshire coast only came into the championship rota late and then for the Amateur only in 1961. This was the year when Michael Bonallack won the first of his five victories in ten years. Turnberry was also used for the disastrous Walker Cup match in 1963 when, after leading six to three on the first day Britain crashed to ruin on the second. It was only in 1977 that the Open came to Turnberry for the first time.

Turnberry was originally part of a British Rail holiday 'complex', with a large – and good – hotel on the cliff overlooking the linksland, and its two courses, and also the southern end of the Firth of Clyde with the granite dome of the island of Ailsa Craig predominating out to sea; the island of Arran can be seen further off, then the Mull of Kintyre and sometimes the far coast of Antrim near Portrush in Ireland. Of course, all these are only visible in exceptional circumstances and we had better recall the rather dour local pronouncement: 'If you can see Ailsa Craig it's going to rain and if you can't see it it's raining.'

Before Hitler's war there were two holiday courses here. Then an RAF Coastal Command station flattened out the fairways and built concrete runways. At the end of the war it all looked a dead loss. But British Rail refused to accept defeat and the courses were reconstructed, one by Mackenzie Ross, the other still a holiday circuit; the big course, the 'Ailsa', gives the full treatment. I must say that the only time I played it, off the back tees, on a windy autumn day I found it extremely long and tough, but there were some beautiful shots to recompense you. Thus after a modest up-and-down start on the flatter ground inland from the big sandhills you come to the splendid 170-yard fourth cocked up in the dunes, with the shore in between you and the green which has that characteristic of all difficult holes – it looks much farther than it is. After a par five fifth there is another heavy one-shot into the hills of 245 yards, beyond my reach against the wind. So up we go hitting to the seventh and eighth – half a mile between them – so that we can be ready to tackle the drive at the ninth to a 425-yard hole. The back tee is a rocky pinnacle out to sea, and we must hit the ball over the cliffs and surging in-running tide to a fairway and green by the lighthouse, the apotheosis of seaside golf. The tenth along the cliffs is another exhilarating two-shotter. From then on it is rather less exciting until the short fifteenth, a hole with a minute green perched up in the hills with nothing but it to shoot at. Then comes the attractive par four sixteenth, 385 yards downhill but with a deep, deep unrecoverable-from burn in front of the green. Downwind the second shot is hard to hold on the small green; in still or adverse air it is fatally easy to be short, ditched and doomed. A par five seventeenth follows, before a milder finishing hole. So ends a great links in a great setting – don't miss it.

For the 1977 Championship the weather was perfect almost, too perfect, for the four days there was hardly a breath of wind and the sun shone continuously throughout. Furthermore, through unfavourable spring weather, the rough was very thin and undemanding. With a par of only 70 that year there was every expectation that the course would be mercilessly eaten up by the very strong field of American professionals. In the event there were many scores in the sixties, but apart from the results of the tremendous duel between Tom Watson, the ultimate winner, and Jack Nicklaus, the scoring at the end of the day was not quite what was expected. Indeed, apart from these two giants only one other player, Hubert Green, beat par over four rounds and that by only one stroke.

For Britain, the Championship was a humiliation as the United States took the first eight places and eleven out of the first twelve. But all eyes were on the two leaders, who, as Herb Wind reported, 'produced what many people

on both sides of the Atlantic consider the finest and most dramatic stretch of golf ever played in a major event.

'In the third round the two leaders pulled away from the field with a pair of sensational 65s. In the fourth round Nicklaus added a 66 but it wasn't good enough; Watson had a 65. Far ahead of the pack, the two leaders were engaged virtually in match play. The duel was not decided until the last hole which both of them birdied'.

The finish was dramatic enough for those of us who witnessed it. At the comparatively easy eighteenth, a 430-yard par four, Watson, who was one shot up, hit his second shot with a seven-iron to within two feet of the pin. Nicklaus from a bad lie in the rough belted the ball just on to the green; he then holed it for a three, fully 35 ft it was reported, leaving Watson to hole his missable short one to win, which he did.

The championship of 1986 was a very different matter. A cold, wet year had produced a rich crop of rough and the course had been lengthened somewhat, although par was still 70. It started with one of the most testing first days anyone could remember with a 40 mph gale off the Atlantic 'numbing of the nerves and sending the scores rocketing' as *Golf Illustrated* reported.

Greg Norman, the Australian, who ultimately won said: 'It was extremely rough. Some of the players are being humiliated out there. It was the kind of day when you walk off with a headache with the concentration and just fighting the wind'.

Many other complaints and sad stories were heard. Jack Nicklaus, who had a 78, said, 'Everything that could happen to me did so. I am just pleased to get off the course without breaking a leg'. Sandy Lyle took 78 and Tom Watson 77. Altogether, it could have been said that it was Turnberry's revenge.

On the second day things were easier and Norman sailed into the lead with an astounding 63 and there were altogether fourteen scores in the sixties. This put Norman ahead while such dangerous competitors as Ballesteros, Sandy Lyle and three other previous winners, Tom Watson, Lee Trevino and Jack Nicklaus, were struggling to make the cut.

On the third day the weather was shocking again, with heavy winds accompanied by squalls of rain driving in from the sea. The scores were back in the 70s and once again nobody beat par. On the last day the weather at last relented with a little watery sunshine and the scoring looked more like championship standard. Ballesteros had a 64 but it was too late. He voiced his dislike of the conditions saying, 'The fairways are too narrow and there is too much rough. The R & A should not set up a course as difficult as this . . . add that to the British weather and it just becomes crazy'. Jack Nicklaus on the other hand said: 'It's a fine course. You only get criticism from the players with high scores. It can't be that bad if Norman shoots 63. There will be other good scores and Turnberry will produce a good champion.'

The final scores showed how much the leaders of the game have changed in the years since 1977: there were only two Americans in the first ten in 1986 and neither of them within striking distance of the winner.

The scores in the John Player Classic held here at the end of September 1972 exhibit perfectly the effect of wind on the best professional game. Here was a field of 31 players, the best of the British and some distinguished overseas players as well – Arnold Palmer, Gay Brewer, Bob Charles, Gary Player, Billy Casper, Peter Thomson, Doug Sanders, Roberto de Vicenzo, and several others; just about the top except for the great Nicklaus and Open champion, Lee Trevino. On the first day conditions were as near perfect as you could ask, with warm, still autumn weather and plenty of run on the ball. The pros just about murdered the course with ten scores under 70. At the end of the day, eleven players were under par and six more were on par. Huggett had a 64, which was notable for his taking wood no less than nine times to play for the green, at the short sixth and fifteenth, and seven times from the fairway, showing that Turnberry was not playing all that short for everybody.

Next day, 'with a restless wind stirring from the south all day', things were different with

---

Turnberry, Ailsa Course: Medal and Championship Cards

NAME	M	C	PAR	NAME	M	C	PAR
1 Ailsa Craig	365	365	4	10 Dinna Fouter	405	460	4
2 Mak Siccar	390	440	4	11 Maidens	145	180	3
3 Blaw Wearie	405	475	4	12 Monument	395	395	4
4 Woe-be-Tide	170	170	3	13 Tickly Tap	385	385	4
5 Fin' me oot	405	490	4/5	14 Risk-an-Hope	405	440	4
6 Tappie Toorie	245	245	3	15 Ca Canny	180	220	3
7 Roon the Ben	480	520	5	16 Wee Burn	385	415	4
8 Goat Fell	405	440	4	17 Langwhang	485	515	5
9 Bruce's Castle	425	475	4	18 Ailsa Hame	390	430	4
	3290	3620	35/36		3175	3440	35

Total 6465 or 7060: par 70/71

only four scores under 70 and only nine players in all below par at the end of two rounds.

On the third day, when the wind 'blew hard and firm, but not at gale strength', the course began to show its teeth and as Peter Ryde said 'the wind joined hands with Turnberry's 7060 yards to make the contestants pay for their fun on the first two days'. There was only one round under 70, Bannerman's 67, and no one else beat par. At the end of that day only five players were below par for the three rounds.

On the Saturday, the last round was played in an even tougher wind and some of the tees were moved forward. Scores again rocketed and no one beat or equalled par except for a splendid 70 by Gay Brewer. A last round of 76 was good enough to give Bob Charles the first prize with an aggregate of one over par for the four rounds. Peter Townsend's scores reflect the conditions perhaps better than anyone's – 65, 70, 75, 80. There were twelve rounds of 80 or more on the last day and Gary Player had the distressing experience of an 85. So did a big course grab back what it had been forced to yield on the first two days.

According to the pro, there are some local characters among the caddies with such romantic names as Long John, the Wasp, Happy and the Lawyer. Once Long John was caddying for an American visitor who asked if the lighthouse at the ninth worked; he replied, 'Yes, sir, but only at night.'

Royal Dornoch

My friend Rush and I, with our wives, made a special pilgrimage to Dornoch in July 1966 and I am glad we did, for this introduced us to a most famous links. At that point Dornoch was not well known except to a discerning few, like the regular visitors before World War I who were a distinguished band of amateurs. The reason for this is easy to understand – remoteness. For Dornoch is 220 miles from Edinburgh and even when you get to Inverness, and you think you ought to be near, you still have sixty miles of road to travel. It seemed far into the North, a sort of Ultima Thule, alluring but unattainable.

Now all has changed and already it has hosted the Amateur Championship and the 100th at that. There is almost a cult of Dornoch today for which we can, I think, thank Herbert Warren Wind, the American writer, who is such a perceptive observer of golf in the British Isles and such a charming writer of the game, who said this on his first visit in 1964:

While no one expects the pro shop at a Scottish club to resemble our temples of merchandising, the shop at Dornoch, close by the first tee, turned out to be nothing but a glassed-in booth with a roof of corrugated tin painted brownish red. There was no one on duty when we arrived. We tried the clubhouse, a small two-storey building in which, except for a new bar, everything must be quite as it was in 1904, when the club celebrated the official opening of its extended eighteen holes . . .' [If I may interpose: there is a fine new clubhouse now.]

I could not help thinking that on such a glorious morning – and Saturday too – the Old Course at St Andrews was probably overrun with golfers, yet here, at what one might call the St Andrews of the North, there was not a soul to be seen except a big grey cat with one blind eye. He is called Nelson, and prowls placidly round the first tee from morn to night – the reincarnation, unquestionably, of some old golfer who never got his fill . . . However, this same remoteness explains the unique position that Dornoch has long held in golf; for over half a century it has been regarded as one of the outstanding courses in the world by men close to the heart of the game, yet very few of them have ever played it.

One had heard so much of Dornoch that it would not have been surprising if reality had been a disappointment but for once it wasn't so, for this is a magnificent natural links with some of the most beautiful sites for greens on natural plateaux that you could imagine. Moreover, it turned out that it included a hole, and not a very good one, about which over many years I had had a recurring dream, a hole going up and up, intensely green, with heather in the rough, uphill into a sky of driving wet clouds and fleeting sunlight as the mists blew across. Always in the dream it was the same and I knew that one day I would find it. The sixteenth at Dornoch, the first time we played it, was just like that, except that we saw no heather in the rough, but like enough for me to say at once 'This is it'; there was an absolute sense of *déjà vu* – and I've never had the dream again.

If you could pin a couple of defects on Dornoch it is that it is a straight out-and-home course and that it has four short holes of much the same length, for I have used a four-iron at each of them in one round. But this is very minor criticism for what otherwise earns lyrical praise.

The links lies along Dornoch Firth and from every hole there is a view of the sea, by no means a characteristic of seaside links, witness Birkdale, for example, Deal or St Andrews, where a sight of the sea is fleeting indeed. Dornoch links is on two levels: the upper holes on a ridge of sandhills and the lower holes down in among them close to the beach, so close in fact that at the short tenth a moderate pull will put you on the shore. A most ingenious feature of Dornoch is that in changing levels you play downhill three times – at the third, eighth and seventeenth – and only play uphill once, at the sixteenth; the other changes of level are made by walking up to the tee, vastly preferable to beating a golf ball uphill, the most tedious of all forms of the game. Capilano in Vancouver has the same pleasant characteristic.

It is a matter of possible interest that the last witch to be hanged in Britain suffered at Dornoch and before the last grisly deed was ducked in a pond on the short course here at the hole now called 'The Witch'.

You start the main links at Dornoch with a short par four of 336 yards, where the ground runs kindly for you and a birdie is always a possibility; after that there is a stiff, tough par three with a bunker at the left edge which grasps your ball all too readily. You then transfer to the lower level with an exhilarating drive downhill at a 414-yard hole with a shot to the green which is not easy; the green doesn't gather the ball. The fourth is much the same length with the green on a plateau, a fine shot. The fifth, too, has a plateau green, a real beauty, so moulded that although the hole is only 361 yards it's a tough, difficult four. The green lies well in from the front of the carry. This hole is called 'Hilton', no doubt after Harold of that name rather than Conrad. Six is a short hole among the sandhills, again the green is on its plateau. So then you walk uphill and play a rather mild, uninteresting 465-yarder along the upper level.

This is, however, taken care of by the lovely eighth, where you drive over a precipice towards the northern sea, then probably off a hanging lie, a stiff iron shot down, down over a lot of humps and bumps and a little dead ground to a green in a little dell.

Then at the ninth you turn for home, and probably into the wind, starting with a mild and helpful par five. After that all mercy is done with and you have to play for your life against the prevailing wind. The tenth is a short hole, set among the bents and bunkers and the shore just off line to the left.

Eleven is a very tough 445-yard par four, out of my reach, only redeemed by twelve, which is a shortish par five. Thirteen is another stiff iron shot into the wind, par three. Fourteen is 'Foxy', a famous double dog-leg or double-banana hole of 448 yards, which needs a big, drawn drive, followed by a big, faded brassie along a shallow valley up to a plateau green, all without a single bunker. This hole is splendid for bigger golfers than I am, but too far for me as a four hole. The fifteenth is a short par four with a big sandy hill to carry and sixteen is long and uphill and in spite of being the 'hole in the dream' the dullest on the links. The seventeenth, though, is a gorgeous hole, a big drive downhill and downwind, with a firm iron shot over the protecting bunkers in the face of the ridge on which, fifty yards on, the green is moulded. After that the walk up to the eighteenth tee and the subsequent hole of 457 yards along the top of the ridge, with a swale in front of the green, are only moderately interesting. Altogether, the 6577-yard course has a par of 70 and if you can match that – gross or net – you have achieved something.

Few international tournaments were at Dornoch until the Amateur of 1985, won by Garth McGimpsey from Northern Ireland, the first from there since Max McCready in 1949. After all, it is about 58 degrees north of the Equator and only about 70 miles from John O'Groats – but in its day, which goes back to 1616, some distinguished players have been nurtured by it. Donald Ross, one of America's great golf architects, came from Dornoch. Sir Ernest Holderness, Amateur champion of 1922 and 1924, developed his game there, and very good it was; Roger Wethered, who won the Amateur in 1923 and so nearly won the Open in 1921, was another pupil of Dornoch, and so was his sister Joyce Wethered, perhaps the greatest woman player of all time. After all, didn't Bob Jones reply to the question put sixty odd years ago, 'How does it feel to be the greatest player in the world?': 'I don't know; the greatest player in the world is a woman.'

It is especially agreeable to find that Herbert Warren Wind at the end of his round was delighted by Dornoch just as I was; he says:

. . . I played an exceedingly solid round, for me, and that was important to me. Dornoch was one course I wanted very much to like, and, say what you will, you cannot like a course unless you play it reasonably well. I should imagine that Dornoch usually elicits a golfer's best game. It doesn't overawe you with its length. It supplies plenty of gorseless 'lebensraum' to err in. It keeps you on your toes by making it clear from the outset that it rewards only shots that have been well thought out and well executed. And it encourages you to hit decisive shots by providing vigorous, close-cropped turf on which the ball sits up beautifully, and very true greens, which are a joy to putt. In a word, I found Dornoch all I had hoped it would be – a thoroughly modern old links with that rare equipoise of charm and character that only the great courses possess.

NAME	YARDS	PAR	NAME	YARDS	PAR
Royal Dornoch Golf Club: Medal and Championship Card					
1 First	336	4	10 Fuaran	148	3
2 Ord	179	3	11 A'chlach	445	4
3 Earl's Cross	414	4	12 Sutherland	504	5
4 Achinchanter	418	4	13 Bents	168	3
5 Hilton	361	4	14 Foxy	448	4
6 Whinny Brae	165	3	15 Stulaig	332	4
7 Pier	465	4	16 High Hole	405	4
8 Dunrobin	437	4	17 Valley	406	4
9 Craigliath	499	5	18 Home	457	4
	3274	35		3303	35

Total 6577 yards: par 70

Chapter 3
MORE SCOTTISH COURSES

This chapter presented some problems, for if I were to stick to my original resolution and write only about courses on which I had played myself, many famous Scottish courses would have been omitted which would have been unpardonable in a book like this.

However, as I have said, Sam McKinlay, the noted golfer and writer on the game for many years, came to the rescue by allowing me to use some recent articles of his which were printed in the *Scottish Field* to fill the five serious gaps in my own list. For this kindness I am indebted to Sam himself and to the *Scottish Field*.

North Inch

The North Inch, in the city of Perth, like the South Inch, is public parkland lying along the bank of the River Tay. Golf has been played on this spot for centuries.

It would be reasonable to suppose that 500 years ago, when golf was being suppressed in Scotland for interfering with archery, this was a golf course, but records are silent. However, the Perth Kirk Session records pin-point one tolerably early date:

Nov. 19, 1599 – John Gardiner, James Bowman, Laurence Chalmers and Laurence Cuthbert confessed that they were playing at the golf on the North Inch at the time of the preaching afternoon on the Sabbath. The Session rebuked them, and admonished them to resort to the hearing of the Word diligently on the Sabbath in time coming, which they promised to do.

The clubhouse of the Royal Perth Golf Club overlooks the North Inch. This is the oldest of all the Royal clubs, older in its title even than the Royal and Ancient. The honour was conferred on the club in 1833 by King William IV. St Andrews was not 'canonised' until 1834.

Today there are eighteen holes on the North Inch, together with football and hockey fields, with a total length for the course of 5000-odd yards. There is nothing really to show that it is indeed historic turf. The ground is flat, there are a few trees; the river is on one side, with perhaps a man in waders trying for a salmon, and solid citizens' houses on the other. Various games are played, numerous golfers are on the move and dogs are being exercised; it looks not unlike Clapham Common. The length of the course has varied; in very early days there were only six holes, then nine, and for quite a time ten; thirteen holes next made the round and

---

North Inch Golf Course: Medal Card

NAME	YARDS	PAR	NAME	YARDS	PAR
1 Muirton	379	4	10 Palace	302	4
2 Witches	392	4	11 Brae	225	3
3 Fauld	411	4	12 Haugh	327	4
4 Mid Bunker	150	3	13 Tayside	417	4
5 Pond	330	4	14 Sand Hole	215	3
6 Cottars	149	3	15 Peninsula	369	4
7 Annie's Well	259	4	16 Chance	81	3
8 Burnside	246	3	17 Brig	219	3
9 North Road	276	4	18 Home	434	4
	2592	33		2589	32

Total 5181 yards: par 65

---

finally eighteen; the holes have also moved away from the city, which would be easy enough with their simple layout.

The start of the round is dreary in the extreme, flat, featureless and without rough or hazards, three holes up and down the common. As the Rev. T. D. Miller wrote at the turn of the century: 'To a stranger, at the first glance, the Inch seems sadly lacking in hazards. In the park part there is ample scope for the wildest of drives. But it is when we leave the Inch and gain the peninsula that the real sport begins.'

And that is so today, bunkers shrewdly placed, small greens and the proximity of the river, all make for good fun once out beyond the parkland. The holes at the end, the long one-shot fourteenth up to the river's edge, the 369-yard fifteenth all along it with the easy possibility of a hook into it, the short trickly little sixteenth right by the water, all these make good sport. So after a dull start and a dreary eighteenth we find we have enjoyed ourselves more than we expected, but, of course, we have not played the actual *holes* which King James VI played, but have played on the *ground* where he and his predecessors played.

The holes must have altered many times, but no matter, it is good to have visited such an historic spot. After all, the great players of a hundred and more years ago all competed here: Young Tom, Allan Robertson, Willie Park, and the most famous of the players in the town, Bob Andrews named 'The Rook'.

Nairn

Leaving Dornoch with regret and turning our backs on the links of Golspie and Brora, which might well have detained us, we retire through Inverness and then along the eastbound road which parallels the south shore of Moray Firth to the resort town of Nairn for our next game. Here I will with pleasure hand you over to Sam McKinlay as this is one of the courses I only know by hearsay from those ardent golfers Kenny Cameron and my American friend Charlie Yates. Sam writes:

Where else in Scotland, where else in the world indeed, is there a course where the line from the first tee is a mountain 60 miles and more distant? Where else can a player swing his eyes through 150 degrees and see a headland 40 miles away? And in between the peak and the headland lies a vista of mountain and foothills, of seashore and estuary, that is a rare refreshment and a solace to the player whose game has turned sour.

That is the prospect before the golfer standing on the first tee at Nairn on a fine day. To be sure, all of the first fairway and the green 400 yards away are in full view, and the more single-minded player will sight on the flag and rifle his shot down the trim track, which is comfortably wide, though the beach is near enough to the slicing side to send a shiver down the timid spine. But I am an incurable romantic on the links and would prefer to be told to aim on the left-hand peak of the Five Sisters of Kintail on the blue horizon. There is no more attractive first tee in all Scotland and he would be a dullard indeed who failed to find inspiration thereon.

Perhaps at this point I should, as the parliamentarians have it, declare my interest. I am a country member of Nairn, but only a very new newcomer, and the course captured my heart years ago when I was first a casual visitor and only later a regular if sporadic player on the links.

Nor did my affection breed on immediate if petty triumph. The course handled me very roughly indeed when first I sought to solve its problems. The whins, which are gorgeous gold in May and June, took heavy and expensive toll of my crooked tee shots. The greens, subtle in slope and variation of pace, perplexed me as they have perplexed my betters. I searched for my ball among the beach pebbles at the third and fifth, two glorious holes where at high tide you can toss a cigarette end into the sea from the tee, and I have fished my ball out of the Alton Burn which guards the seventeenth green.

In short, as must be apparent to any golfer of sensibility, here at Nairn is God's plenty for the golfer – true linksland lying within sight and sound of the sea, heather, whin, burns, the typical hazards of the best seaside courses, and all in a setting miraculous in its beauty and in a climate more favoured than most parts of these islands.

You may, if you are unlucky, be thoroughly soaked in July and August, you may, in the Spring, be seared by the east wind (though that makes the outward half easy and at least gives you a flattering start to your round); but you may also have the great joy of choosing a fine April or September day, or even a day only a few weeks on either side of Christmas, and you will play round in your shirt sleeves, marvelling at the mildness and thinking not unkindly of the man who christened Nairn the Brighton of the North.

Nairn golf course is not without its faults. Though some may claim that the ideal course is nine holes out and nine holes home, which is roughly the pattern at Nairn, as at St Andrews, that can make for two such disparate halves as to induce exasperation. And exasperation may turn to wrath and dismay when, as can happen, you slog your way out against a west wind and find, on the ninth green, that the wind has changed and you have to slog your way home against a rising nor'-easter.

All the holes at Nairn except three – the thirteenth, fourteenth and fifteenth – run either east and west or west and east. That can make for monotony and also for too kindly treatment of wild shots which find a haven on a parallel fairway (though that always happens to my opponents, never to me). There are, too, a few holes of no great distinction, and even the building of new 'tiger' tees at some holes has added only length, not quality. Again, some of the greens, such as the eleventh, are flatteringly ingathering; others, such as the thirteenth, have slopes so severe that in dry weather even the best putter plays a sort of ping pong before he finally pops his ball into the cup.

But these are small imperfections which add only savour to the round. Against them can be set some excellences not commonly found on links of even greater renown. All in all, Nairn is a fine course, wonderful alike for the holiday golfer who does not want to be examined too strictly and for the championship aspirant who expects to be put to the most severe test of his power and putting . . .

It took the Scottish amateurs a long time to find Nairn, but the Scottish professionals were more discerning. They have played their championship at Nairn frequently, but it was not until 1956, when Eric Brown won the title for the first time, that a score of

Nairn Golf Club: Medal Card

NAME	YARDS	PAR	NAME	YARDS	PAR
1 Sea	400	4	10 Cawdor	500	5
2 Achareidh	474	4	11 Gate	161	3
3 Nest	377	4	12 Table	445	4
4 Bunker	145	3	13 Crown	430	4
5 Nets	378	4	14 Kopjes	206	3
6 Ben Wyvis	183	3	15 Sutors	309	4
7 Long	494	5	16 Road	418	4
8 Delnies	330	4	17 Burn	361	4
9 Icehouse	325	4	18 Home	500	5
	3106	35		3330	36

Total 6436 yards: par 71

less than 292 was produced – and Brown, as was his wont, smashed the previous best in style by doing the 72 holes in 281. The Northern Open Tournament has, inevitably, been played many times at Nairn, the most recent occasion being in 1986, and each time the course has produced the man – J. T. Henderson, Jack McLean, John Panton, Eric Brown and Lew Taylor after a tie with Ryder Cup player George Will . . .

Nairn is a driver's course, and it is no accident that the local player with the longest record of consistently good scoring is one of the straightest hitters in the game. He is Kenny Cameron, for long in northern golf and a regular collector of my half-crown tribute. But Cameron, like other Nairn members, is notable not only for his own excellent golf. He is one of the greatest supporters of an enterprise that is unique in Scottish golf – Nairn Golf Week – which is held each year in May and is now run by the Nairn Golf Club.

The Golf Week committee bring to Nairn, at the cost of some hundreds of pounds, famous professionals who for a week give lessons to groups and to individuals, play exhibition rounds, attend and give talks and films in the clubhouse and generally stimulate interest in the game among the participants who travel to the town, often from places in England, to share in the instruction and the fun.

Of course, it is good for the town, for the hotels, the shops, the public services. But it is only splendid entertainment for the golfers, some of whom have come back year after year. This is a tribute to the quality of the professionals, such as Henry Cotton (who was in at the start), the late Dai Rees and Max Faulkner (great favourites both), Mrs Valentine, and the Nairn Club's own ex-professional, Gregor McIntosh, a Fifer with a giant frame and a sense of fun, a wonderful eye for a golfer's errors and for a golf club's good lines. His death in 1986 was a great loss.

But the success of Nairn Golf Week is a tribute also to the club members of Nairn, to the warmth of their welcome, to the comforts of their snug clubhouse nestling on the shore, and to the enduring qualities of the course itself. There is no better place for golf and golfers.

Leaving Nairn and by-passing Lossiemouth and its fine links with sorrow, we must make for Aberdeen for there are two fine links to be visited there.

Cruden Bay

The first of these is 23 miles north of the city on the coast at Cruden Bay. Originally the course was one of the attractions of a big railway hotel here, established in the days when seaside holidays in Britain were fashionable. It belongs now to a private club. It was laid out by the great Tom Simpson who regarded it as one of his major successes, so much so that he put three holes, the first, eighth and eighteenth among the best eighteen holes in the British Isles. In the words of Frank Pennink:

The first is a long two-shotter with hummocks to the right, requiring a well-placed drive, and then a second on to an angled green, bunkered in front and to the left. The safe line from the tee gives a harder second shot. The eighth, a long par three, Simpson describes as an outstanding jewel of a hole, mischievous, subtle and provocative, the element of luck with the tee shot being very high. Its green is triangular, the ground sloping away on each side, so the direction of the shot must be exact; recovery work round it is very tricky. The third of Simpson's great holes is the eighteenth, 405 yards, but seeming to play longer. Out of bounds to the left, it has a burn running at right angles across the right hand side of the fairway, and disappearing underground. The carry is a furlong from the tee; the green is severely

	Cruden Bay Golf Club: Medal Card				
	YARDS	PAR		YARDS	PAR
1	416	4	10	385	4
2	339	4	11	149	3
3	286	4	12	320	4
4	193	3	13	550	5
5	286	4	14	372	4
6	529	5	15	239	3
7	392	4	16	182	3
8	258	4	17	428	4
9	462	4	18	416	4
	3329	36		3041	34

Total 6370 yards: par 70

bunkered on the left and has a steep drop to the right.

I only wish I knew the links myself for it sounds like a wonderfully natural and secluded layout with such anachronisms as a blind par three, the fifteenth hole, and in other rather old-fashioned ways like two par threes in succession. A Tom Simpson course at its best and that is not only fun but challenging.

Royal Aberdeen, Balgownie

For a description of the Royal Aberdeen Golf Club's links at Balgownie I gratefully retire in favour of Sam McKinlay once again, for alas this piece of coast is unknown to me and judging by what we hear, more's the pity.

It was with some apprehension but also the most lively expectation that I returned to Balgownie to refresh my memory for the purpose of this piece. Was it really the great course I had thought it to be? Were the Aberdeen folk as kind as they had been to me in 1929, when a total stranger gave me a Tom Stewart mashie because, when he asked my opinion

of it, I answered truthfully that it was a beauty? Above all, would the weather be as kind as it had been in mid-winter 1927 and mid-winter 1929?

It was, they were, and it was. I chose a glorious day in mid-March, with brilliant sunshine and enough wind to be testing, and if, to be honest, the greens were altogether too keen and kittle for my rather ham-handed putting, I had a thoroughly rewarding day in the company of two excellent golfers, J. K. Hall, captain of the club, and an old university opponent from Buchan, J. A. S. Glennie.

In one respect my memory had played me false – the course was even better than I had remembered it

Left: Jack Nicklaus – 1966 Muirfield, 1970 St Andrews, 1978 St Andrews (seen with Simon Owen – 1978 St Andrews)

Gene Sarazen – 1932 Prince's

Bobby Locke with Peter Thomson – 1949 Sandwich, 1950 Troon, 1952 Lytham, 1957 St Andrews

Arnold Palmer – 1961 Birkdale, 1962 Troon

GALLERY OF OPEN CHAMPIONS

Left: Fred Daly – 1947 Hoylake

Max Faulkner – 1951 Portrush

Tony Jacklin – 1969 Lytham

Left: Sandy Lyle – 1985 Sandwich

Right: Peter Allen – At Merion where Bobby Jones won the Grand Slam in 1930

Henry Cotton – 1934 Sandwich, 1937 Carnoustie, 1948 Muirfield (seen with Lloyd Mangrum – Ryder Cup Wentworth 1953)

Gary Player – 1959 Muirfield, 1968 Carnoustie, 1974 Lytham

to be. At least – and Aberdonians appreciate candour beyond sycophancy – the first nine holes were better, much better, and the second nine not quite so good as I had thought. I would go so far as to say that there are few courses in these islands with a better, more testing, more picturesque outward nine than Balgownie. It has everything – good two-shot holes, two excellent one-shotters, one two-shotter that is only 'a kick and a spit' but both must be plumb accurate, and a par 5 second hole that must be one of the best long holes in the country.

What adds enormously to the charm of the first half of the course is that the player is never out of sight or sound of the sea except when he is in the valley. Some of the tees stand high on the dunes overlooking Aberdeen Bay, and if you have an eye for the other beauties of nature you may see and hear a raft of eider duck mewing just off the shore or a flight of whooper swans heading north for the Ythan sanctuary.

Happily, on my visit the wind was behind us going out and the worst rigours of the links were slightly reduced, but it was a different matter coming home, into the eye of the wind and sun, and I was glad that in total the second nine measured some 300 yards less than the outward nine. Even so, there were at least three holes where it was a case of 'wuid for length', and at the last, only 443 yards and a par 4, I would have liked to see the great Palmer get up in two against the breeze we encountered.

Again, as on the first nine, there are some excellent two-shot holes, one short hole (the eleventh) that demands nerve and accuracy, and another short hole (the seventeenth) that must be uncommonly easy because it surrendered to me in 2. But that will be the last 2 I have there, for a new, better short hole has taken its place. The old green was semi-blind and generously bunkered; the new green lies in full view of the player, and is ringed around with traps, also in full view. Woe betide the man who is looking for a 34 finish to break 70 – he'll have to work for his figures.

The par of the course is 70, and if there is any wind at all he would be a prudent man on a medal day who would settle for 72 and stay in the comfortable clubhouse wasting his substance on the one-armed bandit that, at Balgownie as elsewhere, is now seemingly an indispensable part of the furnishings.

Yet a few years ago, on a day of stiffish wind, one of the members, John P. Grant, so far forgot himself as to hole the course in 63 strokes in a medal competi-

tion. As the old professional whom I never tire of quoting said – 'It's no' possible, but it's a fac'.'

The previous amateur record was 68, and when I record that Grant had a putt for 61 and took three I only add to the wonder of the occasion. You could put the world's professionals on Balgownie for a whole week, aye a whole year, and Grant's record would stand fast at the end. [After Sam McKinlay wrote this, a young American college boy, John Fought, holed in 63 on the present course; he subsequently became US Amateur Champion in 1977, and later a professional.]

The course is the heart and core of any golf club, but Royal Aberdeen has distinctions that are independent of the great links at Balgownie that lie only a mile or so north of the city on the other side of the River Don. It is one of the oldest golf clubs in the world, having been founded in 1780 by the Society of Golfers at Aberdeen. But golf had been played on the links (between the city and the sea) – and on a Sunday at that – in the late sixteenth century. Half a century later the Town Council gave 'licence and tollerance' to John Dickson of Leith to make golf balls within the burgh, so the Society of Golfers might almost be accused of being dilatory in taking until 1780 to organise themselves.

Still, the date makes the Aberdeen club the sixth oldest in the world, though it was not until 1815 that the club as we know it today, without the Royal prefix, came into existence. Some of the society were original members of the Aberdeen Golf Club, so continuity was preserved, along with the original ballot box bearing the date 1780 and the president's chair, now the captain's, dated three years later.

There was, therefore, an ancient and honourable tradition lasting well over a century before that day in August 1903, when the secretary, Colonel M. M. Duncan, was informed that King Edward VII had been pleased to accord Royal recognition.

He, who was not the most patient of men, would have relished Rule XII in the Laws of Golf drawn up in 1783 by the Society of Golfers at Aberdeen – 'The Party whose Ball is amissing shall be allowed Five Minutes to search for it, after coming to the Spot where the Ball appeared to drop.' Was time, I wonder, more valuable in Aberdeen than elsewhere, that this rule, which is now universal should have been established there before it was thought of by any other club?

Aberdonians have always observed the rigour of

Royal Aberdeen Golf Club, Balgownie Links: Medal Card

NAME	YARDS	PAR	NAME	YARDS	PAR
1 First	409	4	10 Shelter	342	4
2 Pool	530	5	11 Short	166	3
3 Cottage	223	3	12 Plateau	383	4
4 Valley	423	4	13 Blind	375	4
5 Road	326	4	14 Dyke	390	4
6 Scotston	486	5	15 Well	341	4
7 Blackdog	375	4	16 Hill	389	4
8 Ridge	147	3	17 Pots	180	3
9 End	453	4	18 Home	434	4
Outward nine	3372	36	Inward nine	3000	34
			Outward nine	3372	36
			Total	6372	70

the game in a manner that would have delighted Mrs Battle, and to this day there is chuckling over an incident in that 1929 Scottish championship. The fourteenth hole at Balgownie has a ditch running athwart the fairway just about the range of a long drive. In one tie in the championship an Anglo-Scot hit a long one from the tee which his opponent, perhaps too young and too eager, chose to recall because, he said, the Anglo-Scot had teed his ball in front of the markers.

'Surely, I'll play another,' said the unwitting offender, 'but I think I ought to tell you I'm probably in the ditch.' 'No matter,' was the stern rejoinder, and the other drove again, this time to a safe place – and the first ball was in the ditch. But the upholder of the rigour of the game had the last laugh, for he won on the home green.

That championship was only one of many played at Balgownie. Many times it has housed the Scottish amateurs, the Northern Open is regularly played there in April, and the British Boys were there in 1935. I insist that it deserves to be better known because it is a great golf course belonging to a club with its roots deep in the best traditions of the game. Besides, the sun always shines there.

There is an attractive short course also with a par of 62 for those who want to pause from 'the full rigours'.

Montrose

The links at Montrose is like many in Scotland, a public course on common land with a number of private clubs, four here, with their clubhouses near the course. The playing of golf at these places – and St Andrews, North Berwick and Carnoustie are similar – is far older than the banding together of groups of players to form clubs.

Golf has been played at Montrose, 'from time immemorial' and in 1785 the golfers of the town successfully induced the burgh council to stop the ploughing and enclosing of the common land which was encroaching on their rights to play golf. The oldest of the Montrose clubs, the Royal Albert, was formed in 1810, and maintains a close relationship with Royal Blackheath with a match played each year, home or away. There are two courses at Montrose but it is with the medal course that we should concern ourselves, the other being a relief course on flat land. The medal course on its present site is comparatively new; a much older layout to the west in the days when golf was less stereotyped than now had a round of no less than 25 holes.

Like many seaside links, the medal course gives hardly a sight of the sea as the coastline is shut off from the flatter ground inland by a range of tumbled sandhills and dunes covered with rough coarse grass. The outward nine is laid out in, as it were, the foothills of the coastal range and provides links golf at its most typical, with narrow rolling humpy fairways, greens in dells or on plateaux provided by nature and supplemented by man with a liberal sprinkling of pot bunkers. The inward nine is on much flatter ground nearer the town and, as so often happens, is the longer and the harder half.

There are only three par threes, one of great quality and menace and one of almost extreme length and difficulty. On the other hand there are two short par fours which in favourable circumstances can be reached from the tee, but not on the same day.

A drive at the first encounters a minefield of bunkers on the flat and then you go up into the sandhills with the second shot. Next is a two-shot hole with a quite prodigiously tumbled billowy fairway. The third, at 156 yards from a tee in the sandhills across a wasteland to a green perched on a summit above a deep hollow, with no vestige of what could be called fairway, is one to make the best of us scratch his head if there be any wind across, indeed any wind at all. The green gives positively no welcome. After a brief descent into the plains, we go back into the hills at five with a hole of 288 yards with the green hidden in a hollow, where a following wind gives hope of driving the green. But as so often happens on the folded ground of linksland we may get a bad break which denies the shot what we think it deserved. But that's why we play golf. By the seventh we are at the end of the course with two holes, a par five and a four with again fine

---

Montrose Golf Course: Medal Card

NAME	YARDS	PAR	NAME	YARDS	PAR
1 Scurdy	393	4	10 Girdle	382	4
2 Bents	390	4	11 Mid Road	440	4
3 Table	156	3	12 Pouderie	153	3
4 Butts	363	4	13 Gates	323	4
5 Hillock	288	4	14 Curlie	416	4
6 Sandy Braes	478	5	15 Wilderness	524	5
7 Whins	372	4	16 Gully	234	3
8 Valley	331	4	17 Rashie's	415	4
9 Jubilee	444	4	18 Dean's Drive	349	4
	3215	36		3236	35

Total 6451 yards: par 71

seaside fairways. Turning with the eighth we can get home here in one, but the favouring gale needed is almost the opposite of that we have to have at the fifth, and a bunker guards the entrance. The half ends with a long tough par four towards the prevailing wind.

We now head away from the hills towards the town on the flatter ground, but the tenth with its domed green does anything but gather the ball and eleven is a long, long way. The twelfth could, I suppose, be said to be the easiest of the short holes but a huge cross bunker lies across the entrance and a small pot gathers anything with hook. There is a cross bunker in front of the green at the thirteenth also, but the shot here is not very long.

After working back towards the hills we have to face a gruelling finish. The sixteenth is no less than 234 yards; it is against the prevailing wind, there are three pot bunkers guarding the entrance on the right and one on the left. Then if you do succeed in hitting the green, a three is by no means assured, for the green is full of severe folds and slopes. A big brute this one. So is the seventeenth, for that runs in the same direction; the green is quite small for a hole of 415 yards and lies on a steeply-banked plateau or rather shelf as the ground to the left, which contains some menacing whins, rises slightly. The eighteenth looks more innocent but the green is surrounded by five bunkers, all too close to the 'prepared surface'.

So ends a fine course, not too well known outside Scotland, but after all, it is within an hour's drive of St Andrews, which everyone visits. The Scottish Professional Championship has been played here, victories going to Harry Bannerman and in 1970 to Ronnie Shade, whose death at the age of 47 in 1986 was a great loss to golf.

Rosemount

Still keeping to the east of Scotland, I am calling again on Sam McKinlay, this time to do justice to what he calls the best inland golf course in Scotland at Rosemount near Blairgowrie. I played here myself, but so long ago that the course has been altered by an entirely new second nine and so is not the one I played on then and memory, too, is dim after sixty years. So an up-to-date description by Scotland's leading golf writer is a far better account than I could render.

It was with something of the feelings of the poet Wordsworth visiting Yarrow that I recently returned to Rosemount after a lapse of seventeen years. Would the course be as good as I had thought on that day of unexpected felicity? Would the very short fifteenth hole still be the only real weakness? Would there be the same sense of wonderful isolation as between the hole you were playing and the holes fore and aft of it, for it has been one of my cherished memories of Rosemount that even when the course was comparatively busy you saw only the couple in front and the match behind? Each hole was played in its own avenue between the pine and birch trees – the hole behind and the hole in front were a world away.

None of the illusions was shattered. It was, admittedly, a golden August day, with not a breath of wind, a hot sun beating down from a blue sky, with the heather at its best, with the birches just beginning to run, a red squirrel busy at the second hole gathering its winter store of fir cones, a cock pheasant whirring into flight only a wedge shot from the fourth tee, and all the world placid and benign. And when I drilled two woods on to the green at the 450-yard first hole and began with a model four I would have been almost content to cry 'Hold, enough'.

That, of course, would have been to deny myself a very great pleasure. To be sure, I putted like the auld sweetie wife of legend and my score was many strokes more than that I had recorded in 1947. My partner, Gordon Kinnoch, the local professional, was kind enough to suggest that the greens were not at their best. After all, almost all of them had suffered so severely in the winter before that they had to be lifted and re-sown. But they have fared wonderfully well and, apart from a little meadow grass that should not be difficult to eradicate, they present an excellent putting surface and are quite up to the standard of the crisp moorland turf that constitutes the fairways.

This turf is a most important ingredient of the course. It makes for easy walking, and 6600 yards is really quite a long walk. It never dries out as hard as seaside links or parkland clays and although my visit came at the end of three weeks without rain the ball did not scamper along the fairways like a scalded cat. The par fives – and there are at least three – needed 'twa guid paps wi' wuid' and a bit more. The long two-shotters, of which there are about half a dozen, demanded wood or a big iron for the second shot. In all I played wood for my second shot six times, and this, if you please, on one of my good driving days.

So Rosemount is a man's course, all right, but it is not so demanding as to be a misery for frailer vessels. There are no severe carries from the tee so that the man – or woman – who can knock the ball out a respectable distance encounters no difficulty at all, provided he steers clear of the odd lofty pine which a wise designer has left growing in mid-fairway at some holes.

The fairways are generously wide, which may account for my having had a good day with the driver, and the greens are accommodatingly large, which may have had something to do with my puny putting. If the course has a serious weakness it lies in the short holes, which are well spaced through the round but are rather unequal in quality.

The most difficult is the former fifth of 219 yards, which needs either a very big iron or a wood, and the most attractive is the 168-yard seventeenth, played across a valley to a two-tiered green on which it is possible to bring the ball squirming back the way Gary Player does in the TV matches. The sixth is a straightforward shot of 189 yards to a comfortably big green and the fifteenth is only some sort of pitch to a half-hidden green that has no particular merit.

But there are so many glorious holes that it would be churlish to lay too much emphasis on the lack of character of the one-shotters. More than half of the holes, excluding, of course, the short ones, are dog-legged, some of them quite sharply. This naturally puts a premium on accurate driving, and the man whose eye is in can greatly reduce the rigours of the second shot – and its length, too – if he can park his tee shot on the appropriate spot. There are no blind holes, no hills to climb (the course is quite flat but has enough small undulations not to appear flat) and the orientation is such that a wind has to be mastered from many points of the compass.

Rosemount lacks something of the grandeur of the Gleneagles Hotel courses. It is only about 200 feet above sea level, compared with its rival's 500, and it does not have, therefore, the glorious vistas of the other. But I for one would willingly surrender the distant scene for the nearer beauty; there is a peculiar charm in playing each hole down its own green avenue flanked by the heather and pine.

My preference is widely shared. Rosemount attracts golfers from a wide area, and the club very wisely has set itself out to cater for them as for its own myriad members. Situated only a mile or so south of Blairgowrie, it is fourteen miles from Perth, less than twenty miles from Dundee, and therefore draws its membership from a populous and prosperous golfing district. It has a handsome clubhouse, much better appointed than most, excellent changing rooms, dining and lounge accommodation, and Gordon Kinnoch's shop is a model of what a pro's should be but rarely is.

This concern for the creature comforts of members and visitors is part of an old tradition. When the club was founded in 1889 on land leased from the

	Blairgowrie Golf Club,					
	Rosemount Course – Medal Card					
	YARDS	PAR			YARDS	PAR
1	444	4	10		507	5
2	339	4	11		500	5
3	220	3	12		293	4
4	408	4	13		401	4
5	551	5	14		512	5
6	189	3	15		129	3
7	371	4	16		475	5
8	368	4	17		165	3
9	326	4	18		390	4
	3216	35			3372	38

Total 6588 yards: par 73

Meiklour estate of the Marquess of Landsdowne, after whom the original nine-hole course was named, the committee of the day not only put up what was at the time described as 'a pretty rustic club-house', but they also 'had the foresight to include stabling'. The stables are gone, needed no longer, but there is today a spacious car park, and the registration numbers proclaim the diversity of places from which the players have come to match their games against the green and to refresh their spirits among the pines. I swear I won't wait another seventeen years till I return to Rosemount. It is, I am persuaded, the best inland course in Scotland.'

A tough new 18-hole course, the 'Landsdowne', was added in 1974 to the design of Alliss and Thomas. The first, and sixteen through eighteen are holes from the old Rosemount course.

Lansdowne Course, Blairgowrie					
	YARDS	PAR		YARDS	PAR
1	486	5	10	379	4
2	375	4	11	366	4
3	454	4	12	407	4
4	367	4	13	371	4
5	167	3	14	211	3
6	391	4	15	440	4
7	448	4	16	363	4
8	533	5	17	552	5
9	153	3	18	402	4
Out	3374	36	In	3491	36
			Out	3374	36
			Total	6865	72

Gleneagles

We must not leave this part of Scotland without a visit to Gleneagles, if only that to the golfers of the outside world it is better known and more visited than anywhere in the British Isles except St Andrews; every American golfer has heard of St Andrews and 99 per cent of them have heard of Gleneagles.

Well, there are many things in its favour, first of all a superb setting in a shallow valley between the Ochill hills to the south and foothills leading up to the Grampians to the north. On a fine day in early autumn there is no more beautiful place in the world to play golf, none, not any. Then there is a spendid hotel – that is if you can afford it – with excellent food and service, shops and all the amenities. Incidentally, you can eat at the Dormy House down by the courses at half the price.

But how about the golf, or should we say gowff? It is not especially difficult, but it is not meant to be, either on the King's or the Queen's course, and the same can be said of the new shorter courses, the Prince's, par 63, and the Glendevon, par 67. On the big course, the fairways are wide and smooth, the greens large and the bunkers do not intimidate. It is fairly long and the pull uphill on the King's from the second green to the sixth can be a weariness of the flesh if the wind is in your teeth. The *look* of the courses is excellent and they are beautifully kept; they flatter you delicately. Nevertheless, there are some highly picturesque and delightful holes on the King's, where the tournaments are played, like the exhilarating drive downhill at the second, the blind shot over the hill at the third, the long pull up to the fourth, the short fifth, with a domelike green like a man's bald head amid bunkers and the drive and iron at the ninth. Coming in, there's the big 260-yard belt over the hillocks and hazards to the green at the fourteenth and a superb big-two-shotter immediately preceding it.

To end on a sour note, I must declare that I find the Scottish ballyhoo with which Gleneagles is larded revolting. The holes have

---

Gleneagles, King's Course: Medal Card

NAME	YARDS	PAR	NAME	YARDS	PAR
1 Dun Whinny	362	4	10 Canty Lye	445	4
2 East Neuk	405	4	11 Deil's Creel	230	3
3 Silver Tassie	377	4	12 Tappit Hen	387	4
4 Broomy Law	465	4	13 Braid's Brawest	446	4
5 Het Girdle	160	3	14 Denty Den	260	4
6 Blink Bonnie	476	5	15 Howe o' Hope	457	4
7 Kittle Kink	439	4	16 Wee Bogle	133	3
8 Whaup's Nest	158	3	17 Warslin' Lea	376	4
9 Heich o' Fash	351	4	18 King's Hame	525	5
	3193	35		3259	35

6452 yards: par 70

---

been elaborately named with such efforts as the 'Heich o' Fash', the 'Warslin' Lea', the 'Wee Bogle', and others which you can't bring yourself even to try to pronounce.

Gullane

Moving now to the east coast of Scotland east of Edinburgh, we should spend a week if we can, for there is a rich profusion of beautiful links, of which, after Muirfield, which came into the previous chapter, the best is perhaps Gullane No. 1 (pronounced Gillan by the way), though proponents of New Luffness, with its superlative greens, or historic North Berwick might not agree.

However, I have to come down for Gullane No. 1, if only that I had a flashy lucky round there some years ago with three birdies in the first six holes. The No. 2 course is rather shorter than No. 1, though both of them have been used for Open Championship qualifying rounds, while No. 3 is distinctly shorter. They all have this in common, though, excellent turf and greens and a climb up Gullane Hill. This is well worth the effort, for the view from the top on a fine day is a wonderful sight; Muirfield links spread out like a map on the right, the Firth of Forth ahead, with distant hills beyond to the north, Aberlady Bay running away to the left towards Edinburgh, of which the main features and even the Forth bridges can be seen in clear weather. And all around at your feet acres of fine turf, emerald greens with their flags and links merging with links for miles.

The course is a good deal hillier than many seaside links because of the great hump of Gullane Hill, but, apart from the second, fifth and sixth, the climbing won't bother you too much and you have some enjoyable shots downhill to compensate, like those at the seventh and the seventeenth. There are four short holes, of which two stick in my memory, the 142-yard fourth, where I hit the stick with an outrageously overhit shot over the guarding cross bunker and so got an undeserved two,

---

Gullane Golf Club No. 1 Course: Card

NAME	YARDS	PAR	NAME	YARDS	PAR
1 First	304	4	10 Thucket Knowe	470	4
2 Windygate	378	4	11 Maggie's Loup	472	4
3 Racecourse	498	5	12 The Valley	478	5
4 Island	142	3	13 Hole Across	165	3
5 Murray's Hill	445	4	14 The Shelter	430	4
6 Roundel	325	4	15 Pumphouse	538	5
7 Queen's Head	400	4	16 Traprain	187	3
8 King's Chair	364	4	17 Hilltop	384	4
9 Corbie	152	3	18 Kirklands	359	4
Out	3008	35	In	3483	36

Total length 6491 yards: par 71

---

and the attractive plateau green of the 165-yard thirteenth cocked up in the sandhills.

Another memorable hole is the seventeenth, where you drive downhill and quite probably downwind and then find yourself confronted by three huge bunkers in a ridge guarding the green with no way round.

North Berwick

Moving along the coast from Gullane past Muirfield and Dirleton, with its castle and excellent restaurant, we must pause for a round on the West Links at North Berwick, a private club with a charter that requires it to permit visitors to the town to play at a reasonable fee, and good and famous golf it is. Some of the qualifying rounds of the Open Championship are played here.

You start with a tricky hole, 'Point Garry Out', for although it's only 324 yards long you can drive too far and get into an unattractive gully about 210 yards from the tee leading down to the shore, so you must be careful or you will spoil your pitch up to a high green once shared with the seventeenth, 'Point Garry In'. The green is a malevolent one, sloping to the sea. The second hole, the 'Sea Hole', along the coast is alarming for if you go for a proper line to enable you to get home in two, and you slice it ever so little, you are on the beach again. Then follows a long par four which necessitates hitting your second shot over a stone wall, a rather dull hole this.

The fourth is 'Carl Kemp', a stiff iron shot to a green amid bumps, humps, bunkers and even a few rocks. Then a moderate length two-shotter bending to the right, followed by another short hole, the 'Quarry', over a great pit with bunkers in it. So to number seven, a difficult 354-yarder, for the green is guarded very closely by the Eil or Eel burn, for which the hole is named; don't underclub here – I did the first time and paid dearly for it. With two rather moderate holes, a par four and a par five, we are out at the end of the links.

We turn for home with a tightly-bunkered par three, hitting down from a tee in the sand-hills. Then a 515-yarder hugging the sandhills on the left-hand side of the fairways leading to a small plateau green. A dog-leg 374 yarder takes us back close to the shore and after that the fun begins. The thirteenth, the 'Pit', is 348 yards long, the second half of it flanked on the left by a stone wall about three feet high. The fairway is on one side of the stone wall and ultimately the long narrow green on the other. If you have driven cleverly up the left side of the fairway your pitch will be almost along the line of the wall and up the length of the green, very good. But if you drive right of centre, then you are pitching more or less across the line of the green, which is all too near the beach for comfort. Then you have to do something clever or else exceedingly skilful. I had beginner's luck here, for on hard ground my ball bounced over the wall and on to the green, which annoyed my friend Gibb exceedingly, as well it might.

The fourteenth is 'Perfection', a drive-and-iron hole of 377 yards. You drive on to a fairway, which cants to the right off the slopes of a big sandhill; if you hit a bad slice you may be among 'Carl Kemp's' rocks. However, if you are on the fairway then you blaze away with a completely blind shot over a big hill running across your front, aiming at a tall marker on the very beach itself. The green looks perilously near the shore and no doubt people have been known to putt into the sea, certainly hit their approach shots into it.

The fifteenth is the most famous hole at North Berwick, the 'Redan', a big thump of 191 yards over a hill to a plateau green set diagonally across the line of play and guarded by a huge deep bunker under the left-hand side of the escarpment of the green and lesser bunkers on the right. This hole has been copied, or rather imitated, innumerable times in the United States, notably at the National, at the Links Club and at Merion East, always with the feature of the green on the plateau or shelf at an angle to the line of play with the deep encroaching bunker lying under its flank. Well, I don't know what's the matter with me, but I found the hole at North Berwick totally unsatisfactory, as it is masked by a great hump about 125 yards from the tee which completely spoiled the look of the hole as well as blinding it. If the hump were bulldozed away the hole would be no easier and far better. Alas, for one of the great disappointments of a golfing life! Indeed I

North Berwick, West Links: Medal Card

NAME	YARDS	PAR	NAME	YARDS	PAR
1 Point Garry Out	324	4	10 Eastward Ho!	161	3
2 Sea	453	4	11 Bos'ns Locker	515	5
3 Trap	459	4	12 Bass	374	4
4 Carl Kemp	171	3	13 Pit	348	4
5 Bunker's Hill	378	4	14 Perfection	377	4
6 Quarry	161	3	15 Redan	191	3
7 Eil Burn	354	4	16 Gate	383	4
8 Linkhouse	467	4	17 Point Garry In	423	4
9 Mizzentop	489	5	18 Home	270	4
Out	3256	35	In	3042	35

Total 6298 yards: par 70

found the so-called 'Redan' at the National Golf Links of America, while barely recognisable as an imitation, a much better hole.

The sixteenth is a curious hole, with its green close under the windows of the Marine Hotel. You drive over the wall and have to watch that you don't go into the ditch about 210 yards out; you then play over some bunkers with about a five-iron to a green which even Trent Jones would think was eccentric in shape; two little plateaux joined by a narrow neck formed by a deep gully, but all mown putting surface; how you putt from one plateau to the other I wouldn't know.

Seventeen, 'Point Garry In', is a long, long par four, uphill at the finish, of 423 yards; the hole has a reputation for terror as the small green slopes sharply towards the sea and there is a big cross bunker seventy yards short of the hole.

Finally, we hit home to a plateau green 270 yards away and, of course, hope here for a three to finish; however, the slopes of the plateau tend to shrug you off, so you may be disappointed. There's a story of a young pro in his first tournament saying to his caddie, 'I don't need a driver; I'll go over the green if I hit it', to which the caddie replied dourly, 'Ye'll no hit it'.

Among the charms of North Berwick is the scenery, the coastline being enhanced by the Bass Rock and several rocky islets and the Forth with its shipping.

Southerness-on-Solway

It is now time to cross to the western side of Scotland and start our tour there right on the border, on the Solway Firth over which we look south to the links of Silloth and the hills of Cumberland beyond. Here we must make a brief reference to the links at Southerness-on-Solway on the Dumfries shore; not only is this a beautiful place with views along the coast of Galloway and inland to the mountain of Criffel, but also across the Solway to the mountains of the Lake District, and on a clear day even to the Isle of Man. It is also an attractive natural links; more distinctive, it is one of the few golf *links* to be built since World War II.

It was laid out on a flat area of sandy soil with some heather to the design of Mackenzie Ross and it gave the impression that not much money had to be spent on it. It is all the better for that, for like the old links of the last century, use has had to be made of natural hollows and dells and plateaux and shelves for greens and tees and the bunkers are often scars and scrapes occurring naturally in the thin turf. Wind-eroded bunkers are not uncommon and sometimes give you a bad lie. But it is a delight-ful, natural golf links with some absolutely charming holes.

The erection of a new clubhouse in 1974 on a new site meant that instead of the course going straight out and back, it is now virtually in two nines, with what was the sixth hole becoming the first.

The present sixth hole of 407 yards is crossed by a burn and with a strong east wind many drives end in the water. Look out also for the twelfth, an outstanding par four of 419 yards, a dog-leg to the right presents a tough drive, with a bunker on the left and two on the right, and, having escaped these, the approach is to a green in a hollow, with the sea beyond, and for too bold a shot, the chance of finishing on the beach, which is not out of bounds. In the Scottish Amateur in 1985, a gentle breeze gave way to gales, and the green was unreachable in two. Experience told as David Carrick took the title.

This is a fine finishing stretch. A dog-leg sixteenth calls for an accurate drive, with whins on the left and heather on the right, and a prevailing wind coming in slightly from the left, leaving a long second shot, with a ridge ahead of the green, making the distance deceptive, with many approaches short. It is followed by a fine short hole to a long plateau green, and then a par five to end the round. Don't miss a game here if you are in the neighbourhood.

Near Southerness, indeed within less than a mile of the links, John Paul Jones, Admiral and sea rover, was born. He threw in his lot with the American revolutionaries in 1775 and during the ensuing war harassed British shipping off our own coasts as far afield as Lowestoft. Later he took service with Catherine the Great of Russia as Kontradmiral Pavel Ivanovitch Jones and eventually died in reduced circumstances in France. He also gave his name to a dance which is practised to this day.

Southerness Golf Club: Medal Card

	YARDS	PAR			YARDS	PAR
1	396	4		10	166	3
2	453	4		11	392	4
3	408	4		12	419	4
4	169	3		13	467	4
5	494	5		14	458	4
6	407	4		15	218	3
7	214	3		16	433	4
8	368	4		17	174	3
9	430	4		18	485	5
	3339	35			3212	34

Total 6551 yards: par 69

Western Gailes

Working our way north to the famous links of Turnberry, Prestwick and Troon, we must include at least one more of the slightly less-known links, which gives us a hard choice. The one I would finally pick is Western Gailes. The links of the Western Club at Gailes on the Ayrshire coast lies between Troon and Irvine, hard by the Glasgow club's links also at Gailes, with which it is sometimes confused. Both of these are among the finest courses in Scotland, though less renowned than some, for few major titles, other than the Scottish Amateur and Professional Championships, have been contested here, though in 1972 the British Ladies played the United States at Western Gailes for the first time. Since 1973 it has been a qualifying course for Open Championships played at Troon and Turnberry.

Western Gailes runs in a big loop out from the clubhouse, first to the north, then with a long run to the south among the dunes close to the shore, and then a final turn back northwards for the last five holes to the finish. There is an abundance of fine sandhills, and several of the greens, like the first, are in delightful natural dells or saucers. There are only three short holes, but none of them easy; the seventh is a tough shot through a gap in the sandhills to an unwelcoming green, while the thirteenth has a

Western Gailes Golf Club: Medal Card

	YARDS	PAR			YARDS	PAR
1	318	4		10	334	3
2	441	4		11	454	4
3	392	4		12	456	4
4	398	4		13	151	3
5	461	4		14	562	5
6	503	5		15	197	3
7	204	3		16	408	4
8	392	4		17	449	4
9	327	4		18	386	4
	3436	36			3397	35

Total 6833 yards: par 71

burn to call to the aid of all its bunkers. The third, fourth and fifth were rebuilt on new land in recent years after the erection of a bridge across the railway, giving two holes just under 400 yards, and the fifth of 461 yards running south, a testing hole, with sand dunes down the right.

Sam McKinlay, our well-known helper, wrote: 'Western Gailes occupies a place in the affections of Scottish golfers that cannot be explained solely on the grounds of its undoubted quality, its superb situation, or the creature comforts which it furnishes. To the connoisseur of the game it represents something approaching the ideal in golf.'

When on the pilgrimage to Troon, Prestwick and Turnberry, try to spare time for a round at Western Gailes; you will be repaid.

Prestwick St Nicholas

Prestwick St Nicholas is a fine seaside link's, right down by the shore in fact, to the south of the town with as old a history as that of its famous neeighbour to the north.

The club has an interesting story, of which more in a moment, having originally shared the use of the Prestwick Club's links. Then after a number of moves the club came to rest on its present site in 1892. Since then Charlie Hunter's layout has altered comparatively little and for today's hitters its length of 5926 yards looks much too short. But many of the holes are of full length and the par of 68 was not made to look more ridiculous by Tony Johnstone's 63 in the qualifying rounds for the 1986 Open than Turnberry's full length by Greg Norman's 63 in the Championship itself. I think this bears out the belief, which I share, that for tournament play, great length for a course is no protection against low scores. The conspicuous holes are those around two worked-out quarries now full of water, the seventh, the eighth recently lengthened, the ninth and the tenth. The sixteenth has a formidable bunker in front of the tee and a

Prestwick St Nicholas: Medal Card

NAME	YARDS	PAR	NAME	YARDS	PAR
1 Well	342	4	10 Lady Isle	165	3
2 Bruce	172	3	11 Pladda	414	4
3 Maryborough	281	4	12 Pans	217	3
4 Dyke	420	4	13 Tam Jack's	456	4
5 St Nicholas	406	4	14 New Prestwick	412	4
6 Bellrock	326	4	15 Kingcase	276	4
7 Midfield	454	4	16 Coila	379	4
8 Quarry	360	4	17 Grangemuir	301	4
9 Cock O'Bendy	318	4	18 Home	227	3
	3079	35		2847	33

Total 5926 yards: par 68

full blooded all-carry par three eighteenth is reckoned one of the toughest in the West of Scotland.

Originally named the Mechanics Club it was formed in 1851 four months after the old club with Tom Morris, who had come to Prestwick from St Andrews as Head Green Keeper, as a moving spirit. It was intended to cater for golfers who were not elected to the exclusive Old Club. The artisan nature of the club soon disappeared and the name was changed to St Nicholas, after the Patron Saint of Prestwick, in 1858.

Up to 1877 the two Prestwick clubs shared the same links but congestion increased and the St Nicholas Club was given five months to move out. A new course was laid out, but two days before opening the title was found defective and the club had to leave its new abode – though it was allowed to play its opening competition before leaving. Another site was found at once and a twelve hole course was laid out, subsequently to be one of the first full-scale Ladies' Courses, when St Nicholas moved in 1892 to its present site.

Machrihanish

We near the end of this chapter with reluctance and the sure knowledge that much more should have been included, but one more true links we must have and that is Machrihanish, one of the most remote courses in Scotland, situated on the open Atlantic at the toe of the great peninsula of the Mull of Kintyre, lying between Arran and the Hebrides. Alas, I don't know it, so once more I have appealed to Sam McKinlay, who knows it well, to allow me to use one of his articles for the *Scottish Field*. Here is what he says:

Old Tom Morris is said to have remarked of Machrihanish that 'Providence assuredly designed this part of the country as a special earthly Paradise.' He was a pillar of respectability so no one could accuse him of being influenced by the fact that in Campbeltown nearby a score of distilleries were then operating, to the benefit of local employment and the larger refreshment of the wider world. Old Tom took all his refreshment on the links, in the laying out of which he had a hand. Today Machrihanish is still a paradise for golfers, and although Campbeltown's distilleries have shrunk in number, there is no part of Scotland where a golfer can find greater contentment than at the south end of Kintyre.

To be sure, some of the social glories of Machrihanish have departed. In the years before the First World War and immediately afterwards it ranked

almost with North Berwick as the most socially acceptable golfing resort in Scotland. In those days it had the special charm of remoteness. Except for the rare and adventurous motorist who was prepared to face the rigours of the old Rest and Be Thankful climb and the less spectacular but hardly less exacting hills at Clachan and Whitehouse, every golfer heading for Machrihanish had to go by sea to Campbeltown and then make his way across the peninsula by hired vehicle or, for a period, by a light railway that served the village. It was a long and costly journey compared with which today's trip by plane or motor car is swift and cheap. Now that we have a much better road it is possible to reach the course, play and return in a day to central Scotland. Yet such was the fame and appeal of Machrihanish in those far-off days that the Scottish women golfers held their championship there as long ago as 1909, and they were back again four years later. Twice again they went to Machrihanish after the First World War, but after their visit in 1927, they did not return until 1966, but they are due back in 1990. The Scottish professionals broke new ground for them by taking their championship to Machrihanish in 1964 – and were enchanted, alike by the course and by the hospitality of the members and indeed the whole Kintyre community. So much so that they returned in 1969.

There has always been something in the air of this part of the world that makes for enjoyment. As early as 1881, when the course was only five years old and was still known as the Kintyre Golf Club, it was reported that 'the links have been visited by parties from all the chief headquarters of the game who have pronounced the turf and course excellent'. Before the end of the century Machrihanish was proclaiming itself 'the finest of all links' and one chronicler recorded that 'Poet after poet has sung its charms'.

So far, I, a diligent admirer of the place, have been unable to trace the laudatory verses, but no doubt they exist, although any poet might be hard put to find a rhyme for Machrihanish. That name, by the way, came into golfing currency a dozen years after the club was founded. Kintyre, it was felt by some members, was a rather dull name for a romantic and exciting golf course, and the change was effected at the September meeting in 1888 'in consequence of some members preferring the sonorousness of the word Machrihanish'. How right those members were, and if you doubt me take your stance on the first tee at Machrihanish on a fine summer morning and look around you.

Already, I have eulogised the first tee of the Nairn course, but Machrihanish wins the palm for beauty and excitement. The hole itself is a wonderful two-shotter, and fit to be included, as it has been, in some wise observers' symposium of the best holes in golf. The tee is on a modest eminence overlooking a small burn that runs into the sea only a duffed drive distant. The Atlantic rollers pound on the rocks immediately behind the player's back as he takes his stance. On his hooking hand runs the start of six miles of strand, one of the finest beaches in Britain. If he is brave and skilful he can bang straight at the flag a quarter of a mile away, but that means a carry of nearly 200 yards over beach and bent. If he is timid, or prudent, or just one of the weaker vessels, he has an easy if longer way round.

Let him hit a good one and then he can lift his eyes to Gigha lying to the north, or to Jura and Islay to the north-west and west. If he has eyes only for golfing country and is a stranger to the links, he will be enchanted by the lure of the terrain. To be sure, he will find as he makes his way round that what seems the best and most obvious golfing country is hardly utilised to the full. There is lots of wonderful territory lying between the course as it now is and the sea, and no doubt if there were money enough the energetic people who run the club would take in some of this country and make a course fit for golfing heroes to play on. But what they have at their disposal is good enough in all conscience – a course that, as one

observer has put it, is 'beautiful golfing ground full of hills and dells which has not been overmuch modernised, and is perhaps none the less lovable for that'.

This observer has put his finger on the strength and weakness of Machrihanish. There are too many blind holes to satisfy the purist, who likes to know precisely where he is going, and that is a weakness, albeit an engaging one. There are humps and hollows which produce some awkward stances and lies, another weakness by modern thinking but, to my mind, a pleasing test of a man's spirit and skill. Then there are some greens with slopes so severe, as at the second, as to make putting something of a lottery, especially when the putting surfaces are keen and kittle. There are others, such as the third, which are so in-gathering as to reward many an ill-directed stroke. And that's another weakness, but, again, a delightful one, especially if your own play has been flattered thereby.

Again, you can drive at some holes across a whole parish and find an excellent lie, and so the wild hitter profits when, by rights, he ought to be penalised. That, I am assured, was one reason why R. T. Walker won the Scottish championship with a sparkling last round of 65. On many another course his crooked tee shots would have left him struggling: at Machrihanish he was merely inconvenienced to the extent of having to attack the green from an unusual angle.

Machrihanish, then, is not a severe academic test such as Muirfield, or so demanding of accurate tee shots as Nairn, or so majestic as Dornoch. But it has charm and romance and beauty overlaid on turf so naturally perfect for playing golf that no wonder one nineteenth-century writer, who was skilled in these matters said, 'the turf in its nature is an improvement on that of Westward Ho! Every ball is teed, wherever it is.' That was true 90 years ago and it was true when I revisited the links after an absence of several years.

One particular quality of the turf is that the course, being spared the tread of thousands of feet that beat down St Andrews, for example, into something like concrete in high summer, has retained its spring even in a dry spell. The ball sits up asking to be hit, and when you clip an iron shot up comes a divot the size of a small pancake, not a sheet the size of a crumpet.

In short, golf at Machrihanish is holiday golf at its best, difficult enough to test the tiger with ambitions to break 70 but not so difficult as to reduce to tears of frustration the tiger's wife who plays off 24 or more at Little Mudheap. And Mrs Tiger, whether her husband likes it or not, can play the live-long day, for, although the course is reviving in popularity, Machrihanish is only a tiny village with two or three small hotels, a few boarding houses and only a little private accommodation. Thus, if you present yourself on the first tee around 9 o'clock even on a sparkling morning in July you will be singularly unlucky if you have to wait more than a few minutes before driving off. In any case, the first tee is within clear view of every bedroom in Machrihanish that has an outlook to the sea and you can time your arrival on the tee to the appropriate minute.

The evenings are a different affair, for the club has a very lively local membership drawn in the main from Campbeltown, and there may be some congestion after tea, but only for a short time. This local interest has endured from the earliest days. Indeed, the manner in which the club was founded is in itself remarkable. A meeting of eight people was held on 11 March 1876, at which it was resolved that a club should be formed for the purpose of playing golf in the vicinity of Campbeltown. It was also agreed that the 15th should be the first day for play. Has any golf club, I wonder, come into existence one day and begun playing on its own course four days later? Exactly four weeks later the club played its first

medal competition, the medal having been presented by the first captain, Captain John Lorn Stewart.

All down the years there is evidence in the minutes of the club of the same energy and liveliness of spirit. I like in particular an entry for October 1888, only a month after the club changed its name and a year after Tom Morris had been called in to advise on improving the lay-out. It is reported that, in addition to the medal, 'the following prizes were reported to be played for at the autumn meeting next day'!

Silver butter cookers from the Captain
Grouse, hare, and rabbits from Captain Macneal
Five pairs rabbits from Mr McKersie
Cigar case from Mr Greenlees
Two clubs from Mr Pearson
Club from Mr Chalmers
One dozen balls each from ex-Provost Greenlees, Mr S. Greenlees, and Mr D. McCallum

Then there follows the intriguing comment which conceals untold treasures of fun and games – 'In view of such an attractive list the committee revised the handicaps with, if possible, more than usual anxiety.'

There have been only three professionals at the club in more than 100 years, all of them of the local Thomson family. The most famous son, Hector

---

Machrihanish Golf Club: Medal Card

NAME	YARDS	PAR	NAME	YARDS	PAR
1 Battery	423	4	10 Cnocmoy	497	5
2 Machrihanish	395	4	11 Strabane	197	3
3 Islay	376	4	12 Long Hole	505	5
4 Jura	123	3	13 Kilkivan	370	4
5 Punch Bowl	385	4	14 Castlehill	442	4
6 Balaclava	315	4	15 The Hut	167	3
7 Bruach More	423	4	16 Rorke's Drift	233	3
8 Gigha	337	4	17 The Burn	362	4
9 Ranachan	354	4	18 Lossit	315	4
	3131	35		3028	35

Total 6159 yards: par 70

Thomson, won the Amateur Championship at St Andrews in 1938. He is now a professional in Greece.

That most estimable Scottish lady champion, Belle Robertson, nee McCorkindale, comes from these parts, winner of every important international event and a pillar of the British and Irish teams.

Killermont

Near the close of our circuit of Scotland, I feel that one of the many urban courses of renown should be included and where better to go than to Killermont, the urban home of the Glasgow Golf Club, and how better than to draw for the last time on the kindness of Sam McKinlay:

Your true golfer is a romantic at heart, if only because he is heir to an ancient tradition. Yet for me, the most romantic association of the Glasgow Golf Club is not with the great golfers of the past but with one of the greatest non-golfers of our own time. The association is in a sense tenuous and an accident of geography, but for me it is real enough.

When the golfers of Glasgow in 1904 ended their long pilgrimage at Killermont, their delightful parkland course on the north-western outskirts of the city, they had reached their fifth home. In the earliest days they had played on Glasgow Green, their golfing endeavours broken from time to time by the harsh realities of the wars with Napoleon and the prior claims on their energies and golfing ground of volunteering and drilling. Then, after a long interregnum, the revived club played on Queen's Park for a year or two before moving across the city to Alexandra Park. Later they moved farther east and north to Blackhill, now covered by a rash of houses, and finally they settled at Killermont.

The choice was in its own way romantic. In the early years of the century the committee thought the time had come to seek fresh fields. Various open spaces were inspected without success until on Sunday two of the prospectors, Daniel Sinclair and Charles Murray, on an afternoon walk along the banks of the Kelvin beyond Maryhill, saw across the turgid waters of what used to be a salmon-bearing stream, 'a far stretching sward, diversified by graceful groups, and handsome single specimens, of oaks and beeches'.

This was the promised land, and negotiations were begun forthwith with the laird, the Rev. J. E. Campbell Colquhoun of Garscadden. He was not at all well disposed towards a project of turning his beautiful estate into a golf course, but the persistence of Sinclair and the more tolerant views of the laird's son combined to make him relent. The deal was clinched, and the ancient Glasgow Golf Club came into possession of a course worthy of its long history.

Now here is the ring of romance. To the list of honorary members of the club were added the names of the laird and his son, and the laird's address is given as Chartwell, Westerham, Kent, famous as the home of Sir Winston Churchill. We golfers of Glasgow may therefore claim to have had some influence, however slight, on the life of the man who, more than any other, made it possible for us still to enjoy the delights of golf at Killermont and all around the world.

True, the Killermont which was opened in 1904 with splendid ceremony by the Lord Provost of the day, Sir John Ure Primrose, Bt, with a silver-mounted cleek and a new Haskell ball teed by the famous 'Fiery' of Musselburgh, was different from the green and pleasant course we now know. There were more trees, especially around the clubhouse, though visitors may be ill to persuade of the truth of that claim. The avenue leading to the clubhouse was fenced on either side, a hazard which no longer exists to ruin a good score at the last hole. The course was shorter by some hundreds of yards, but Old Tom Morris, who laid it out, made a fine job of the last work of the kind he undertook.

The pattern of the course has remained essentially unchanged. A new tee here, a new green there, may have added length, variety, and a slightly different orientation; but Old Tom clearly had a fine eye for country, even for country so different from St Andrews, and although it is possible to fault the layout of Killermont, it is beyond question a most agreeable course and not nearly so simple as it looks. Even the professors, the gladiators of the game, have never succeeded in making a fool of the course on the rare occasions when professional tournaments have been played here.

Maybe the flanking trees are intimidating. The 'graceful groups and handsome single specimens' of oaks and beeches have been rattled down the years by thousands of golf balls. They have tried tempers and ruined scores, and though some have had to be removed for safety's sake, more than enough are left to justify the original description of the scene that so captivated the discoverers of Killermont more than half a century ago.

My own acquaintance with Killermont goes back a very long way, to a notable day in the history of sport – none other than Derby Day 1919. As a small boy I trekked across the city to see the first day's play in a professional tournament organised as part of the golfing victory celebrations to mark the return of peace after the First World War. And, because, on that day I saw for the first time Vardon and Braid, Taylor and Duncan, and many others besides, golf became my game, and Killermont my most cherished course; and so it has remained.

Killermont does not set itself out to be a great golf course, a supreme test of golf, a breeding ground for giants. Rather is it the perfect course for the business-man-golfer seeking refreshment in an evening round or mild week-end exercise. If he is of sterner stuff, he can flex his muscles at Gailes, where the Glasgow club have had a course since the nineties of last century. Gailes can be very fierce, especially in a wind out of the south-west, for there is flanking heather at nearly every hole, making the course a fine test of driving, and the greens are smallish and often perched on plateaux, putting a premium on accurate approaching.

Gailes is a most useful corrective to the mellowness of Killermont. Though equally well groomed it has in its very nature asperities unknown at Killermont, and the younger members of the club in particular do well to submit themselves to the examination it sets.

It is not, however, for its golfers of distinction that the Glasgow Club is namely in the annals of the game. Great players there have been, as might be expected in a history stretching back to 1787, which year the club modestly claim to be the date of origin. As early as 1780 the town council gave official permission for the playing of golf on Glasgow green, the directory of 1783 lists the members of the Silver Golf Club, and the club records show that in 1786 a

player named John Gibson made a series of measured drives with a feather ball, the longest being 222 yards and the shortest 182 yards. There are many members of the club today who would gladly do equally well with all the modern appurtenances that lend adventitious inches to our golfing stature.

The first really great player in the club's history, I suppose, was James Robb, who won the Amateur Championship in 1906, but truth compels me to admit that he was entered from Prestwick St Nicholas. There has been no other Amateur champion till Reid Jack won the title at Formby in 1957, but there has been no lack of famous names. Around the turn of the century the Bone family were renowned, George Hutchinson (later to become captain) was a mighty player, and probably the best of the lot was Robert Scott, one of six members of the club who have played in the Walker Cup match.

Scott had the distinction of matching shots with the great R. T. Jones in the foursomes at Garden City in 1924. He and his partner, another Scott, the Hon. Michael, were square with Jones and W. C. Fownes with one hole to play. The last at Garden City is a one-shotter, and it was Robert Scott who played a tee-shot that Jones could not equal.

I have left to the last the greatest of all – William Doleman – born in 1838 and therefore well into middle age before the Amateur Championship was established, but he played in nearly every championship until 1911, and in 1910, when 73, won his first-round match at Hoylake. By that time his eyesight was so poor that he carried field glasses with which to pick out the flag on the green, and then he relied on a wonderful memory and a true swing. In his early years he was a sailor and was a combatant in the Crimean War, which may have accounted for his resolution and physical resilience. He was a small man, but he had a handsome head, and his grave, bearded face looks down on the beardless members of today from an honoured place on the clubroom walls.

It is difficult, therefore, especially at Killermont, to escape the sense of history pervading the club. The silver clubs with silver balls attached, the true mark of an ancient golfing foundation, are handsomely housed in special cases. The trophy cabinet has something of the magnificence and diversity of its counterpart in the Royal and Ancient clubhouse at St Andrews. But there is one trophy the like of which is to be found nowhere else in the world. It is the

Tennant Cup, the oldest golfing trophy in existence for open competition among amateurs under medal conditions. It was presented by Sir Charles Tennant in 1880 to mark his captaincy the previous year. That was five years before the Amateur Championship was first played for. Small wonder that every right-thinking golfer in Scotland would almost as soon win the Tennant Cup as win the national title – and several have done both, including a recent holder, Dr Frank Deighton. [Sam McKinlay modestly refrains from telling us that he won the Tennant Cup in 1932. So here it is for the record.]

I like to think that the original 22 members who played on the miry Green, dodging the lines of washing, would feel at home on the manicured perfection of Killermont and the equally trim links at Gailes. The stately mansion house which serves as clubhouse is a good deal more palatial than the changing hut they used, but they would not feel ill at ease, for some of them must have lived handsomely in spacious homes. But they were gowfers a', and that is what really matters.

I can't resist adding the following quotation in the austere prose of the *Golfers' Handbook* to Sam's account:

A magnificent beech tree with a trunk five feet in diameter, which governed the approach to the fifth green at Killermont collapsed when hit by a ball driven by one of the members. It occurred during the 1939–45 war. There was hardly any wind to disturb the tree. When the ball hit the tree it was in full foliage and, for a moment or two the tree trembled and then slowly collapsed. The story is told that it was the ball that knocked this tree down, but it may have been top heavy. During the German blitzing of Clydebank, two land mines came down about two hundred yards away, the tree was in the direct line of the blast of one of them and the windows and doors of that side of the clubhouse were blown in. Bombing may have affected the tree, but certainly it was immediately following the blow by the ball that the tree fell down.

To mark its bi-centenary in 1987, a comprehensive history of the club is to be published.

Glasgow Golf Club, Killermont: Medal Card

	YARDS	PAR		YARDS	PAR
1	273	4	10	424	4
2	244	3	11	173	3
3	405	4	12	423	4
4	158	3	13	252	4
5	525	5	14	383	4
6	439	4	15	476	5
7	336	4	16	141	3
8	302	4	17	295	4
9	346	4	18	373	4
Out	3028	35	In	2940	35
			Out	3028	35
			Total	5968	70

Glasgow Golf Club, Gailes: Medal Card

	YARDS	PAR		YARDS	PAR
1	344	4	11	419	4
3	427	4	12	178	3
4	414	4	13	324	4
5	528	5	14	483	5
6	143	3	15	152	3
7	410	4	16	414	4
8	341	4	17	365	4
9	304	4	18	437	4
Out	3251	36	In	3961	35
			Out	3251	36
			Total	6447	71

The Royal Burgess Golfing Society of Edinburgh

The Royal Burgess Society, founded in 1735, is accepted as the oldest golf club in existence, as, although its records only go back to 1773, there is every reason for believing the earlier date is correct. It therefore takes precedence over the Honourable Company of Edinburgh Golfers who date from 1744 while the Royal and Ancient at St Andrews can only claim the bronze medal with its foundation in 1754. When the Edinburgh Burgess' Society had reached its two hundredth anniversary in 1935 the captain of the club was the Prince of Wales, although it had attained the Royal title six years earlier.

In the early days, Edinburgh clubs, the Royal Burgess, the Royal Musselburgh and the Honourable Company, used to play on public ground on Bruntsfield Links beneath the rock on which Edinburgh Castle stands. This is indeed historic turf and an even earlier golfer, Mary, Queen of Scots, played here in the sixteenth century. There is still a primitive form of golf played on this ground in the form of a rather dreary pitch and putt course. Later the founding fathers of Edinburgh golf moved out to old Musselburgh Links where there were and still are nine holes laid out inside the racecourse. This became too crowded and indeed disagreeable, so the clubs migrated further out and built their own courses.

In the 1890s, the Edinburgh Burgess club built a fine inland course at Barnton on the parkland of the Cramond Regis estate near the Edinburgh city boundary which was once a Royal hunting lodge. The Royal Musselburgh club moved out to a park course at Prestongrange House at Prestonpans and the Musselburgh club, a different society, moved to Monkton Hall, a parkland course nearer to Musselburgh. Also at this time the Honourable Company of Edinburgh Golfers abandoned Musselburgh links in 1891 and moved to Muirfield.

Robert Clark, who wrote *Golf, a Royal and Ancient Game* in 1875, was tenant of Barnton House before the Edinburgh burgesses acquired it. He had some holes cut, including one which required a drive right over the house. As Bernard Darwin said:

Barnton is pure golf, still it has undoubtedly many merits, and not least among them is that the greens are as good and true as any in the world . . . The course lacks nothing that the hand of man could do for it. Nearly all the holes want good straight accurate play; but as is the case with this type of golf, they make no passionate appeal to the imagination.

The Edinburgh Burgess Society were the founders of the Boys' Championship played for the first time in 1921; the winner Donald Mathieson is, we hope, still going strong; his brother, I remember, was in the Oxford team when I was at the University myself.

In the post-war era, Bernard Gallacher won the Scottish Professional Championship here in 1977 with a score of 282 which implies that the course is no flatterer.

			Royal Burgess Club: Championship Card			
	YARDS	PAR			YARDS	PAR
1	396	4		10	385	4
2	322	4		11	366	4
3	440	4		12	320	4
4	465	4		13	205	3
5	175	3		14	395	4
6	484	5		15	435	4
7	440	4		16	482	5
8	169	3		17	454	4
9	420	4		18	252	4
	3310	35			3294	36

Total 6604 yards: par 71

Chapter 4

LONDON, TO THE SOUTH

The problem of this chapter and indeed of the whole book is how does one decide what to leave out. The *Golfer's Handbook* lists over 50 clubs in the London area without venturing much beyond Kingston and Croydon, and the Society of London Golf Captains, which is particular in keeping its boundaries to a distance of twenty miles from Hyde Park Corner, admits the captains of over 100 clubs.

I have to say that, for my choice, the courses most worthy of admission are those farther out, amid the heather and pines of the sandy stretches of otherwise useless heath, with which Surrey and Berkshire are so liberally provided. Just as I enjoy golf most of all on the linksland by the sea and think that here the best

golf is to be found, so, inland, the heather-and-pines courses are to my mind supreme. This chapter, therefore, will embrace few courses in the London area itself, but cover a number which are within easy reach of town, allowing a day's golf – once 36 holes, now I suppose 18 – and give the visitor time to get back to change for dinner or the theatre. By this choice, we shall alas lose the classical parkland course of the Royal Mid-Surrey club in the Old Deer Park of Richmond, once the home course of the famous John Henry Taylor who did so much to raise the status of the golf professional in the early years of the twentieth century, as well as winning his share of the Championships.

Royal Blackheath

We must, however, lead off with Royal Blackheath, as it is without question the premier club in Britain outside Scotland, if not in the world. It is a strongly-held tradition in the club that the Society of Blackheath Golfers was formed in 1608 by the Scots who swarmed into England when the thrones were united in 1603 under James I. There is no reason to doubt that golf was played on Blackheath about this time or even earlier, the difficulty is to establish the

date of formation of the *Club*. Records were destroyed in a fire at the end of the eighteenth century and the earliest facts that can be established are that on 16 August 1766 a silver club was presented to 'the Honourable Company of Goffers at Blackheath', while written records start with a list of subscribers of 'The Goff Club at the Chocolate House at Blackheath' for 1787. This list shows almost all the members to be Scots though the treasurer bears the sound Sassenach name of Kensington.

Golf on the stony common land of Blackheath survived in the old primitive form well into my lifetime and only ceased when the first world war broke out. Originally, there were five holes which avoided the gravel pits then being worked on the heath, but from 1844 a new layout of seven holes which traversed the worked-out gravel pits was made. These holes, bearing in mind the powers of the feathery and later the gutty ball, must have been a sore trial for they measured 170, 335, 380, 540, 500, 230 and 410 yards. It is small wonder that the course record made by Mr A. S. Johnston in 1910 with a rubber-cored ball was 95, or eleven over fours for twenty-one holes, at a time when most 18-hole course records were below seventy.

The best professionals of the day, J. H. Taylor, James Braid, Harry and Tom Vardon, played a medal competition over 21 holes at Blackheath in July 1908. JH won the prize with a score of 96 – equivalent to 82 for 18 holes – Braid and Tom Vardon took 97 and brother Harry scored 99. In the afternoon in a fourball Tom Vardon did one round in 28, a remarkable score.

When golf became impossible on the open heath, the club amalgamated with the Eltham Golf Club and withdrew to its present site on Crown land in Eltham Park. Here the club, with its incomparable collection of trophies, pictures and china, is suitably housed in Eltham Lodge, a superb seventeenth-century house built by Hugh May for Sir John Shaw, banker to Charles II in 1663. This gives a proper atmosphere which so important and historic a club should have, for the course, a good parkland circuit with fine trees and a lake, laid out by James Braid, cannot with the best will in the world provide it.

It is for this reason that attention and interest are inevitably aroused more inside than outside the clubhouse.

The club's trophies are a splendid array, including the Spring Medal, originally the gold medal of the Knuckle Club (the old Blackheath Winter Club) which dates back to 1792, the silver club of 1766 and the newer one to accommodate the silver balls affixed by the captains after the old one was full. There is also a fine collection of eighteenth-century china, including punch bowls and four joram jugs which hold about a gallon, used no doubt for claret to pay the fines, forfeits or bets of the members.

The pictures are attractive, including the almost lifesize portrait of Henry Callender by Lemuel Francis Abbot in red coat, white knee breeches and silk stockings which is found in reproductions in many parts of the world. He was captain in 1790, 1801 and 1807.

The most famous of all golfing pictures, that of William Innes, captain in 1778, painted by Abbot in 1790, is lost, and if it turned up one day, and stranger things have happened, what a find that would be for the club. Meanwhile, like thousands of golf clubs all over the world, Royal Blackheath has to be content with a print. Who hasn't seen it: Innes with a proud look in the uniform of a past captain, red coat, white knee breeches and silk hose, buckle shoes and a fine big black hat worn at a jaunty angle with a club over his shoulder? Behind is his 'college man' or caddie in a tricorn hat with a bundle of clubs under his arm and a bottle in his pocket, wearing the dress of a pensioner of the Royal Naval Hospital; in the background is a windmill. One theory is that the picture still exists immured in a private collection in Fife; another belief is that it was destroyed in the Indian Mutiny.

Most appealing is the painting of Old Alick, born in 1756, who served under Nelson at Trafalgar. Alick Brotherson was a caddie until it was minuted in October 1833 that 'it was proposed and carried that poor old Alick's allowance be increased to 2s 6d per week and that he be restrained from carrying clubs and confine himself to taking care of the holes'. Here is the dear old man in breeches and a top hat carrying two iron clubs with windmills and players in the background.

The most famous player at Blackheath was

George Glennie from St Andrews, who was captain in 1862–64 and hon. secretary from 1868 to 1886. Glennie, who presented a medal to the club, which in turn presented a replica to the Royal and Ancient, held the amateur record at St Andrews from 1855 to 1879 with a score of 88.

Glennie and Lt J. C. Stewart of the 72nd Highlanders won the first golf championship ever played when eleven clubs – Blackheath the only English one – competed in a foursomes knockout tournament at St Andrews on 29th, 30th and 31st July 1857. The results were these:

FIRST ROUND

Royal Blackheath beat Royal Perth by 8 holes
Edinburgh Burgess beat Montrose Royal Albert by 12 holes
Edinburgh Bruntsfield beat Prestwick by 3 holes
Royal & Ancient beat Dirleton Castle by 10 holes
Innerleven beat Musselburgh by 2 holes
    North Berwick, a bye
The Honourable Company of Edinburgh Golfers and Panmure failed to turn up and scratched

SECOND ROUND

Royal Blackheath beat Innerleven by 12 holes
Edinburgh Burgess and Edinburgh Bruntsfield halved
Royal & Ancient beat North Berwick by 4 holes

THIRD ROUND

Royal Blackheath beat Edinburgh Bruntsfield by 6 holes
Royal & Ancient beat Edinburgh Burgess by 3 holes

FINAL

Royal Blackheath beat Royal & Ancient by 7 holes

Thus the fine silver claret jug came south, though there is no record of whether the winning pair played each other for the trophy and the champion's title. Next year a singles tournament was played at St Andrews and the youngest entrant, Chambers, beat the oldest, Wallace, in the final.

While we are still at Blackheath it may be of interest to list those golf clubs which were formed in the eighteenth century. The palm for the oldest golf club seems to go nowadays by common consent to the Edinburgh Burgesses, who have a firm date of 8 April 1773 from written records but the club is known to have existed earlier, its Chronicles claiming 1735. The Honourable Company of Edinburgh Golfers is next with the date of 1744 and The Royal and Ancient at St Andrews comes third dating from 1754. The Edinburgh Brunstfield Club dates from 1761 and takes next place and then comes Blackheath with its silver club of 1766.

Remaining dates are:

Musselburgh	1774	Glasgow	1787
Aberdeen	1780	Dunbar	1794
Crail	1786	Burntisland	1797

Here is the card for Royal Blackheath today, with which I would like to record the exceptional help given me by Royal Blackheath's captain, secretary, field marshal and members, with lavish hospitality.

Royal Blackheath Golf Club: Medal Card

	YARDS	PAR		YARDS	PAR
1	473	4	10	349	4
2	386	4	11	376	4
3	428	4	12	180	3
4	197	3	13	523	5
5	348	4	14	377	4
6	482	5	15	348	4
7	374	4	16	174	3
8	158	3	17	400	4
9	357	4	18	284	4
	3203	35		3021	35

Total 6224 yards: par 70

Addington

After Blackheath we will next play Addington, a bare ten miles from the centre of London and two from bustling burgeoning Croydon with its skyscrapers. I had hoped to somehow be able to work in the couplet:

'Pitt is to Addington
What London is to Paddington'

but have failed to find a good excuse. Addington is a true sandy, heather course, with pines and birch and an astonishing air of solitude for its location. It was laid out by J. F. Abercromby, one of Britain's greatest architects, in 1914, and a second course, alas no more, was added after World War I. Many proclaim that the New course was the better of the two, but I have only a hazy recollection of it in the 'twenties and in any case it has gone now to make a housing estate and we must content ourselves with the fine course that remains.

Abercromby liked short holes and Addington has no fewer than six, starting the round with quite a difficult but not very exciting one uphill. The others are splendid, notably the elusive seventh and the full hearty thump of 225 yards from a high tee across a 'vale of tears' up to the rising bunker-beset green at the thirteenth. Henry Longhurst, in the club handbook, swears it to be 'with the exception of the fifth at Pine Valley, near Philadelphia, the greatest one-shot hole in inland golf. To see a full shot with a brassie, perfectly hit and preferably with a new ball, sail white against a blue sky, pitch on the green and roll up towards the flag, is to know the sweetest satisfaction that golf has to offer. The fact that this may not happen more than once in twenty times is irrelevant!'

For my taste, the long two-shot twelfth, which many dislike, is a fine and attractive hole at which you have to hit a really big second across a valley and up to the plateau green and, again quoting Longhurst, 'if you happen to hit it, you will never forget'. The drive, though, is awkward; the fairway slopes gently down and then more steeply to a level platform. Too short a drive gives you a hanging lie and too long a one puts you over the platform and into possible trouble. The hole has the attraction to me of relying entirely on the humps and folds of the ground without a single bunker.

One day in the mid 1950s we were entertaining a Japanese mission to discuss 'Terylene' licensing, led by the venerable septuagenarian, Mr Takahata. At lunch he said, 'Twenty years ago, before the war, I used to be a member at Addington; how I would love to see it and play it again.' My friend Todhunter said, 'That's easy, I'm a member, we'll go tomorrow', which they did. As they entered the bar, the steward without a moment's hesitation said, 'Ah, Mr Takahata, how nice to see you again; it must be some years now since you were here.' The day was made.

The Addington Golf Club: Medal Card

	YARDS	PAR		YARDS	PAR
1	166	3	10	385	4
2	557	5	11	134	3
3	212	3	12	472	4
4	437	4	13	225	3
5	442	4	14	362	4
6	387	4	15	432	4
7	150	3	16	496	5
8	412	4	17	185	3
9	358	4	18	430	4
	3121	34		3121	34

Total 6242 yards: par 68

Royal Wimbledon

Golf has been played on the stony heath of Wimbledon Common since the officers of the London Scottish Regiment formed their club with a seven-hole course in 1865, a year after Westward Ho! There they play to this day on a hard uncompromising piece of common land amid the gorse and birch trees, sharing the course with the Wimbledon Common Club, who have to play in red coats lest the public be alarmed. Each club, however, has its own premises at opposite ends of the course, the only example I know of such an arrangement. Oxford met Cambridge here for the first time in 1878 and the match was played here sixteen times in all.

The Royal Wimbledon club also played on the common until 1907 when they migrated to their own grounds next door, to a more kempt course designed by Willie Park although they continued to play on the common as well until 1915. H. S. Colt modified the new course in 1924; there are fourteen holes laid out on higher ground with gorse heather and trees, including the dell and rampart of Caesar's Camp, where the Roman Army had a garrison, into which we play at the sixth and tenth and out of it at the seventh and eleventh. The other four holes are on lowlier meadowy ground which is less attractive.

The upper holes have an extraordinary seclusion, seeing that they are only eight miles or so from Hyde Park Corner. The holes that appeal to me most at Royal Wimbledon are the first, a

Royal Wimbledon Golf Club: Medal Card

	YARDS	PAR		YARDS	PAR
1	405	4	10	476	5
2	426	4	11	455	4
3	382	4	12	455	4
4	401	4	13	161	3
5	164	3	14	455	4
6	261	4	15	421	4
7	500	5	16	390	4
8	221	3	17	138	4
9	282	4	18	341	4
	3042	35		3258	35

Total 6300 yards: par 70

very sharp dog leg to the right and a mighty difficult opening four, three of the short holes and the 261-yard sixth into Caesar's Camp which, it was believed, was holed in one for an albatross by the Prince of Wales when he was captain of the club in the twenties. This, in fact, turned out to have been a hoax by the caddies involved in the game and a confederate lurking out of sight near the green.

The short holes of special merit, I think, are the fifth, thirteenth and seventeenth, each of which has a carry with substantial difficulties for a missed shot and attractive bunkering round the greens.

Coombe Hill

Just across the valley, and the Kingston by-pass, about a mile from Wimbledon heath is Kingston Hill, which harbours hidden amongst its trees and slopes the Coombe Hill course, another surprise at this close distance to London; heathland again, with many fine trees and rhododendrons and some rather severe slopes. The course is another of J. F. Abercromby's and most enjoyable I always find it. It is not too tough except for some of the climbs. Bing Crosby said it was 'perfect for those of us without the physical strength of yesteryear'.

The club has always had a distinguished pro in its shop, Sandy Herd, Arthur Havers, Henry Cotton and Dick Burton, all Open champions, Archie Compston, Ken Bousfield and many others. I once had the pleasure of a round here with Arthur Havers many years ago. He gave me six shots and beat me by one hole in 2 hours 20 minutes, holing the course in 70 to my 78. I dare say he could have won more easily if he had needed to.

You lead off with two par fours, both downhill, which gives you a cheerful start; neither is very long and you really ought to start four, four. And so you should, for the going now gets much tougher. Three is a longer par four on the flat with an elusive plateau green and this is followed by a dog-leg five out to the end of the course. Then uphill with a big heave and immediately we come down again with a par three to a green well below the tee.

A shortish par four on the flat follows and then at eight it's uphill work again for a difficult 418 yarder towards the clubhouse. The half ends with the short ninth across a valley with a bunker in front ready to grab a short one.

The tenth is another tough par four, but at least it is downhill and immediately after comes an excellent four hole whose slight plateau green is hard to find.

The twelfth is a good stiff iron shot with a bad

			Coombe Hill Golf Club: Medal Card		
	YARDS	PAR		YARDS	PAR
1	320	4	10	440	4
2	368	4	11	408	4
3	407	4	12	186	3
4	510	5	13	314	4
5	452	4	14	341	4
6	180	3	15	494	5
7	346	4	16	400	4
8	418	4	17	145	3
9	184	3	18	390	4
Out	3185	35	In	3118	35
			Out	3185	35
			Total	6303	70

fall to the left of the green, a hole I have always made a mess of, but the next two, short par fours both, I have always liked, especially the pitch to the fourteenth with its small green among the humps. Fifteen, driving downhill, is a big one with trees on the right to carry if you want a chance to beat home in two. The sixteenth is sharply uphill again, very tough to make in four; seventeen is a short shot across a hollow and the last, home on the flat.

St George's Hill

It is now time to get on down the Portsmouth Road, leaving out, alas, that fine park course at Burhill, and make for Weybridge and St George's Hill. The course is one of the first combinations of golf course and private residential estate in this country and the golf, like that at its neighbour Burhill, was laid out by Harry Colt in 1913. I find it a most admirable course – though some do speak a little of hilliness – with two well-balanced loops ending outside the clubhouse and a third shorter loop of nine for lesser occasions. The only criticism I

make is of the clubhouse itself, which had the misfortune to emerge after reconstruction as a battlemented castle in red brick replacing a three-storeyed thatched building of some distinction.

Big events have taken place here in the old days. In 1924 the *News of the World* professional Match Play Championship was played here and it was then that I first saw professional golfers at work. I remember being much impressed by their practice swings with the sole of the club slapping the turf in a brisk and assured manner. Like a fool I omitted to follow Harry Vardon in the play – though I saw him plain – and went after newer and lesser heroes like George Duncan, Abe Mitchell and Charlie Whitcombe. Ernest Whitcombe won that year, beating George Gadd in the final.

Also in 1924 at St George's Hill was the first half of the 72-hole challenge match in which Duncan and Mitchell beat Hagen and Macdonald Smith for a stake of £200 a side. In 1925 Mitchell beat Archie Compston over 72 holes for £200 and in 1926 was the famous £1000 Hagen and Mitchell match. Abe had been four up after the first day's play at Wentworth. Hagen kept Mitchell waiting next morning, knowing, I suspect, how nervous a man his opponent was, and then took command of the game and won by two and one.

Now for the golf; the first hole takes us over a dip with a roadway and some rough to a high rising fairway, from which we pitch up to a green on a saddle in the hills. Then comes a big tough two-shot hole with some help downhill on the drive. The third is not the most spectacular of the four short holes, but I suspect it is the most difficult as the green is divided by a ridge so that a ball on the wrong side is very difficult to put close to the hole. When the hole is cut on the side of the green near the big bunker on the left, the hole can be a very difficult three.

The fourth is a very short par four with a triangular green surrounded by sand over which you must hit a most delicate pitch; you can easily lift your silly head and fluff it into the bunker.

Five is a modest par four uphill to a corner of the woods and then come two big holes, the sixth of 466 yards downhill towards Brooklands motor track of immortal memory and the Vickers works where the 'Wellingtons' were built. The seventh is uphill all the way to where a big lone pine marks the site of the green.

The short eighth is one of the most spectacular holes in golf. You can play down over a valley of rough to a hill in the face of which are four of the most alarming bunkers you can imagine – the dominant one on the left side of the entrance of extreme size. Above these sits the green which doesn't look big enough for its job. However, a well-hit four-iron will do it all right. The club handbook says that Bernard Darwin was believed to have included this hole in his symposium of an ideal eighteen-hole round. At any rate, it is fit to be included with those at Pine Valley, which St George's Hill so much resembles. The ninth, a modest dog-leg par four, comes rather as a relief.

Driving off from the clubhouse again we have a really good two-shot hole of 431 yards to a partly masked green and then another spectacular short hole of a mere 117 yards with the green on a shelf with hill to the left, a fall to the right and a ravine in front and behind. At this hole I once nearly achieved the supreme fluke as I hit my tee shot full pitch into the hole; the ball left its mark in the rim of soil just above the tin and below the green surface, but the clank with which it hit the pin was ominous and sure enough the ball kicked out and lay dead.

The twelfth is an attractive drive-and-pitch hole with a beautiful line of pines threatening on the right. A longer par four takes us out to

St George's Hill Golf Club: Medal Card					
	YARDS	PAR		YARDS	PAR
1	380	4	10	431	4
2	465	4	11	117	3
3	197	3	12	348	4
4	269	4	13	424	4
5	385	4	14	210	3
6	466	4	15	537	5
7	480	5	16	436	4
8	175	3	17	414	4
9	370	4	18	388	4
Out	3187	35	In	3305	35
			Out	3187	35
			Total	6492	70

the end of the course and then a short hole comes across before the run-in. This consists of a big par five of 537 yards, two very tough fours, the sixteenth with a plateau green and finally another shot uphill to the 388-yard eighteenth rather like the ninth in front of the clubhouse.

Of all the inland courses of Britain, I think I like this one best and I believe that Colt said that this was his favourite work. It is not the toughest inland course – Walton Heath is that – or as well known as Sunningdale, but for variety and beauty to my mind it has no equal.

Walton Heath

I think we might turn now to what I believe to be the toughest of our inland courses, Walton Heath, which was my home club for more than ten years. It lies twenty miles due south of London and is 650 feet up on the North Downs, so that every breeze that blows is on hand. It is open heathland golf in the widest sense, even more now than a few years ago, as a lot of intrusive thorn trees and bush have recently been cut down to restore its former bareness.

There are two very fine courses here, and, as happens so often, the New course, good as it would be anywhere else on its own, is just slightly inferior by comparison with the Old – and about three shots easier – so that it gets scant praise and less than it deserves.

Both courses at Walton Heath were laid out by Herbert Fowler, the Old in 1904. The Old course has been altered many times and I believe that only seven of Herbert Fowler's original holes survive. Nevertheless, from what I remember of the course in its earlier state, the style has remained the same. The most recent changes have been forced by the construction of the M25 road which encircles London. This has made it necessary to provide two new holes at the top of the course.

Walton Heath sets out to be, and is, totally uncompromising: the fairways are narrow when they should be narrow and the rough is rough. Walton Heath's heather has been notoriously tough for years, with encroaching bracken at times providing an even worse rough and killing the heather as well. Cross bunkers are plentiful, and all, including those that don't compel a carry, are deep and steep

faced. The greens are often just cultivated and mown terminations to the fairway, full of subtle slopes and borrows, difficult to judge and approach to, fast and hard to read. Luckily, they are as true as velvet. Altogether, Walton Heath sets as strict an examination in golf as any course in the United Kingdom.

It is also very good for your golf; you don't have to fear it, just respect it. If you can drive straight you won't do too badly; you just have to learn to drive straight. One thing is certain: if you play regularly at Walton Heath, any other course you go to will seem easy. In the evening of my golfing life, when I was in my fifties, it had a most invigorating effect on my poor game, so that for about five years I was playing as well as I ever had in my life, which I attribute entirely to this course and some tough games there.

The name of James Braid, five times Open champion, is indissolubly linked with Walton Heath, for he was the professional there for forty-five years until he died in 1950, aged eighty. He used to go round regularly and ritualistically in his age or less on his birthday and his vigorous austerity was a good match for that of the course.

Patric Dickinson put this well:

Perhaps it is fanciful, but Walton Heath itself seems to be very like James Braid, for it is strong and modest, positive and forthright, yet never ostentatious. Walton Heath, by saying nothing, will give an opinion of your golf. If you ask for an opinion you will get one and there will no mincing matters.

Many tournaments have been played here,

the English Close Championship twice, and the *News of the World* Match Play Championship many times; indeed it came to rest here until the new owners of the newspaper abolished it.

More recently, the European Open Championship was played at Walton Heath in 1978 and 1980 with wins for the USA, with winning scores averaging around 71, and again is back in 1987. The Ryder Cup, Europe against America, was here in 1981. The Americans were exceptionally strong that year and although we were slightly ahead at the end of the first day they took a commanding lead on the second day and finished us off in the singles.

Well, then, praying for a good day of driving straight, let us go out and sit the examination. The first hole, unfortunately, is soon to be abandoned, which is a pity, but keeping it in the round does not fit in with modern traffic conditions on the main road, which you have to cross from the green to present second tee. It was, and for the moment, still is a very short par 4 of some 300 yards in a little annexe to the heath; there is a pond in front of the tee, but most people don't know it's there. However, unless you hit your drive to the right spot on the left, you have a tricky pitch to a green that runs away from you, over the protecting bunkers.

It is a less innocent hole than you'd expect and makes a good nineteenth in a match, as I well remember one evening in the Heathens' Foursomes competition. Our opponents on leaving the fifteenth green had unwisely said, 'That makes us dormy three, I think', to which my friend and partner, Maurice Allom, replied, 'Oh no; it makes you three up and three to play', and he then proceeded to hole four putts of highly doubtful length, one a long one, to win the match for us at the nineteenth.

The second was a most difficult hole, a par four of 445 yards or more off the back tee, for it had a great gully of humps and heather right across the fairway about 250 yards from the tee; you played short, of course, and then usually had a full wood shot off a hanging lie to get you anywhere near the green. Now two thirds of the gully has been smoothed out and mown and, in my opinion, it is not nearly as challenging for the ordinary player as it was.

The third can be driven, but usually isn't unless the tee is forward; it is flat with the green merging into the fairway. Flat, too, is the fourth and it can be reached in two, but very often is not.

The golf now begins with full rigour. The fifth is a lovely two-shotter, driving downhill to play up to a bunkered green on a slight plateau, a very pretty hole. The sixth isn't pretty, it's just long and straight, with a bunker to catch a slightly pulled drive just where you don't want it. You can always feel delighted if you do this and the fifth in four.

The seventh, soon to be the sixth, is one of the hardest short holes I know, especially with the greater length of the new tees; for me it is a five-wood played to fly high and pitch right on, for if you pitch in front to the right you're in one trap or another, while the other half of the entrance and the rim of the green kicks your ball down into a little valley running round the green, or even into the rough.

The eighth hole has been completely remade although some of the old fairway has been used. The original green would have been almost in the middle of the M25, but by hauling back the tee and building an entirely new green, the hole of the same length, namely a short par five, has been created. The hole is still a climb to the top of the course and now about 800 feet up. The ninth is now an entirely new hole, as the old hole, which I reckoned pretty difficult, is now completely buried under the new highway.

The tenth is a pretty two-shot hole, curving up to the right to a green on an up-slope. Then another short hole, the 174-yard eleventh, which is much more from the back tee. The hole is guarded on the left by a big bunker and the shot across a vale of heather is all carry.

A few years ago I had the supreme pleasure of hitting a number four-iron shot which holed out from the tee which put my score of 'aces' just one ahead of Harry Vardon's. Later in the clubhouse Harry Muirfield Braid, the great man's son, and a very distinguished amateur golfer, said a kind word of congratulation, so I asked how many he had done and he replied, 'None', which only goes to show that holes in one don't go by merit. Not only did Vardon, our greatest golfer of all time, do only one 'ace', so, too, did Walter Hagen, and I believe that Bob Jones, the greatest ever, did only two holes in one. Compare this with the figure of thirty-seven holes in one by Art Wall Jnr; it doesn't make sense.

I am sorry to say that the eleventh will be scrapped when a new short hole almost at right angles is built followed by a new shortish par four using the present eleventh green. This new construction will enable the first hole at last to be abandoned.

The twelfth, which will still be twelfth, is a drive and a pitch hole, a real round-the-corner-to-the-right hole, though Henry Cotton in a big challenge match once drove right across the chord to the green. However, you and I drive downhill to the fairway like good boys and then come up with a seven-iron. The thirteenth, a long curving par five, and the fourteenth, another par five, downhill, cover over 1000 yards and we should be satisfied with ten for the pair.

Fifteen is a tough par four into the prevailing wind with the second over a cross bunker. The green is particularly unmoulded and slopes evilly to the right. A new bunker has been built to the right of the green to make things harder.

So to the par-five sixteenth, which is a great hole whether we can or cannot get up in two shots; the fairway slopes from right to left and cross bunkers menace the way; the cream of it, though, is the shot to the green, a big bold plateau, or rather shelf, with a bunker under the right-hand side of the ascent into which any poorly hit shot inexorably rolls. On a favourable day the smack of a wood shot held up properly to the left, but not too much, which breaks right towards the pin, gives a supreme pleasure.

The seventeenth, a shot of 181 yards, has recently been altered by closing the small gap, by which you might just run on, and putting bunkers all the way round the front of the green.

The last hole is a splendid one. You drive over a gully full of scrub on to a perfectly flat wide fairway; the second shot – the hole is about 400 yards – has to cross a full-size deep cross bunker, so deep that small ladders assist your egress. What's more, the green is apparently hard up to this grave, but it isn't in fact, so the shot always needs one more club than you are prepared to give it. The cross bunker is uncompromising, you've got to go over it sooner or later; there is no way round. What the pros make of it from the new back tee when the hole becomes nearly 480 yards I can't guess, but anyway they never make a fool of Walton Heath.

New Course

The New course suffers, I think, from a rather spotty start with two very short par fours, a short hole and two very tough par fours indeed, one of them 469 yards, in the first five. My friend Shipley, later the Canadian Seniors champion, took off, I remember, with birdie, birdie, double bogey, eagle, par – or 3 2 6 2 4.

While the fifth takes it out of us on sheer length, the third is a really difficult par four with a central fairway bunker which can catch a really good drive and a bunker right up to the green at the right side of the entrance and a deep pit, said to be a Roman stable, in the rough close by the entrance on the left.

The sixth is a good short hole, again with a bunker right up close, and a plateau green. The half ends with a par five and a long four so that if we are out under 39 we have done well.

The key holes in the second half are the attractive eleventh, masked on the left by a hump and protected by another Roman stable, if that is what these pits are, on the right, then the tough par-four twelfth and the beautiful par-four fourteenth sweeping downhill and then up to a shallow plateau green.

Fifteen, a moderate length par four, is fun with the green on two levels, above and below ground, and sixteen is a long five sweeping down off the moor, as it were. The seventeenth is a short four, but with a small shelf green demands that your drive should be steered to the left side of the fairway or you have an almost impossible pitch.

The last hole runs parallel to the eighteenth on the Old, is like it but shorter and less uncompromising. As I have said, if this were not alongside the Old course, how we would admire it. Some changes are planned for the New course for future years.

'Championship Course'

When the big events are played at Walton Heath, a combination of holes is used to give a rather tougher layout and fit it in with the needs of the crowd. This layout starts out on the heath at the present second on the Old course, omits the rather insufficient third hole and continues out on the Old as far as the par-five thirteenth. At that point, two holes are played on the New, the twelfth and thirteenth, then the tournament circuit returns to the fourteenth, fifteenth, sixteenth and seventeenth on the Old and, rather to my surprise and sorrow, to a strengthened eighteenth on the New.

Walton Heath Golf Club: New Course

	MEDAL TEES		FWD TEES		MEDAL TEES		FWD TEES
1	310	4	304	10	189	3	158
2	140	3	125	11	389	4	371
3	424	4	416	12	426	4	416
4	260	4	255	13	489	5	476
5	469	4	429	14	408	4	395
6	169	3	161	15	410	4	386
7	385	4	370	16	511	5	491
8	499	5	488	17	353	4	314
9	455	4	442	18	373	4	363
	3111	35	2990		3548	37	3370
					3111	35	2990
				Total	6659	72	6360

Walton Heath Golf Club: Old Course

	MEDAL TEES		FWD TEES		MEDAL TEES		FWD TEES
1	298	4	263	10	395	4	386
2	439	4	427	11	189	3	181
3	289	4	279	12	371	4	343
4	443	4	430	13	507	5	488
5	391	4	381	14	517	5	482
6	422	4	390	15	404	4	371
7	174	3	160	16	510	5	478
8	489	5	476	17	181	3	165
9	390	4	367	18	404	4	397
	3335	36	3173		3478	37	3291
					3335	36	3173
				Total	6813	73	6464

Walton Heath Golf Club: Championship Course

	YARDS	PAR		YARDS	PAR
1	410	4	10	341	4
2	513	5	11	521	5
3	391	4	12	462	4
4	422	4	13	470	4
5	174	3	14	517	5
6	489	5	15	404	4
7	390	4	16	475	4
8	395	5	17	165	3
9	189	3	18	432	4
Out	3373	36	In	3787	37

Total 7160 yards: par 73

Coming back to Walton Heath to discuss these matters recently with the most helpful secretary, it was a real pleasure to meet again Harry Busson, from whom in years gone by I had many a lesson, and to find him after 25 years as pro happy and wonderfully successful in the art of club making. Working with the best persimmon wood, the only suitable material for wooden clubs, he makes, in James Braid's old shop, the most beautiful clubs you can imagine, the last practitioner in all but a dead art. Yet, so good are his works of art, that they are in demand by the best tournament golfers, to name only Nicklaus and Norman, and at a price that brings a gasp of surprise to the ordinary player and of joy to the national balance of payments; Harry said that he was nine months behind with his orders. He works quite alone and it is sad that no one has beaten a path to his door imploring an apprenticeship.

I asked Harry who were the great club makers in the old days and I was pleased to hear him say at once Frank Frostick, of St George's Hill, whom I used to know, and Fred Hedges, the pro at West Byfleet, who taught me to play 65 years ago. Fred, a wiry little terrier of a man, was a beautiful club maker and iron player; he hit his iron shots as Bernard Darwin used to say with a click 'like the shutting of a knife'.

Reigate Heath

While in this district, I would recommend as a complete change a couple of rounds on the nine-hole course at Reigate Heath, a pleasant layout below the escarpment of the North Downs. It has fine views to the north and west, of the chalk downs above Betchworth along to Box Hill and further off beyond the gap in which Dorking lies, to Ranmore Common with its spire, and Leith Hill.

The golf course circles a small hill crowned with the clubhouse and a fine old windmill. There is heather, bracken and gorse enough in the rough to make you keep straight and some good bunkering, including a couple of old fashioned cross bunkers in front of the greens.

Alterations to the course since my last visit have been described very kindly for me by the hon. secretary, Mrs Doreen Howard, in the following paragraph:

You walk down the hill to drive off over a stretch of heather to the first fairway, sloping left to right, and thence to a tree-backed plateau green. The second comes back almost parallel on the lower level; then after an uphill short hole you have the newly formed par-five dog leg to a green sheltered by a dense pine wood. Up through the trees is the elevated tee for a completely new hole, the 405-yard fifth, a splendid

hole with a fairway rising to a stepped green, once the site of a gallows. Six is a long par three played over a water hazard, while the second shot to the seventh green has to clear a severe cross bunker. At the eighth the drive must be threaded between trees barely a cricket pitch length apart, while the approach needs to be only three or four yards too long to be out of bounds. The difficult par three ninth brings you back to the clubhouse – and the second

Reigate Heath Golf Club: Medal Card

	YARDS	PAR		YARDS	PAR
1	389	4	10	363	4
2	389	4	11	380	4
3	181	3	12	181	3
4	487	5	13	450	4
5	405	4	14	405	4
6	190	3	15	165	3
7	307	4	16	306	4
8	324	4	17	324	4
9	154	3	18	154	3
	2826	34		2728	33

Total 5554 yards: par 67

nine holes to the same greens but nearly all played from different tees.

This course, although of no great length, is not only beautiful but difficult and few indeed are the scores under 70 returned in competition.

Mrs Diane Bailey, one of three former Curtis Cup players in the club, is perhaps its most distinguished present member, having led the 1986 Cup team to a 13–5 victory in the United States – Britain and Ireland's very first victory at golf on American soil.

Sunningdale

Invigorated by the bracing air on Walton Heath and with our golf sharpened and honed by its difficulties, it is appropriate now to call in at Sunningdale, where the golf is rather less severe, and its neighbours Wentworth and Swinley Forest. Sunningdale somehow seems to have become the leader and certainly the best known of all the clubs near London; others might not agree, but at least all will accept that it offers you a very fine game of golf.

As at Walton Heath, there are two full-length sandy heather courses, but the New, which is less highly regarded than the Old, is out on the open heath, while the Old is almost entirely among fir trees. On both there is plenty of good heather in the rough.

Many events of major importance have been played at Sunningdale and it even had a connection with the Open Championship when qualifying rounds were held there in 1926 and Bobby Jones played the perfect round – perfect with one small flaw like an emerald – of 66, 33 out and 33 in, 33 shots and 33 putts, twelve fours and six threes.

Recently, the European Open has been played here and some pretty low scores have come from the list of overseas winners. In 1987 the Walker Cup is here, for the first time away from the seaside.

No resident professional at Sunningdale has matched Braid's fame, though Jack White won the Open Championship at Sandwich in 1904 with four rounds each lower than the one before. The fame rests more on the former caddie-master, the late James Sheridan, as salty and forthright a character as ever left Scotland, who showed, too, that he knew how to write a book.

Although the New, laid out by H. S. Colt and remade after the devastations of World War II, is a very fine course, with many magnificent holes, it is to the Old, laid out by young Willie Park in 1900, that we must go if we've only time for one round.

Old Course

The 494-yard first hole on the Old course is undemanding, slightly downhill with no rough or bunkers of great import. The second, with a semi-blind shot to the shelf green – it runs down sharply at the back – is a tougher proposition if you want a four. The third insists that you carry a cross bunker on the right-hand side of the fairway if you want the easiest pitch into the green, but at 296 yards you should get a four.

The fourth hole, 161 yards rather steeply uphill, doesn't give me any pleasure, but it is followed by three superb par fours, each 400 yards or slightly under. At the first two of these you drive over a thick belt of heather, downhill at the fifth, and at the seventh you have to hit over a high, menacing mound right in front of the tee. The second shots are all a delight, the fifth has an absurd little pond on the right which becomes an infuriating great lake when you get in it; at the sixth, which is a two-island hole, you have to cross a second heather belt to get to the green – and there is dire trouble to the

Left: Gleneagles: on the King's Course

Prestwick, the original home of the Championship

At Turnberry in the 1986 Championship; the winner, Greg Norman, at the 9th

St Andrews: Tom
Watson, five times
winner of the Open
Championship in
trouble at the Road
Hole, 1984

Royal Troon: the
difficult 'Railway Hole'

Muirfield: the fifth hole

Western Gailes: a fine
links in the West of
Scotland

Castletown: a fine
course in the Isle of
Man

Royal Lytham and St Annes: the 18th hole

Carnoustie: the 15th hole

Royal Liverpool, Hoylake: Greg Norman in the European Open

right. The seventh gives a lovely shot home to a plateau green with a protecting mound on the right flank. Three fours running for these is grand golf.

The eighth is a prosaic short hole, but the ground in front and the green itself slope considerably to the right, more than you think, and the bunker on that side works overtime.

You can drive the green very nearly at the ninth and it is not a hole of great character or joy. The tenth, however, is a charmer, with a great tee shot needed off high ground right down and down to a wide fairway below; it is 463 yards on the card, but you can get home or near if you keep out of Braid's bunker on the left, from which he once hit a prodigious iron or cleek shot to the green and holed for a three round a half stymie to wipe the smile off Ted Ray's face.

The eleventh is only 299 yards, but the fairway is narrow and the little plateau green, small and hard to hold. The drive is across a cross bunker and a hook into the heather or a fade into the trees makes a four very difficult.

Next comes a very fine two-shot with the second shot uphill to a rising green, a handsome hole too. The thirteenth is a rather indifferent par three, a downhill shot. The distinction it has is that Jones's only flaw was here as he got into a bunker, but he chipped out and holed the putt.

We are now faced with a very fair, just and stiff finish starting with the 477-yard fourteenth; I like this hole because, off a lenient tee, I scored my last eagle here, probably the last I'll ever do, which is a sad thought.

Fifteen is a very tough par three, 226 yards out of the trees to the edge of the heath. It is also the best of the par threes by far, I think. On the Old course they are the weakness and the two-shotters the strength.

Three of these carry you to the finish and difficult they all are. The sixteenth is a hole where you can never seem to drive far enough, for your second shot is uphill, with cross bunkers to carry, some way short of the green; I

have had to use wood recently and the hole has stretched me exceedingly.

At seventeen you drive downhill and length is not such a problem, but for some absurd reason you tend to fade the drive, to keep it out of some trees at the bottom, I suspect, and then you're trapped and bang goes your four. The green is closely bunkered at this hole.

Finally, at the eighteenth you have an uphill drive and woe betide you if it is at all cut, for then you're in dire rough while a pull bunkers you. Then home over the cross bunkers, aiming at the great oak tree by the green for a tough finishing hole. A splendid course and one where you hardly see another game except at that long vista from the fifth tee over to the sixth green or from the hilltop at the tenth tee.

New Course

The New course, as I have said, suffers by comparison with the Old and it does have some rather weak holes, notably the first and last. On the other hand, it has five short holes, and while the second and seventeenth are nothing

Sunningdale Golf Club: Old Course: Medal Card

	WHITE TEES	PAR		WHITE TEES	PAR
1	495	5	10	463	4
2	456	4	11	299	4
3	296	4	12	423	4
4	161	3	13	178	3
5	400	4	14	477	5
6	388	4	15	226	3
7	383	4	16	423	4
8	172	3	17	421	4
9	267	4	18	414	4
Out	3017	35	In	3324	35
			Out	3017	35
			Total	6341	70

Sunningdale Golf Club: New Course: Medal Card					
	WHITE TEES	PAR		WHITE TEES	PAR
1	466	4	10	213	3
2	175	3	11	453	4
3	396	4	12	400	4
4	436	4	13	553	5
5	190	3	14	194	3
6	492	5	15	446	4
7	383	4	16	385	4
8	402	4	17	175	3
9	440	4	18	477	5
Out	3380	35	In	3296	35
			Out	3380	35
			Total	6676	70

to get excited about, the other three – particularly the fifth with its isolated plateau out on the heath, the tight difficult fourteenth and the long and hard-to-find tenth – are all great, better than anything on the Old, I think. Among the two-shot holes, where the Old course has the edge, the spectacular ninth with a blind drive and a tight second between hills and traps, and the twelfth with its uphill second shot to a shelf green and the attractive pretty third hole, are my favourites.

If you have time, don't fail to go across the road and play a round at the Sunningdale's Ladies Club, a separate club, by the way, and requiring another green fee. This is a most amusing little heather course of about 4000 yards with a par of 61. The shots are not long, the longest hole is 335 yards, but the greens are small and you don't race away with such a low score as you might imagine; one enjoyable exercise for the handicap player is to try to play twenty-seven holes in under 100 strokes. There are plenty of narrow shots, an occasional out of bounds and carries of heather off the tee. I've played dozens of rounds here and thoroughly enjoyed them.

There is one story of an irascible and unpopular member of Sunningdale who did the first seventeen holes of the course in three apiece, a really great performance; he then hit a prodigious drive and reached the eighteenth green – where he took three putts. Arthur Lees, formerly the pro next door, has been round in 52!

Wentworth

On our road down to Sunningdale we probably passed the gates of the Wentworth estate, although the golf courses are hidden from the road by trees and masses of rhododendron bushes. Inside the gates are many fine houses and gardens, three golf courses, two of full length and a short nine for fun, in the best heather and pine country and one of the few country clubs of the American style in England, with ballroom, squash courts, tennis, swimming and all the clubhouse facilities you can ask for.

An even more lavish layout is under construction with a new clubhouse and a third full-length golf course to the design of Gary Player, John Jacobs and Bernard Gallacher, the resident professional.

The older, shorter East course is now less famous than its big brother, the West course, the Burma Road, but it has had its days of fame in the past, for the first Curtis Cup match against the ladies of the USA was played here in 1932, which we lost, and in 1926 the British professionals beat the daylights out of their American visitors and paved the way for the Ryder Cup series of matches.

I have an affection for the older East course as I once won a very minor scratch prize there after starting with an eight. To play your handicap against the par value of 68 on the East Course is certainly no easier than on the West with its formidable par of 72, for the West, to be sure, is not quite so tough as you might suppose. All this, I fear, is being put to rights on the East course by lengthening the twelfth, thirteenth and fourteenth holes by no less than 400 yards. Oh dear, always more length.

At any rate, the Burma Road is now the more famous course and the one to play if you can only manage one round. Here the Ryder Cup match of 1953 was played, which we so nearly might have won but didn't, and here the Canada Cup, now the World Cup, was played in 1956 when Snead and Hogan beat the world hands down. This was Hogan's only appearance in England in competitive golf, although he had won the Open at Carnoustie three years before, and he certainly gave value for money. He started his first round with an eagle, followed by a two at the second and holed the first nine in 31, following this by another deuce at ten, making what might be called a promising start towards winning the individual aggregate prize, which he did with a score of 277. I followed the American pair for most of a round and of the two, the slow majestic full swing of Snead looked the better and made Hogan's flat style look almost slashing. But style at golf isn't always decisive, though it is a great deal.

In later years the Burma Road has been the home of many professional tournaments, especially the World Match Play tournament, which has become a world-famous event. This has been won five times out of nine by Gary Player and twice by Arnold Palmer. More recently the mighty Spaniard Seve Ballesteros has won the trophy four times in five years and now Greg Norman the Australian is muscling in. In this tournament some very low scores have been accomplished, notably Tony Jacklin's 63, with an outward half of 29 in 1972, and Lee Trevino's 32 in, in this most notable match between them that year. The spectacular golf to which this course so lends itself was also shown in the match in 1986 between Sandy Lyle, our British winner of the Open the year before, and

Tommy Nakajima, whom we last met in the Road bunker at St Andrews. Both of them were no less than 15 under par for 36 holes and Lyle won at the 38th.

We start the West course with a long par four, formerly par five, with two valleys to cross and we then go over the second of these for the

Wentworth Club, East Course: Medal Card

	YARDS	PAR		YARDS	PAR
1	391	4	10	187	3
2	421	4	11	462	4
3	337	4	12	157	3
4	192	3	13	402	4
5	327	4	14	303	4
6	353	4	15	332	4
7	229	3	16	458	4
8	458	4	17	213	3
9	531	5	18	423	4
Out	3239	35	In	2937	33
			Out	3239	35
			Total	6176	68

Wentworth Club, West Course: Medal Card

	YARDS	PAR		YARDS	PAR
1	471	4	10	186	3
2	155	3	11	376	4
3	452	4	12	483	5
4	501	5	13	441	4
5	191	3	14	179	3
6	344	4	15	466	4
7	399	4	16	380	4
8	398	4	17	571	5
9	450	4	18	502	5
Out	3361	35	In	3584	37
			Out	3361	35
			Total	6945	72

short second hole and then along it for the long par four third, with its two-tier green. We then move out to the heath and have as the finest hole the 399-yard seventh, with a difficult uphill second shot to a two-tiered green, on which four putts are not unknown in the best company. The second nine has some fine holes, notably the curling attractive eleventh up a valley and the twelfth with a menacing line of pines across the fairway to clear with your drive. The finish is tough, an uphill par three, a long par four, a mid-length par four and two curving fives to finish you off, the seventeenth with its opportunities to go out of bounds on the left being very tough.

The East course is shorter, but has some very attractive holes, notably the eighteenth with its plateau green guarded by a diagonal line of bunkers and the downhill fourteenth, where a great bash and some help from run and wind could get you a 'bird', though sadly this hole is to be lengthened.

Swinley Forest

The next call in this district should be at Swinley Forest, near Ascot, with its course hidden in the pines a mile or so beyond Sunningdale. The club is a very private one and I have a great liking for it and the course. There is never a crowd, you can get a caddie, the golf is fun and it used to serve what I thought was the best plain lunch in England. The course is not demanding but enjoyable to play with some splendid holes, especially the par threes and the two-shot holes in the second half. It is very beautiful as well, particularly when the rhododendrons are out at the back of the twelfth green in June, or when the heather is in full flower in September.

The holes I would pick as the best are the uphill par-three fourth hole, a Redan hole par excellence with a big bunker under the flank of the green, and the uphill two-shot fifteenth where you, or rather, where I, need wood to get home after a good drive. It also has one of those short par fours, the eleventh, where favourable conditions will allow you to get on with your absolute best from the tee.

Yes, lots of fun, Swinley Forest, but you do require a written invitation from a member to play the course.

	Swinley Forest Golf Club: Score Card				
	YARDS	PAR		YARDS	PAR
1	370	4	10	210	3
2	350	4	11	286	4
3	305	4	12	480	5
4	165	3	13	160	3
5	465	4	14	375	4
6	437	4	15	433	4
7	410	4	16	430	4
8	155	3	17	180	3
9	430	4	18	360	4
	3087	34		2914	34

Total 6001 yards: par 68

Berkshire

Now that we are in the Ascot area, we might as well move over and play the two courses of The Berkshire club, built on Crown land at the end of the 1920s to the design of Herbert Fowler.

The golf here is of the highest quality, heather, pines, open heath and plenty of slopes and variations of levels. Frank Pennink describes the courses as 'among the finest inland of the

British Isles' and providing golf of 'spectacular grandeur'.

I suppose the Red Course could be regarded as the major layout – though the Blue is just as good, it is rather different, on a lower level of the ground and a hundred yards shorter. The courses, I think, were laid out to provide contrast, the Red being 'all fives and threes' as it were, and the Blue 'all fours'. This isn't quite so with the modern par ratings but it has some truth in it. I find it hard to choose which of the two courses I prefer and can only suggest that you must try to play both of them.

I hope I may be excused if I report that at the Berkshire at the age of fifty-three I had my one and only great day – this, in a competition of the Plastics Industry Golfing Society, known always as the PIGS – winning the scratch prize and the handicap on the Red in the morning and the foursomes, or rather greensomes, in the afternoon with my friend John Lennard as partner on the Blue, where we holed the course in 71 strokes, so returning home with all the prizes – and that after a night in the train. Well, that was once in a lifetime, for nothing like it has happened before or since.

On a higher plane, the 72-hole medal competition for amateurs, which was instituted after World War II as the Berkshire Trophy, has become, with the Brabazon, the most important amateur event of its kind. It is an interesting commentary on the progress of British amateur golf to look at the winning scores on record which in forty years have come down from the 300 level to below 280.

There are some great holes on both courses, my prizes going, on the Red course, to the extreme dog-leg sixth and the curving two-shot eighth with its encroaching group of pines on the right, the death or glory short tenth with a drop to perdition on the right front and the 477-yard fifteenth with the huge lone pine behind it; the long par-five seventeenth is a good hole, too.

On the Blue, I like especially the short par-four fifth, the difficult ditch-beset eleventh and

two of the par threes, the first a most troublesome opening hole and the downhill tenth which has recently been shortened from par four.

We are near the end of our pilgrimage to the great heath-and-pines courses of Surrey and

Berkshire Golf Club, Red Course: Medal Card

	YARDS	PAR		YARDS	PAR
1	518	5	10	187	3
2	146	3	11	338	4
3	481	5	12	328	4
4	394	4	13	484	5
5	182	3	14	436	4
6	353	4	15	477	5
7	201	3	16	221	3
8	427	4	17	529	5
9	477	5	18	177	3
Out	3179	36	In	3177	36
			Out	3179	36
			Total	6356	72

Berkshire Golf Club, Blue Course: Medal Card

	YARDS	PAR		YARDS	PAR
1	217	3	10	200	3
2	340	4	11	478	5
3	477	5	12	360	4
4	152	3	13	159	3
5	316	4	14	365	4
6	481	5	15	406	4
7	363	4	16	452	4
8	405	4	17	375	4
9	310	4	18	402	4
Out	3061	36	In	3197	35
			Out	3061	36
			Total	6258	71

Berkshire except for a most important trinity, perhaps even the most important of all in the area, that is Worplesdon, West Hill and Wok- | ing. These three courses are in the closest juxtaposition and all but share boundary fences with each other.

Worplesdon

The Worplesdon club is perhaps the best known of the three because every autumn the Amateur Mixed Foursomes Tournament has been held here and in its early days the most frequent winner was Miss Joyce Wethered, perhaps the most accomplished of all golfers, with a succession of male partners, including her brother, Cyril Tolley, J. S. F. Morrison, 'the Cambridge triple-blue', and Bernard Darwin, who wrote so charmingly about it in 1933.

Worplesdon was laid out by J. F. Abercromby of Addington fame in 1908, and for the last fifteen holes he is seen at his best, only the first three on more meadowy ground than the remaining heathland being rather less good. The fourth, for instance, which some think resembles the 'High Hole' at St Andrews, though I can't see it, is a fine uphill par three to return us to the clubhouse and the best heathery country. In this, the eighth is notable with a sharp two-tier green modelled on 'Pandy' at Musselburgh, which makes the second shot a teaser and so is the curving two-shot ninth along a row of silver birches.

The tenth is as pretty a short hole, across a pond, as you will find, and eleven has all you need as a par five against the prevailing wind. The next is a big two-shot hole for the experts with a cross bunker to carry with the second shot, and thirteen is a tough sand-beset par three. There is another short hole at sixteen and two fine two-shotters to see us in, the eighteenth, with its encroaching bunker on the right to catch the tee shot, most exacting.

Worplesdon Golf Club: Medal Card

	YARDS	PAR		YARDS	PAR
1	365	4	10	138	3
2	414	4	11	520	5
3	385	4	12	478	5
4	168	3	13	175	3
5	412	4	14	405	4
6	476	5	15	500	5
7	183	3	16	193	3
8	387	4	17	400	4
9	372	4	18	451	4
	3162	35		3260	36

Total 6422 yards: par 71

West Hill

It is no distance now to move over to West Hill hard by the railway station at Brookwood. This is another most attractive heathery course amid birch trees and pines enlivened by a stream which comes into play at the first four holes and the sixteenth and seventeenth before wandering off through the fence to neighbouring Woking. The club was founded in 1910 by Mrs Lubbock, one of the few clubs started by a woman and all the better for that.

The course is blessed with five short holes, among which I rate the fourth as attractive and difficult, the seventh in a private clearing in the woods as charming and the full-blooded 212-yard fifteenth with its minefield of bunkers and curvaceous green as great; to smack a spoon shot in there or in favourable circumstances a two-iron boring into the wind is to achieve a great feeling of satisfaction. Bernard Darwin rated this hole as the best in the world of its kind.

Of the longer holes, the opener, with the stream never quite out of mind, and the third, with the same stream in front of the apron of the green, are both good and so is the attractive sixth with an elusive green in a corner of the woods. Coming in, the tenth and eleventh, the latter with a belt of heather across the fairway and the fourteenth with trees all along the right-hand side make a fine trio to hole in twelve shots – and you can add the eighteenth too as a long testing four.

The major open event of the year is the national Father and Son tournament which has been held since 1932. It was introduced by Major Geoffrey Lubbock, who had two golfing sons, in 1929 when the competition was open to members of Surrey clubs only. The event was

	West Hill Golf Club: Medal Card					
	YARDS	PAR			YARDS	PAR
1	393	4		10	422	4
2	368	4		11	392	4
3	454	4		12	297	4
4	193	3		13	149	3
5	532/500	5		14	462	4
6	419	4		15	212	3
7	170	3		16	384	4
8	383	4		17	498	5
9	171	3		18	440	4
	3083/3051	34			3256	35

Total 6339/6307 yards:par 69

made open in 1932 and after Major Lubbock's death at the end of that year, his widow presented a trophy in his memory which is still played for.

Woking

So last, and by no means least, we come to Woking, founded in 1893 and the very first of the many heather-and-fir courses which have been built in this sandy country in Surrey and Berkshire. Once, years ago, I was a member here and a very private and austere place it was then with no bogey or par scores on the card, nor distances given either on the card or on the tees. Ladies' tees did not exist and there was only one club competition a year. Everything was done under the eyes of Mr Stuart Paton and Mr John L. Low with a rather bleak bearded character as secretary.

Bernard Darwin was long a member here and the tale is told that it was at the fourth green by the railway line that, after missing his fourth short putt, he rolled in agony on the turf, biting it as he went, and then made the impassioned cry 'and now God perhaps you are satisfied'.

The course has altered little in general layout,

but ingenious changes in bunkering have been made from time to time and a reconstruction of the ninth and tenth has taken place to convert two poor par fours to one good one and a new short hole. Although the course is not long the bunkering is often very tight and close up to the edges of the greens.

Woking starts you off mildly enough with a very short par four and you can easily roll your second up for a birdie if you have driven to the right spot. But the short second across a valley is a hard three, as the green by no means gathers the ball, and the 413-yard third, back to the clubhouse, is a very tough four indeed, with a bunker bang in front right up to the green and some severe undulations on it.

The fourth is the famous hole along the railway with a bunker, like the 'Principal's Nose' at St Andrews, plumb in the centre of the fairway, just where a good drive gets to. Take the straight and narrow way between this bunker and the out of bounds fence and you have a simple run-up shot, go to the left for safety and you have a difficult pitch home over bunkers to a sloping green.

Five is a pretty hole of no great length, with the green in a half-circle of trees, and six a fine two-shot hole with a stream, the one we encounter at West Hill, but with its strip of heather no longer in front of the green, alas. The seventh is a par three with the green in two sections divided by a ridge; at one time there was a bunker actually in the green but this has now gone. The eighth is a beautiful two-shot hole to a green up a gentle rise with a bunker to be cleared. Nine is now a big two-shot hole, dog leg to the left, instead of the old hole with a blind shot to a hidden green. The new short tenth runs across a slope which used to be the old fairway and we are now again on the upper levels of Hook Heath. A drive and pitch eleventh and a good length par-four twelfth with a row of pot bunkers guarding it takes us along and back, and then the third parallel hole, the 426-yard thirteenth, a pretty tough hole especially if the flag is on top of the narrow strip of the upper tier of the green.

The fourteenth, the first par five, takes us back to the clubhouse and the temptation of stopping there and calling it a day. The green, which can possibly be reached in two down wind, has some severe slopes to deceive us. Continuing on, the fifteenth is 'Harley Street', 511 yards long, slightly uphill, and slightly dull too, I think. We then have an attractive short

Woking Golf Club: Medal Card

	YARDS	PAR		YARDS	PAR
1	278	4	10	155	3
2	201	3	11	383	4
3	413	4	12	409	4
4	336	4	13	426	4
5	360	4	14	510	5
6	381	4	15	511	5
7	161	3	16	156	3
8	433	4	17	421	4
9	450	4	18	338	4
	3031	34		3309	36

Total 6322 yards: par 70

hole over the pond, a five-iron is about it, and a very tight tough par four at seventeen with bunkers eating into the green.

The last hole is a mild enough par four, but you can slice or shank a very bad second into a pond on the right of the green. Shots have been played to this green from the clubhouse roof, notably by C. H. Alison in the university match in 1904, getting him a half. In the London Amateur Foursomes, a third shot has been holed, through a tiny gap in the branches of the huge holly tree which guarded, and still guards, the left of the green. The ball was apparently hit into the heart of the bush, came out and ran slowly into the hole. A subsequent search reported that the hole in the bush had disappeared.

Chapter 5

LONDON, TO THE NORTH AND FURTHER SOUTH

While the fine courses to the south of London are famous, and rightly so, there is good golf to the north and on an outer group of courses which, though less well known, produce some excellent golf, and give you a pleasant day out in lovely country into the bargain.

I think we might start with Sussex, as it is now my county by adoption, so I make no excuse, and say with the old ballad

> You can tell them all,
> That we stand or fall,
> By Sussex by the Sea

as used to be sung with fervour at pierrot shows at seaside resorts in my childhood, along with 'Glorious Devon' and 'Take me back to Yorkshire', and other patriotic songs of the time.

Sussex is a hilly county, with the North Downs along its northern boundary, and the South Downs, for the most part, right along the coast. In between is the 'Massif Central' of Ashdown Forest, a high wilderness of heather, gorse and that maddening encroaching bracken, birch, pine and some hardwoods, and many little streams to make up some grand golfing country.

On this ground lie Crowborough Beacon and Royal Ashdown Forest Golf Clubs and on the rim of this wild heathland, Piltdown, home of the famous Man, one of the great hoaxes of all time.

Crowborough Beacon

Crowborough Beacon has a wonderful location – much of it lies over 800 feet up in the Forest – with spectacular views over the Weald of Sussex, across to the South Downs and even a glint of the sea on clear days through the gap of Cuckmere Haven, more than twenty miles away; moreover it provides excellent golf. Crowborough was also the home of Conan Doyle – and of Sherlock Holmes too, after he retired from the mythical 221B Baker Street to keep bees in his old age. The turf is splendid, the fairways springy, with here and there some shaven heather to give you the best of all lies, and the greens sharp and true.

You start and finish with two rather pedestrian two-shot holes in the big paddock in front of the clubhouse, though heaven knows the eighteenth at 437 yards, slightly uphill, is a tough one. The course really gets going after you cross the road to play the second, as fierce a par four as ever I saw. You drive downhill on to a big sweeping fairway, swinging hard over to the right. When you get to the corner of the dog leg, you can then see that you have got anything up to a full shot to carry a deep gully of rough which eats into the right-hand side of the fairway about 40 yards from the green and get home. On the left is a splendid lone pine on guard.

The next conspicuous hole is the fifth, where again a big gully full of bushes and rough has to be carried, from the tee this time, before you pitch up to a high half-seen green on a hilltop.

Next comes a famous hole, 'The Speaker', named after a former Speaker of the House of Commons. It might well have a rougher name than that, for it is difficult to imagine a much more intimidating one-shot hole than this. There is the green, at a slight angle across the line and a huge rough, stony hollow, an old quarry, under its left flank in true Redan style; to the right of the green and short is a small piece of fairway for the feeble, and then for a good hundred yards back to the tee, a deep gully full of heather and bracken and the certainty of a lost ball from a topped tee shot. For my taste, the hole would be better for even some more thinning out of the gully. Off the back tee at 193 yards, with any wind at all – 'and there's likewise a wind on the heath, brother' – you would pay good money for a three on your card and keep your ball in your pocket.

At the seventh, you have a stiff climb up to the higher ground, and a long belt it is, but then comes relief at the eighth in a shortish par four. At the ninth you come back with a sweeping curved dog leg to the left, with the second shot uphill to a green guarded by heathery bumps, a pretty, natural hole.

The tenth, another par five, takes us out to the top of the course, and its farthest extremity. The green is another Redan type, with a big bunker under its left flank.

Eleven and twelve are two-shotters back and thirteen a short one-shot hole. I like thirteen, with a big bump and bunker guarding the left flank, and two pits to the right and a chance of slicing on to the road from a really awful shot.

The fourteenth is a shortish par five with a downhill second, with which you might just get home. The green is a small saucer at the end of the down-sweeping fairway, with gorse and trouble over the back. There is a superb view across this green to the Weald, and beyond you see 'along the sky the line of the Downs so noble and so bare'. Up here, on a brilliant summer day, with the breeze of an anticyclone sighing in the pines, and the variously coloured heathers just out, the sun bringing out the scent of bracken and pine, I thought what a marvellously lucky lot we golfers were to be able to enjoy our game in such wonderful surroundings; the courts of Wimbledon or the turf of Lord's are like game factories by comparison.

The downhill fifteenth at Crowborough didn't raise much enthusiasm, but the sixteenth, a shortish par four dog leg to the left, has a daunting carry from the tee, that same tree-filled, bush-choked gully which silenced the Speaker, this time about 140–150 yards from the back tee. After that, you pitch uphill and all is well.

Crowborough Beacon Golf Club: Medal Card

	YARDS	PAR		YARDS	PAR
1	393	4	10	492	5
2	457	4	11	335	4
3	144	3	12	415	4
4	360	4	13	136	3
5	358	4	14	481	5
6	193	3	15	365	4
7	497	5	16	350	4
8	325	4	17	145	3
9	396	4	18	437	4
	3123	35		3156	36

Total 6279 yards: par 71

The seventeenth is a poor hole, I'm afraid, a one-shot all uphill – well, the hill can't be avoided – but a featureless, bunkerless half-blind green can. I'd have liked to let the local expert, the late Frank Pennink, have a go at it. Then if we get home with two fine smacks at eighteen, we can climb the steps to the bar with relief, and sit and look out again at that incomparable view, well content.

Recent researches in preparation for the club's centenary have shown that the first US Open Champion after stroke play became the rule (in 1895) was Horace Thomas Rawlins, who, at the time of winning the event, was the assistant professional at Crowborough Beacon and so, contrary to most belief, the first visiting Briton to win the event. He was born in the Isle of Wight.

Royal Ashdown Forest

Still in this area, we come next to Royal Ashdown Forest club at Forest Row, founded in 1888. This is a totally natural golf course without a single artificial bunker on the entire layout, and with one exception, no man-made hazards at all. Streams, heather, bracken, pits and hollows, humps and natural banks, some trees at the lower levels, severe slopes both up and down, and some sandy roads, these are enough to use all the skill you possess, without artificial additives. And surprisingly attractive all this is, especially as the upper holes give you such fine views over the Forest into the bargain.

As Bernard Darwin says 'Nature is a wonderfully good architect when she is in a painstaking mood and she has made few better two-shot holes than the second at Ashdown. First comes a sufficiently frightening tee-shot (uphill), over a big pit and then a long second on to a small green, guarded in front by a stream.' You would have thought that this was enough, but the bank of the stream on the far side is fenced with a palisade of railway sleepers, which looks like some decapitated fortress, or something left over from the 'Cardinal' at Prestwick, hardly in keeping with Ashdown Forest. This wall was erected to stop balls hopping over the stream and I'm glad to say that its appearance has mellowed with time.

A stream also guards the green closely at the 500-yard fifth, but I imagine that those with a really long drive down the hill, which you can

get in summer with the westerly wind, will want to 'have a go'.

The 126-yard sixth is the famous 'Island Hole', with a comfortably large green with a fair-sized step in it; a stream or ditch guards the front and runs halfway round the right flank and all the way round on the left; unless you are playing right off the back tee, I don't find this a terribly exacting hole, and a good prod with a six-iron, or a seven, should do it. But with a most attractive setting, and a backdrop of trees, this hole is a real charmer, and the two I managed there some time ago caused great joy to some ancient limbs. In 1904, this hole, which then was different and more difficult, with a more awkward shot to the width of the green, so pleased a visitor to the club, Mr Lionel Redpath, that he endowed it in the sum of £5, the accumulated interest on which was to go to anyone who did the hole in one at the Easter, Whitsun or Autumn meetings. It was first claimed in 1947 by David Richardson, who drew about £30. A few months later, Charles Frazer, a former captain, did it, too, and got only a few pence for his skill. Since then the club rewards the lucky striker.

Leaving the 'Island Hole', we have a big swinging drive at the seventh to a rising fairway, as we had at the fourth, and from then on we are on the highlands of the course, with all the grand views over Sussex to help us with some tough, severe golf. With lengths from the back tees of 498 yards at the eighth, 485 at the tenth, a 249-yard par three to give you a breather at eleven and finally a 558-yard twelfth, this stretch, well, stretches you. Things quieten down after that for the thirteenth, coming down off the moor, is only 367 yards, but you have to drive from a high tee over a great ravine full of bracken and bushes, through a gap in some trees on to a rising fairway and play up to a green on top of a hill once more.

We then get a long walk and a not too severe par three, and after that a drive from an elevated tee onto a rising fairway to precede a pitch over a deal of hummocky trouble and a big swale, in front of the fifteenth green. I thought this an attractive hole, but my weakness for short par fours must be remembered.

The sixteenth is a long, tough par four, uphill and upwind; it seems inconceivable, sometimes, that it is only 407 yards off the medal tee. The seventeenth, now par four, downhill and downwind, is an altogether more cheerful hole, with good hopes of being on in two.

Finally, at eighteen, we drive over a big ravine and stream. The eighteenth green is perched again at the top of a slope, and has recently been lengthened, an exacting green but not so tough as that laid on at the first, which has a steep, sharp step in it, to provide a difficult pin position on the left for medal days.

So ends our round on a most unusual and unorthodox golf course, even old fashioned, perhaps, but, my oath, if you can score to your handicap here, 'I raises my 'at to you'.

Recently at Ashdown Forest, a second course of 5600 yards has been built to include the ladies' nine, and Frank Pennink, a fine judge, speaks very well of it.

One of the features of Royal Ashdown Forest is the artisans' club, the Cantelupe Club, which has produced many famous players – many of the Mitchell family, including that fine striker of the ball, Abe, who should have won the Open but never did, and Alfred Padgham, one of a large local family, who did win it in 1936. Another famous character was Abe Mitchell's

Aunt Polly who caddied for forty years and kept a terse and splendidly human diary, so delightfully reported by Henry Longhurst.

Poor Abe Mitchell, how he hated the pressure of competitive golf. I can see him now, grey-faced with distress, topping his second shot to the seventeenth at St George's Hill to lose his big 72-hole £1000 challenge match with Walter Hagen, who had played on his nerves by arriving late on the second morning when Mitchell was four up after the first day. Yet, as J. H. Taylor said to me once, 'the best striker of the ball was Abraham Mitchell – not the best golfer, mind you'.

Many years ago, I played much with Alf Padgham at Ashdown Forest when he was a young assistant and unknown. As a youthful slasher I was wholly envious of his easy, lazy swing, which made the game look so simple, and also his placid manner.

There have been some famous members at Royal Ashdown Forest – named Royal, by the way, after the Duke of Cambridge, who had commanded the troops at a review in the forest by Queen Victoria and who had been prevailed upon to drive a ball wearing his full dress. The best-known members were Horace Hutchinson

---

Royal Ashdown Forest Club: Medal Card

	YARDS	PAR		YARDS	PAR
1	332	4	10	485	5
2	384	4	11	249	3
3	327	4	12	558	5
4	356	4	13	367	4
5	509	5	14	200	3
6	126	3	15	310	4
7	365	4	16	407	4
8	498	5	17	472	4
9	142	3	18	352	4
	3039	36		3400	36

Total 6439 yards: par 72

and F. G. Tait, who were each Amateur champion twice. Famous, too, was that great character, A. J. Rowe, who was professional to the club for fifty-five years. He was succeeded by Hector Padgham, who has been at the club nearly as long. There must have been few clubs who have had only two professionals in 100 years.

Piltdown

The third of the heathland group of courses in this part of Sussex is Piltdown and like Ashdown Forest it is a natural course without a man-made hazard on it. I think I have said enough of the fun of playing a course without a single sand bunker in the previous section, so I will only say that it is pleasing and amusing here, too, even if it is not such a tough course as the other two, although the honours board in the bar does not show any scores in the 60s. So don't think this will be an easy outing.

The great views of Crowborough and Ashdown Forest are not quite matched at Piltdown, but to the south the rampart of the South Downs is very fine.

Originally of ten holes, the course is not very long now, just over 6000 yards, but this beautiful heathland turf does not give much run, and the absence of bunkers somehow makes things look longer than they are. Belts of heather across the fairway can give you a rough time, too.

You play at the first to the top of a rise. Then comes a long par five, the only one on the card, sweeping downwards with a big pond on the left, which on Sundays even attracts some navigators. You swing round the pond with a sharp dog leg at three, and then have a big thump at the 204-yard par three fourth, back towards the pond, downhill it's true, but with a big swale to catch a weak shot and roughage in front of it nearer the green.

Crossing the road, two more substantial two-shot holes, more or less parallel, come next and then an attractive short hole, the seventh, with the green a semi-plateau with low ground full of tough rough in front and on the right; there are also a couple of deep ditches for good measure for the really poor tee shot. The seventh green is said to be the site of a mass grave of victims of the Great Plague of 1665. The first half ends with two more fours up and down hill, and then a short tenth across the far end of the course.

You come up the hill again with the attractive dog leg eleventh, and then a shorter four at the twelfth, where you have to mind the sea of gorse to the right and left off the tee.

We have a tough finish to end with the fine dog leg seventeenth at 436 yards, and then we end with a new par three which was designed to keep the play away from the first hole. The hole is downhill and usually down wind to a step green, a pretty hole to finish with.

Near, but not on the course, the parts of the notorious skull of the Piltdown Man, Eoanthropus Dawsoni, were discovered between 1908 and the end of 1911 by a local solicitor, and archaeologist, Charles Dawson. In conjunction with Sir Arthur Smith Woodward of the British Museum, the skull was 'reconstructed' and dated as being some 500,000 years old. It then enjoyed great anthropological renown for forty years. But something was wrong, for its apelike jaw did not seem quite to belong to the human type of cranium, which led some to doubt its authenticity, and as other discoveries were made, the Piltdown Man seemed more and more a misfit.

The proof came from modern scientific testing. In 1953, K. P. Oakley of the Museum established by means of fluorine and nitrogen tests that the jaw was indeed of no great age, which confirmed the suspicion that it was indeed the jaw of an ape and unrelated to the skull, which on the same tests showed entirely different fluorine and nitrogen contents. Moreover, a uranium test on an elephant tooth found nearby and hitherto believed to be of local origin showed that it almost certainly came from Tunisia. Who done it – and why? Dawson, who would have been able to throw light on it, died in 1916, and the secret, if it was his, died with him. If he didn't do it, who did? Someone with greater scientific knowledge than Dawson?

No one knows or knows whether it was done to gain bogus renown, or as a big practical joke which came off too well and so got the author stuck with it. It seems an inconceivable coincidence that these two bones were just lying there together, especially as a piece of a similar skull and a tooth were later said to have been found by Dawson nearby.

Piltdown Golf Club: Medal Card

	YARDS	PAR		YARDS	PAR
1	372	4	10	163	3
2	519	4	11	395	4
3	453	4	12	312	4
4	204	3	13	396	4
5	431	4	14	411	4
6	402	4	15	160	3
7	151	3	16	347	4
8	397	4	17	436	4
9	327	4	18	183	3
	3256	35		2803	33
				3256	35
				6059	68

Pulborough

At the western end of Sussex at Pulborough is the West Sussex Club. This is a modern course and an absolute beauty, laid out to test every shot, in an oasis of sand, heather and pines, so unlike the nearby Sussex clay. The sand, moreover, is of a dazzling whiteness, which adds delightful contrast to the dark or purple heather and the brilliant green of the fairways and greens. I think if I had to choose one example to demonstrate the best sort of British inland course, to explain what it was trying to do to provide entertainment, and why it had to be so different from a links, to some men from Mars or a group of intelligent Americans, I think I would pick Pulborough, much as I love Woking, Liphook, St George's Hill and a dozen others.

There are some unusual features about Pulborough, such as two par threes in succession, even if the second of these is a monster, and five par threes in all. Moreover, there is only one par five on the course. The length is only 6156 yards, so par is 68. Now if you single-figure men think you are in for a nice score in

the low or mid-seventies to take back to London or Wilmington, Delaware, you had better play very well indeed, for the course demands it. It is first-class golf.

The first lets you go off easily enough now that it has been extended to par five. You get in among the pines at four, a dog leg to the left with a humpy fairway, and one dominant bunker on the left near the green, a pretty hole.

The fifth is a short hole of exceptional beauty, even if it is not too abominably difficult. The big bunkers, the pines on either flank and in a clump behind the green, the great grove of Chanctonbury Ring up on the summit of the South Downs as a backdrop, make a picture hole if ever there was one. The green is slightly dished and therefore quite generous, and the right side is free from trouble, so that's the side for my mashie shot.

This quiet spell is followed by an attack on your game as fierce as any I know. There it is, allegedly only 220 yards and downhill from the top marker and I suppose 200 from the lower mark, but about 50 yards short of the green there is a swamp and pond right across the line and extending beyond it to the right; the pond is kidney-shaped, and I suppose about 60 yards long. The run up to the green is uphill and you can go into the woods or even out of bounds with a big drawn shot or else you can slice into one of a big chain of bunkers guarding the right. For the timid or incompetent, there is an obliging piece of fairway on the right, but from there a very difficult pitch over the last of the chain of bunkers on to the steeply sloping green. To add to all this, the hole looks a good deal longer than it is. Of all the par threes I know, this is as tough as they come, and ranks with the sixteenth at Cypress Point or the fifth at Pine Valley.

After this we have to clear a big hill of rough with a vast bunker at right centre, but then the hole becomes a little exhausted and dull, though fully long enough to get us a five.

The eighth, across a valley, is another pretty short hole, followed by a par four out along the same line. Coming home, the tenth is famous for its steep 'left angle' dog leg. After the eleventh, down to the lower level of the course and the 210-yard twelfth, we come to one of the best and most attractive par fours I know. Pause here for reflection: why are thirteenth holes often so good? I can think of six beauties, but why I don't know. Uphill over the heather we drive and then there it is, a long green diagonally across the line, and under its right flank a chain of large white bunkers as well as one in front. To get to the stick you have a big carry, with a mid-iron, a four or five perhaps, for there's no room to run in, a fine hole.

Fourteen, downhill the other way, is another pretty curving hole, and though there are bunkers across the fairway, they are not too near the green, nor should they be at a 434-yard hole. Fifteen is a little one across the pond and then comes an unusual hole of a type you might

West Sussex Golf Club: Medal Card					
	YARDS	PAR		YARDS	PAR
1	481	5	10	405	4
2	411	4	11	448	4
3	371	4	12	210	3
4	351	4	13	363	4
5	146	3	14	434	4
6	220	3	15	132	3
7	442	4	16	365	4
8	183	3	17	441	4
9	350	4	18	403	4
	2955	34		3201	34

Total 6156 yards: par 68

find on a links. You drive onto a narrow fairway, curving to the right, with a fall on the right-hand side, and then punch your iron shot up over a deep gully full of heather to a small saucer of a green, protected in front by two heathery humps with a very narrow gap between. It looks like playing up a bottle neck, but all's well if you pitch well up.

The seventeenth is a fine two-shot hole, with a gully, or perhaps a big swale is a better term, in front of the tee, another rather over halfway and a third in front of the green. The green is flat and not too fiercely guarded and it sits handsomely with its background of pines. We end with a flat eighteenth with much white sand in evidence to the right of the fairway, and a slightly-raised green, with the big clubhouse and the glorious South Downs in front of us.

The British Ladies' Championship was played here in 1986 with a surprise win for the seventeen-year-old New Zealander Marny McGuire, the youngest winner since May Hezlet in 1899.

Old Thorns – Liphook

This is a new course, built in 1981, on the outskirt of Liphook village with several unusual, if not unique, features. First is its Japanese ownership, as it is a subsidiary of the Kosaido Co, a printing and publishing firm in Tokyo. The course, as well as the adjacent hotel and restaurant, is open to all and there is no membership. The layout is the modern American-style conventional package – and none the worse for that – with two loops of nine holes, with two par fives and two par threes in each. A lot of water comes into play on the lower parts of the course and a golf cart is, I would say, essential for the hillier holes; the course is in fact laid out for cart users who would otherwise often have long distances from green to tee, and I don't think you could get round without one, even if you have to pay handsomely for it. Some of the climbs and descents to and from the tees seem prodigious in length and steepness, as much as 1 in 6 in some cases, I would guess.

Some highly spectacular holes caught the eye, notably the long par-four third where a bunker on the right controls the drive, and a long second shot over a deep swale plays up to a small green on the opposite slope. Then at the fifth from a high hill top there is a huge drop – so providing a spectacular view as well as an exhilarating drive. After a long par five and a short hole over a pond comes the 350/370 yard eighth with a big pond, almost a lake, on the right to control the tee shot and then another up to the right side of the green; a narrow and most difficult hole.

Ten you might almost call a horror hole as it is 201/221 yards long to a green protected by water and there is water again on the right of eleven. There is some relief at thirteen and fourteen but then another fierce climb and shot up a steep slope makes the fifteenth play far beyond its card length. The short sixteenth is an attractive hole, easy from the yellow tee at 126 yards and tough from the white at 162. From here is another spectacular view from Selborne Hill to the Hog's Back and Hindhead, and after we have drunk this in, a swishing, precipitous downhill shot to the seventeenth.

The greens, which are entirely artificial, were moulded out of sand suitably enriched with fertilisers and are small and much beset by bumps, folds and hollows. Altogether it struck me as a difficult course which would play its full length; the ground, sandy meadow and woodland, with these furious hills on one side and lakeland below, good for the game. With its manifest man-made features it is hard to conceive a course more different from Liphook.

At the official opening in 1982 Aoki scored 69, Nicklaus 71, Ballesteros and Rogers 72 each.

Old Thorns Golf Course: Normal and Competition Cards

	WHITE	PAR		WHITE	PAR
1	339	4	10	221	3
2	497	5	11	359	4
3	444	4	12	435	4
4	157	3	13	364	4
5	320	4	14	510	5
6	543	5	15	268	4
7	162	3	16	162	3
8	370	4	17	483	5
9	390	4	18	423	4
Out	3222	36	In	3225	36
			Total	6447	72

Liphook

Liphook is on the borders of Sussex and Hampshire. The course lies astride the Portsmouth road and at the Anchor Hotel in the town Nelson stopped to take tea on his last night in England, on his way to Portsmouth to take command of the 'Victory' and the British Fleet before Trafalgar. Amid affecting scenes he left England never to return. As Southey wrote: 'England has had many heroes; but never one who so entirely possessed the love of his fellow countrymen as Nelson.'

Apart from its painful name, Liphook is one of the most charming courses that I know, very natural and unforced, with small difficult greens, and some beautiful short holes. It was laid out at a minimum of cost and so makes the greatest possible use of natural features and the best lie of the land, with few bunkers. About forty miles south of London, it is a good place for a day out. Frank Pennink, the architect and writer, calls it 'an outstanding course, where anyone who can play to his handicap is doing well'.

The course requires accurate placing of the shots and the architects, Arthur Croome and Tom Simpson, who with no mock modesty said 'Liphook is perhaps one of the five best inland courses in this country', set out to make the tigers scratch their heads. Since the war the course has been changed round and you no longer play off from a pub on the Portsmouth road: that hole is now the tenth and the first half is now the old second half and vice versa.

For my money, the most enjoyable holes are the short third, 'Milland', the short seventh to a very folded green, 'The Bowl', and even more the highly-picturesque and photogenic eleventh, a short hole of 157 yards, with a low plateau green and a clump of straight pines behind it on a knoll.

Among the longer holes, one of the best known is the thirteenth where you drive out of Sussex and cross a big ditch to have a go at the plateau green in Hampshire.

There are some shrewd dog legs among the shorter par fours, notably at 'Hollycombe' and the 'Quarry', which run parallel as numbers fifteen and sixteen, and at the 341-yard 'Pulpit'

Liphook Golf Club: Medal Card

NAME	YARDS	PAR	NAME	YARDS	PAR
1 Birch Hill	207	3	10 Fowley	347	4
2 The Old Road	424	4	11 The Clump	164	3
3 Milland	133	3	12 Forest Mere	425	4
4 High View	466	4	13 Two Counties	476	5
5 The Black Fox	484	5	14 The Pulpit	341	4
6 Ripsley	432	4	15 Hollycombe	368	4
7 The Bowl	157	3	16 The Quarry	364	4
8 The Valley	338	4	17 Sussex Edge	163	3
9 Bohunt	438	4	18 Wheatsheaf	480	5
	3079	34		3128	36

Total 6207 yards: par 70

hole, number fourteen. I also like the sixth called 'Ripsley' for its little bowl close in to the green with a small grove of trees in it. The long par fours are long enough for any man and if the total yardage is rather short because of five par threes don't think you will burn it up; I rather think not, for 70 gross or net is rarely beaten here in competition, in spite of its relative shortness.

How enjoyable it is, and rare, when you find something good has been left alone. Thank heavens Liphook is absolutely unchanged. I shall always remember my first visit here, sixty years ago, for a dramatic moment. We had played all day under grey, lowering skies, with a big wind. As we drove back to London over the high ground of Hindhead it was close to sunset and at that moment the grey cloud wrack lifted in the west and the whole sky became a swiftly moving mass of small scarlet clouds racing past us borne on the wings of the gale.

Hankley Common

Hankley Common is not far from Liphook, just inside the borders of Surrey, at Tilford, near Farnham. If we are approaching it from our visit to Liphook, we will have to pass near Hindhead, another fine heather and pines course with some of the deepest valleys and most pronounced slopes that I know. I fear we haven't time for a round here, which is a pity, for I have known the course for many years and it is indelibly stamped on my memory that once, in a university 'A' foursome against the club, my partner Charles Mitchell and I contrived to lose at the last hole by taking five putts – and no fault of the green at that.

Hankley Common, as we know it now, was laid out on a big open heath by James Braid sixty-five years ago, superseding an earlier course, much of which was built by the members' own manual labour. This sandy heathland makes excellent year-round golf and Hankley Common is noted for its crisp dry turf. When I went round some years ago it was burnt dry by a cool but rainless summer and the course looked strangely yellow. The result was to give, perhaps, a false impression of wide fairways and flatness and a lack of memorable features, except at the real three-star holes of which more in a moment.

The inevitable comparison with Liphook at once comes into mind and I must admit that for my choice Liphook came out a winner with more variety, more differences in levels and slopes of the ground and more individuality in the holes. Of the relative difficulty of the two courses I'm not fully able to judge, but I would think that on the whole Liphook is more difficult, but that Hankley Common has a few blockbusters which are tougher than anything that Liphook can offer.

Hankley starts with a loop of four holes, the first a tough par four which gets you going pleasantly enough, followed by a most charming short hole in a glade of trees; the green is below ground level, as it were, with a cross bunker in front, a delightful hole. The third and fourth each give you a cross bunker to carry. So did the present fifth, and right close up to the green at that, but a new green 80 yards further on has just been introduced which will improve the hole but with an easier access. The sixth is a long sweeping par five with quite a small but pretty shelf green, not too big either, as is right for a par five.

The seventh at 182 yards is a real three-star hole. Off a raised tee you play across a shallow valley and up a rising slope to a green quite a bit above you on a hilltop. There are wing bunkers guarding the green and the green itself has a step in it so that a shot from the back tee to the upper level is a real tough, formidable stroke. Between tee and green, or almost, is an unbroken sea of heather.

At the next three holes we get some relief, trouble in front and right and left but nothing to excite us like the seventh. At eleven, however, we have another short hole, this 219 yards with a shallow vale of heath to cross to an armchair green, all fine if you are straight enough so that the rampart around gathers your ball, but if you are wide it shrugs you off to real trouble.

The next three holes are plain sailing with vales and swales in front of the green at each, but shots must be hit to score. At the fifteenth we have a drive-and-pitch hole, to which Tom Scott gives high praise, with a narrow entry to a small green. The short sixteenth seemed to me like the seventh hole-and-water in the drinking sense; uphill too but shorter, less forbidding and less fierce.

The last hole is another absolute three-star hole; as Bernard Darwin used to say 'a hole of alarming excellence'. 433 yards long, you have first to hit a good drive which has to avoid a path across the fairway at a most inconvenient distance. Then you have the supreme choice of whether to hit a 200-yard shot right through to a small green on a shelf, almost without apron, so close is it to a protecting valley full of heather and tough rough, or play miserably short 'and trust to a pitch and putt'. The one thing you can't do is run through the valley and up on to the green. This is one of the most uncompromising and difficult finishing holes that I know. Long may it continue.

I think it would be fair to say that Hankley Common is not nearly as well known as it should be, but the course is now used for qualifying rounds for the Open Championship. There is a brand new clubhouse for the much

Hankley Common Golf Club: Medal Card

	YARDS	PAR		YARDS	PAR
1	436	4	10	428	4
2	136	3	11	219	3
3	350	3	12	394	4
4	319	4	13	500	5
5	383	4	14	386	4
6	534	5	15	315	4
7	182	3	16	150	3
8	521	5	17	366	4
9	366	4	18	433	4
	3227	36		3191	35

Total 6418 yards: par 71

increased membership, but the best traditions of golf are retained by such ordinances as the prohibition of the wearing of jeans, not only in the club but on the course.

If we are following this chapter as a motor tour we are now in for an attractive drive, through Basingstoke and Newbury and over the Berkshire Downs to Abingdon, for we are headed for Oxford. The road will have taken us through as attractive and ancient a part of England as you could wish to explore and within striking distance of the Vale of the White Horse through which the great Isambard Kingdom Brunel laid out his beautifully-engineered Great Western Railway, presided over, like many hundreds of man's works before, by the prehistoric White Horse carved down to the chalk out of the turf of the downs above Uffington.

Frilford Heath

There is good golf around Oxford, with a fine downland course at Huntercombe, on the edge of the Chilterns between Oxford and Henley, and a tough, uncompromising course which the city and university clubs use at Southfields

above Cowley which was designed by H. S. Colt. The best golf in the district in my view, however, is at Frilford Heath, about seven miles west of Oxford at the top of Cumnor Hill and about as far from Abingdon.

I first knew Frilford in the mid-'twenties, when we used to go out by bus from Oxford on Sundays, play two rounds, aided by a simple cold lunch handed out on a plate through a hatch in the unpretentious clubhouse, then back by bus in time to get into chapel with our plus-fours concealed by a surplice.

In those days, there were but eighteen holes and a very sporting and amusing heathland course it was, with gorse both to avoid and carry. And so it remains today, with most of the original holes surviving in spite of radical changes in the course and club. The first change was the addition of a new nine-hole layout, behind the old clubhouse, across the road from the Old course. More recently, nine more holes have been added and the entire layout altered to fit in with the new and more splendid clubhouse a mile or so from the old. So now we have two courses, the Red, a big affair of 6768 yards, and the Green, more lenient at 6006 yards. Much of the original golf survives, as I say, on one or other, all the new nine-hole layout having been incorporated into the Green course *en bloc* and most of the Old course divided between the two.

Thus the Green course, after a new 500-yard opening hole, takes in the old short seventh as its second. Then the old eighth, with the second shot to the saucer green, across that great pit with the bunkers in it, becomes number three, and the original ninth is now the fourth. This was and still is a hole of great difficulty, although of no great length, with an island green with a grassy pit in front, traps and a swale to the left and the chance of getting into a pond on the right. The entrance used to be protected also by a big mound, but that has now gone. The Green course then goes across the road, plays the whole nine there behind the old clubhouse and returns to the old first tee to play the fourteenth, now a long par four with a chance to hook out of bounds over the wall on to the highway. Originally, this hole was rather shorter and dominated by one huge elm tree, lost but now replaced. Fifteen is the old second

with out of bounds also on the left as a threat and sixteen is approximately the old long third; two new holes, a 206-yarder and a short par four finish a most attractive layout.

The Red course has more new holes at the start of the round, but I could see at once that the 486-yard twelfth was the old sixteenth. Next the former and most excellent seventeenth with its sharp dog leg across a shallow depression on the slant, and a slightly gathering shallow

Frilford Heath Golf Club –
Red Course Medal Card

	YARDS	PAR		YARDS	PAR
1	361	4	10	552	5
2	377	4	11	157	3
3	405	4	12	486	5
4	190	3	13	378	4
5	518	5	14	338	4
6	487	5	15	424	4
7	412	4	16	316	4
8	472	4	17	385	4
9	189	3	18	321	4
	3411	36		3357	37

Total 6768 yards: par 73

Green Course Medal Card

	YARDS	PAR		YARDS	PAR
1	500	5	10	179	3
2	202	3	11	361	4
3	347	4	12	333	4
4	357	4	13	383	4
5	335	4	14	442	4
6	153	3	15	411	4
7	446	4	16	444	4
8	336	4	17	206	3
9	273	4	18	298	4
	2949	35		3057	34

Total 6006 yards: par 69

saucer of a green survives as the thirteenth. So does the plateau green of the old eighteenth as the short par-four fourteenth. So it goes as we turn for home down the old tenth as number fifteen.

Much as I enjoyed the old Frilford, I must say that I think the conversion which was inevitable when the clubhouse was moved, has been most skilfully done, and two fine courses have emerged. The country, of course, could hardly be better; sharp sandy soil, crisp turf, beautiful mature greens and to decorate the rough, gorse and birch, pines and heather; woods frame the holes and you have far views over the Berkshire Downs by Wantage.

Berkhamsted

It is now time to turn for London and play two courses in the Chiltern Hills, Ashridge and nearby Berkhamsted. Both of these are worth a visit and it would be hard to find two courses more different in character; Ashridge is the work of man and very skilled work at that, while Berkhamsted is a wholly natural course, like Ashdown Forest or Piltdown, without a single bunker. There is one very conspicuous work of man, however, at Berkhamsted and that of the days long before golf architects. This is the ancient earthwork of Grim's Dyke with its 6 ft heather-clad bank and grassy trench 4 ft deep which comes into play at seven holes, including the first where we have to pitch over it to reach the green. Grim's Dyke also lends a shoulder to support the green at the short second.

From then on we are out on the open heath with plenty of gorse, heather and hawthorn bush to contend with, noting especially the sharply dog-leg sixth of 396 yards where the great Ted Ray, hat turned up in front, no doubt, and pipe going full blast, belted a ball over the corner of the dog leg, a carry of 270 yards. Ray, of course, was a tremendous hitter but he was more than that. Like many big hitters he had a delicate touch near the green and was a fine putter. He won the British Open in 1912 and was runner-up twice. He tied for the US Open in 1913 and lost in the famous play-off. Then he went to America again in 1920 and won at Inverness, Ohio, by a stroke. As O. B. Keeler wrote, Edward Ray won it because he stood 'the gaff best'.

I enjoy Keeler's account of how Ray took the news on the last green that he had to hole that 4-ft putt to beat Vardon and take the lead.

He was preparing to putt when he got the news. He promptly handed his club back to his caddie; removed the habitual pipe from his mouth; and while the assembled thousands fairly sweated blood with anxiety, he calmly refilled his pipe, puffed away two or three times, took back his putter from his caddie, and without any more to-do, sent down the putt that made him champion.

The second half at Berkhamsted is flatter and tougher and Grim's Dyke is still with us, on duty not only at the ninth but also at the front of the green at the huge eleventh, behind the fourteenth green and at the last.

	YARDS	PAR		YARDS	PAR
1	334	4	10	195	4
2	161	3	11	568	5
3	398	4	12	407	4
4	459	4	13	347	4
5	186	3	14	359	4
6	396	4	15	210	3
7	520	5	16	513	5
8	408	4	17	384	4
9	353	4	18	370	4
	3215	35		3353	36

Berkhamsted Golf Club: Medal Card

Total 6568 yards: par 71

Ashridge

Ashridge is totally different golf from the rough, tough simplicities which give us attractive golf at Berkhamsted. Here is a course laid out between the wars in an immemorial park with huge and beautiful trees, the one-time estate of the Brownlow family, whose vast mansion is now a management college. The layout is attributed to Cecil Hutchinson, Guy Campbell and Major Hotchkin with some subsequent alterations by Tom Simpson; the golf is amusing and apt and the condition of the course immaculate. Tom Scott says that of all the inland courses he knows this has 'the most perfect setting and is unquestionably the best kept'.

You start at Ashridge along a pleasant valley which helps to gather the wayward tee shot into line and so make the opening par four and the subsequent short par five no hardship. The third hole had to be repositioned because of the amount of traffic which has grown on the road which originally crossed it. A new plateau green has been built above the level of the tee and the shot has to avoid bunkers on three sides of the green.

The fourth after an exhausting climb to the tee is a big two-shot hole with a strategic bunker on the right of the fairway. I have been short with my second in this hole 'more times than I care to remember'. Then a curving short par five up a valley, a short hole of no conspicuous merit, a narrow seventh on the flat and another par three and we are ready for the ninth back to the clubhouse and one of the best holes on the course.

You drive up, or rather down, a wide tree-lined avenue and then are confronted with a light iron shot, often from a hanging lie, to a heavily folded, small plateau green sloping to perdition on the left, a splendid hole to do in four. This hole which was named 'Cotton's' for the immortal memory of Henry, professional here just before World War II, who devised a line on which he could succeed in driving the green, no less than 361 yards from the teeing ground.

There follows a loop of three holes from the clubhouse which includes a pretty short eleventh.

After an up-and-over short par five at

Ashridge Golf Club: Medal Card

NAME	YARDS	PAR	NAME	YARDS	PAR
1 Devil's Den	391	4	10 Pitstone	355	4
2 Golden Valley	494	5	11 Thunderdell	165	3
3 The Rookery	165	3	12 Deer Leap	405	4
4 Pooks Hill	410	4	13 Queen Elizabeth's Drive	476	5
5 Witchcraft Bottom	492	5	14 Old Park Lodge	431	4
6 Highwayman's Hide	190	3	15 Princes Riding	513	5
7 Ringshall	400	4	16 Willow Pond	167	3
8 Knobs Crook	179	3	17 Hoo	482	5
9 Cotton's	361	4	18 Home	432	4
	3082	35		3426	37

Total 6508 yards: par 72

thirteen we have a supremely attractive and difficult par four of 431 yards, the second shot to a narrow green set across the line of play with a steep bank in it leading to the upper level where the pin invariably is. There is a bunker guarding the left and a road behind the green. I know few holes requiring a more accurate and skilful second shot. I've played Ashridge many times but I can reckon very few pars here. This hole has been likened to the Road Hole at St Andrews but I don't see it; I think it has supreme merit of its own.

You end this splendid course rather dully, with a flat par five, the least good of the five short holes, another par five with an excessively folded little green at seventeen and a big bash downhill at the eighteenth, to be followed by a tough shot up to a stepped plateau green.

Ashridge has only 58 bunkers, but they are most skilfully situated to dictate play. There are no long carries or thick rough here, the golf is pleasant for the average player, but interesting and at times punishing for the more expert. For all golfers there are no more beautiful parkland surroundings in which to enjoy the game.

Northwood

Northwood on the north-western approaches to London, in Metroland indeed, had always appealed to me if only that it had one of the toughest and most uncompromising holes in all golf. Well, alas, the glory has departed from the tenth, 'Death or Glory', at Northwood, though they have left themselves with a difficult enough drive-and-pitch hole; we could all appreciate this if we did not remember the deep cavernous bunker with its dark sleepered black-avised face, over which we used to have to pitch while evading the equally deep sleepered bunker eating into the left side of the green, while the right side was protected by a bank with furze.

This apart, Northwood remains an open, pleasant piece of rolling country with its trees and whins and natural slopes and hollows, all but within the confines of London's urban sprawl. I enjoy it and like to take friends there.

This is one of the first clubs to mark the hole lengths in yards and metres.

Northwood Golf Club: Medal Card

	YARDS	PAR		YARDS	PAR
1	347	4	10	316	4
2	557	5	11	505	5
3	142	3	12	430	4
4	413	4	13	205	3
5	467	4	14	362	4
6	395	4	15	162	3
7	415	4	16	370	4
8	365	4	17	310	4
9	375	4	18	357	4
	3476	34		3017	35

Total 6493 yards: par 71

Moor Park

We end this round at Moor Park, a near neighbour of Northwood on the north-west outskirts of London. The two golf courses, the High and the West, are built in the superb parkland surrounding the great house which with many vicissitudes, first as a Roman villa, then as the manor house of the More, has seen the whole pageant of English history for close on 2000 years. The present house, which dates back to 1678, was built by James, Duke of

Monmouth, the natural son of Charles II who didn't live long to enjoy it as he suffered on Tower Hill for his rebellion against King James II after the Battle of Sedgemoor in 1685; his rebellion indeed against that same James who won the golf match on Leith links with John Patersone the cobbler as partner.

Before that, the manor of More had been in the hands of Cardinal Wolsey and then of Henry VIII who lodged Catherine of Aragon there during the scandalous divorce. Later the manor changed hands several times and the rich and noble owners altered and embellished the house and gardens to their present magnificence. Lord Leverhulme bought it in 1919 and from then on the present public history of the club begins. Golf began in the park in 1923 and the present members' club began in 1937. Many professional tournaments have been played on this impeccable turf.

I have to admit, as a rough generalisation, that in my eyes the best parkland courses don't come up to the heather and pines, which I might call moorland courses, just as the best moorland courses do not come up to golf links. That said, I would at once assert that the courses at Moor Park are second to none in park golf.

The West course is rather short, lots of fun and not easy, but the High course is the big one, laid out by H. S. Colt, and it has the stamp of his bold bunkering amid the groves of beech and oak all over it. Big two-shot holes and a tough finish, although the last hole is a par three, are characteristic. The holes that cling to the memory most I think are the uphill first, a tough starter, the 467-yard eighth with a pond to watch from the tee and the 480-yard ninth with its grove of beeches all the way along the left-hand side.

Of the par threes, the most spectacular and I think the most difficult, is the big thump at the twelfth across a valley to a bunker-beset two-tier green where a ball on the wrong level produces an almost certain three putts. I remember watching the pros play at Moor Park

more than once and to this day I can see a shot played by the mercurial George Duncan in the *News of the World* Match Play Tournament, though it must have been more than sixty years ago, in 1925 indeed. The ground was wet from overnight rain and there was a slight drizzle. George, who I think was playing Jack Smith, the long hitter, drove a very poor half-topped ball at the long sixth and was caught in a bunker in front of the tee about 160 yards out. The ball lay well enough in the wet sand but not more than about six feet from the bank of the bunker, which was a good four feet high. I'd have been glad to get 50 yards out with a niblick. Not so Duncan; he drew out his spoon and with no preliminaries worth mentioning and barely a glance at the ball, he hit a cut-up shot as clean as a whistle which soared in a high curve up the fairway for a good 200 yards, from which he got an easy five and a half. I think this was the greatest shot I ever saw played.

Moor Park, High Course: Medal Card

	YARDS	PAR		YARDS	PAR
1	371	4	10	145	3
2	418	4	11	393	4
3	165	3	12	210	3
4	426	4	13	507	5
5	334	4	14	435	4
6	493	5	15	430	4
7	362	4	16	517	5
8	467	4	17	408	4
9	480	5	18	152	3
	3516	37		3197	35

Total 6713 yards: par 72

The lengths for the Tournament card are as follows:

2	453	14	458
3	191	15	439
6	526	16	445
8	494		

Chapter 6
MIDLANDS AND THE NORTH

There is good golf almost all over the British Isles, and the Midlands and North of England are well-favoured areas. It is only my ignorance that prevents me describing more courses in this chapter, fewer than I have put in for the London district and the south. But here are some of the highest quality.

Little Aston

It is a sad commentary on my golfing education that the sole golfing representative of the real heart of the English Midlands, Birmingham, the homeland of so much that is famous and valuable in the nation, should be Little Aston. But it is so, and I can only add that it is at least a worthy course to include in any anthology of the best. The course starts in parkland, then ventures out rather surprisingly into a piece of heathery country, and returns again to the respectabilities of the parkland to finish. It is, by the way, one of the few courses attributed to Harry Vardon, whose fame was rarely exhibited in course design, but later changes were made by H. S. Colt and then by Mark Lewis when he was club professional.

All commentators, and I agree with them, take note of the excellence of the greens and the richness of the fairways, the siting of the trees and the seeming remoteness of the place.

Starting off with a modest par four, you are given a view of the famous seventeenth hole and its attendant water to muse over during your round, knowing that this must be tackled

Little Aston Golf Club: Medal Card

	YARDS	PAR			YARDS	PAR
1	390	4		10	438	4
2	437	4		11	398	4
3	505	5		12	491	5
4	316	4		13	164	3
5	160	3		14	313	4
6	426	4		15	566	5
7	374	4		16	402	4
8	394	4		17	364	4
9	197	3		18	389	4
	3199	35			3525	37

Total 6724 yards: par 72

when you return. At three and at four, one of the famous features of Little Aston, the great avenue running all along one side of the park, can be involved in the play; a hook into it at the long uphill 505-yard third can be most unwelcome.

After a rather made-up short hole at five, three more or less parallel par fours test you out before you tackle the short ninth, at which you burst out of the parkland into the open moor through a gap in the trees. Similarly, a short hole, the thirteenth, brings you back into the park, this time playing from the open land into the woods.

So, back on the lush turf of Little Aston Park, we work our way up to the famous seventeenth. Of no great length, 364 yards, the tee shot is nevertheless tight with trees, where you would rather not have them, and the hole is made by the plateau green, beset all round by bunkers and, somehow, with rather unwelcoming contours. Away to the left is a lake, and while it should not enter into the play, I don't doubt that all too often it does.

Woburn

The Duke of Bedford was among the first, if not the first, to open his stately home and the grounds of his estate near Bedford to the public for profit, an example widely followed since.

Among the amenities since provided at Woburn (pronounced Wooburn), now the home of his son, the Marquess of Tavistock, and his wife, has been the Golf and Country Club, with two fine courses, the 'Duke's' and the 'Duchess', designed by the late Charles Lawrie. Both courses were carved out of a dense forest of pine, birch, beech and chestnut and are liberally decorated with rhododendrons. The Duke's course was opened in 1976 and the Duchess a few years later, and from this unpromising bush country, with heather, bracken and gorse, two layouts of great charm and beauty, fine examples of what pine and heather courses should be, have been created.

Perhaps the most spectacular holes are the short third where the tee is level with the tops of the trees round the green, and the long fifth, where the second shot needs a big carry over a gully.

I am sorry I have not had the chance to play here, for both courses have earned wide praise. Three years after its opening, the Duke's course attracted its first major professional tournaments, the Dunlop Masters, won by two of

Australia's great players, Greg Norman and Graham Marsh, and since then has staged many events, both amateur and professional, including the English Amateur Stroke Play Championship (the Brabazon Trophy), the British Ladies Open and the women's professional event, the Ford Classic.

For major events, the first hole of 514 yards is made the eighteenth to provide a spectacular finish, and American Lee Trevino, in winning the inaugural Dunhill British Masters, staged

Woburn Golf Club: Medal Card – Duke's Course

	YARDS	PAR		YARDS	PAR
1	514	5	10	404	4
2	358	4	11	502	5
3	134	3	12	193	3
4	395	4	13	419	4
5	510	5	14	565	4
6	207	3	15	432	4
7	464	4	16	449	4
8	409	4	17	425	4
9	177	3	18	229	4
	3105	35		3718	37

Total 6913 yards: par 72

over the Duke's course in 1985, provided the spectators with one of the most sensational shots of his long and distinguished career. He had pushed his drive into the semi-rough and, with 255 yards to go to a green well guarded by bunkers, he manoeuvred a 3-wood in characteristic style out to the left for the ball to fade towards the green and roll steadily towards the hole, finishing just six inches from the cup, for an eagle 3. It gave him the first Masters title of his career – 'I've always wanted to win a Masters . . . but I never expected it would be a British one,' said the player who has never been able to add the US Masters to his successes in the three other major championships of the world.

The Belfry

The Belfry, near Sutton Coldfield, close to the centre point of all England, is the home of the British Professional Golfers Association. The golf courses here are part of a hotel/leisure complex costing it is said, £3,000,000 and while this might be said to be the PGA's home ground they do not own the golf and are tenants of their offices.

The course was created by the former Ryder Cup players, David Thomas and Peter Alliss, the longer course, the 'Brabazon' – named after Lord Brabazon of Tara, England's first aviator and a former PGA president – and the shorter, easier one, the 'Derby' after the present president. The big course can be stretched to over 7000 yards, though it plays normally rather less off the back tees. Both courses are open to the public.

The ground was highly unpromising, flat agricultural land, a series of potato fields in fact, which as Thomas said was 'flat and nearly featureless except for a smallish lake and a stream zigzagging across'. From this has been built a big straightforward American-style park course with water, water everywhere – at no less than fifteen holes one account says – trees galore planted, big greens, mounds for the spectators and space for a tented village. Remote as this is from old-style Scottish simplicity one has to admire the creation from virtually nothing of this great golfing arena by the intervention of modern earth-moving tools, plus a lot of money.

The long narrow eighteenth is perhaps the most difficult hole on the course, for there is a lake to cross from the tee and again with the shot to the green which has three distinct levels; and all this in a hole of 455 yards.

The lake which has done so much to alarm at eighteen also threatens the whole of the right side of the ninth, while the tenth is a water hole of a rare type. 301 yards from tee to green one is expected to play short of the water which runs along the right side and front of the green and then pitch up over it. That is until Seve Ballesteros in the Great Britain v. Europe match in 1978, as it were, took his coat off and hit a huge shot which carried all the way to the centre of the green. Then like the four-minute mile, once

	YARDS	PAR		YARDS	PAR
	The Belfry Golf Course: Brabazon Course				
1	408	4	10	301	4
2	340	4	11	365	4
3	455	4	12	225	3
4	569	5	13	354	4
5	389	4	14	184	3
6	386	4	15	540	5
7	173	3	16	400	4
8	476	5	17	555	5
9	390	4	18	455	4
Out	3586	37	In	3389	36

Total 6975 yards: par 73

The Belfry Golf Course: Derby Course

	YARDS	PAR		YARDS	PAR
1	362	4	10	496	5
2	371	4	11	433	4
3	286	4	12	367	4
4	395	4	13	177	3
5	331	4	14	349	4
6	188	3	15	410	4
7	348	4	16	161	3
8	305	4	17	357	4
9	402	4	18	339	4
Total	2988	35	Total	3089	35
				3185	35
			Total	6077	70

The Belfry really rose to eminence in 1985 when the Ryder Cup matches of Europe v. the United States were played here. The result was a resounding win for the home team, the first time we had won since Lindrick in 1957. It is strange how at golf, an individual game if ever there was one, a side can rise or collapse as surely as a cricket or football team. Our own teams have lost in this way, for example, our Walker Cup side at Baltimore in 1965, but the Americans fail more rarely, but so it was here and at Lindrick last time we managed to win.

There were some complaints by the losers of excessive partisanship amounting to unfairness by the crowd, which I hope were no more than a natural annoyance at losing; certainly our own captain, Tony Jacklin, thought there was nothing in it. Lee Trevino, the American captain, gave the best answer; he told his side that the only way to silence the crowd was with birdies.

it had been done everyone can do it, so others have hit the tenth off the tee and already Greg Norman has scored an eagle two here and Eamon Darcy has holed the course in 63!

One surprise visitor to the Cup matches was the supersonic airliner Concorde, which made a couple of visits and dipped its wings in salute.

Woodhall Spa

Surprises, especially pleasant ones, enlighten life, and it is always a joy to come on fine golfing territory in unexpected surroundings. Often these areas, as at Mildenhall, are extremely small, and others, like those at Pulborough, Sandiway or Frilford Heath, have only a limited space to offer.

Somehow, the flat fertile fenland of Lincolnshire does not seem too promising for inland golf, and yet here in an oasis of sand, heather, birch and pines, Woodhall Spa springs out of the levels with a notable, fine course, one of the best of its kind in the country, and yet perhaps not as well known as it should be. The English Ladies have held their championship here, and the Brabazon Trophy has been played here, so also has the English Amateur Championship. Here in the Brabazon in 1954, in a gale of wind

and rain, the late Philip Scrutton seized the trophy with a wonderful last round, coming from seven strokes behind which pulverised the field. That discriminating judge, Harry Busson, braving the weather, walked round and said afterwards that this was the greatest round of golf he ever saw played.

Coming here on a perfect September day, with the heather, which lines all the fairways and faces all the tees, in full blaze of colour and the sunlight from a cloudless sky only tempered by the smoke of the straw burning in the fields after a magnificent harvest, this seemed a place of calm, charm and quality. It is a splendid golf course and one which I took to instantly. I liked the atmosphere of the place too; the clean little town, the golfers' hotel and the good houses reminded me of that other

resort and golf town, Pinehurst in North
Carolina.

The course at Woodhall Spa was designed by
that distinguished amateur, Colonel S. V.
Hotchkin. It is fairly flat and no hardship on the
feet, but you have got to place your shots in
order not to be penalised as the narrowness of
entrance to many of the greens is severe and so
are the deep uncompromising bunkers. I can't
offhand remember any course where the
bunkers are tougher than here; no ball runs
through them.

There are only three short holes, but they are
all first-class, and any number of exacting par
fours which really make you work. But there
are three par fours of under 350 yards in the
second nine to relieve the player a little.

After a fairly level undemanding first hole,
you get down to business at the second, a par
four of 408 yards over a gravelly road and up a
gentle slope, whence for the first time you see
the characteristic narrow entrance to the green.
The third is another tough four, this time with a
bunker to clear from the tee and a long heave up
to the green close to the ruined tower which
dominates all this part of the course.

At four, we turn back to the west to get
another over-400 par four, this one with a
plateau green with deep menacing bunkers on
either flank.

The first short hole comes next, of 155 yards
down towards the old railway track which is
now lifted, and a real beauty. The shot is
slightly downhill and the green an elongated
saucer, if you can have such a thing, which
helps to gather a first-class stroke; anything less
is bunkered in some grievous deep traps in
front and under the flanks. This fine hole has
recently been improved by lowering the back of
the bunker guarding the front entrance so that
more of the excellent green can now be seen
from the tee.

Six and seven were, I thought, a little
pedestrian without being easy, but the eighth is
another fine short hole, this one facing due
west. At 193 yards it can be a big shot against

Woodhall Spa Golf Club: Medal Card

	YARDS	PAR		YARDS	PAR
1	363	4	10	333	4
2	408	4	11	442	4
3	417	4	12	152	3
4	415	4	13	437	4
5	155	3	14	489	5
6	506	5	15	325	4
7	435	4	16	398	4
8	193	3	17	322	4
9	560	5	18	516	5
Out	3452	36	In	3414	37
			Out	3452	36
			Total	6866	73

the prevailing wind. It is slightly uphill to a
plateau green with a deep bunker to left and
right and a really big one about 40 yards short.
Somehow, the green does not seem to welcome
the shot.

The ninth is a long hole and requires a carry
for the second shot over a belt of rough and
bunkers, and then for the third shot a very tight
narrow pitch which is as it should be.

The tenth out to the far end of the course is a
short par four slightly dog-leg right, with again
a very narrow entrance to the green. At eleven
we have a fine, long, sweeping hole slightly
downhill with a belt of rough and two deep
bunkers right across the fairway about 40–50
yards short of the green. The green lies in a
most attractive semi-circle of trees.

The twelfth is a delightful short hole of 152
yards: you play out of the trees up to a high
plateau green, by no means small, with edges
which help gather a fair shot a little but beyond
the fringes deep, deep sandy trouble.

At thirteen we have a long par-four hole
running down to the far-off green, with rough
encroaching on the right to catch a faded drive

and from the left to catch a drawn second. A par five comes next, short in yards but tight to play, then the famous 325-yard fifteenth, with its saucer green surrounded by bunkers.

Now for the run-in. At sixteen you have the scenery at its best with open heath to the left and a long avenue of birch, pine and hard-woods to the right. If you hit a good drive you have to clear a rampart of heathery knobs with your mid-iron to the green.

At seventeen, though only 332 yards, the drive is tight and the plateau green not easy to capture. You end with a par five into the westering sun and cannot count on a par as the green slopes away from the shot. This hole has recently been lengthened and from either tee it is suggested that the best weapon to use would be a rifle.

After tea you can amuse yourself with the little pitch and putt course in the birch trees close to the clubhouse.

As is fitting for a city of its size, Leeds is well provided with golf courses, but the outstanding ones lie on the northern fringe of the town, on a stretch of sandy heathland known as Wigton Moor, Alwoodley, on one side of the Leeds–Harrogate road and Sand Moor and Moortown on the other.

Alwoodley

Alwoodley lies in a fine piece of natural golf country, with heather and gorse in the rough and pines and silver birches as background. The soil is sandy and light, and the course is never wet. It is, moreover, one of those courses which take the perhaps rather old-fashioned view that there ought to be something in front of the tee to drive over. This, no doubt, can be pinned on H. S. Colt, who was in on the first designs in 1907, and that other famous archi-tect, Dr Alister Mackenzie of Dornoch, the club's first secretary, who afterwards helped lay out the famous Augusta National Course with Bobby Jones in the United States.

In ordinary conditions, Alwoodley is not back-breakingly difficult, though I do remem-ber a day there with hard-baked fairways, knee-high grass in the rough and a stiff wind, when I thought it was almost unplayable.

You start peacefully enough with a flat par four of 405 yards and no particular difficulty. The second is also par four, a short one of 305 yards, uphill, restricted by the road behind it. However, confessing to a liking for short par-four holes, if they are tight and good, I like the second here. You have to clear the gorse in front of the tee and then pitch past the wing bunkers to a small green with a central hollow running from back to front; this may give you a difficult putt.

Three is a great, long, sweeping hole, over 500 yards, and with the prevailing wind behind you, you may hope to be there in two on a summer's day. The fourth, back the other way, although a shorter par five than the third, plays longer very often as you beat uphill into the breeze.

The fifth hole is a terror for the player with any tendency to slice, for the fairway slopes severely to the right, and any mis-hit with fade will be shot into the rough, giving you hard pitch back over the bunkers to make the green; here is a hole I'm always delighted to get away from with a four. After this, we have a 420-yard par four, flat but well bunkered, so that's another you're glad to see the back of.

Seven is the first short hole, a nice 142-yard punch, to big built-up green, with a wood called Wigton Cover as a nice backdrop. Then comes a 546-yard par five, the hole first swing-ing to the left round the end of Wigton Cover; then, after carrying a chain of cross bunkers with your second, you pitch up to an elevated green.

The ninth is a longer par three, 193 yards, also back towards Wigton Cover with bunkers eating into the green. A sharp blow with a spoon or a two-iron is needed here, although the shot is slightly downhill.

The tenth is a fine hole, a short par five of 478 yards; the fairway at the landing point runs uphill and slopes to the left as it swings round towards the green, with out of bounds all along the left side, giving a very testing tee shot. Once there, you can strike for home to the green on a hill beyond a deep gully across the fairway, with a cross bunker in its face. A three here with a stroke allowance and so five whole points in a Stableford competition once was a tonic I well remember.

The eleventh, a par three, needing a four- or five-iron, has an attractive plateau green set amid the gorse and scrub; the slopes on the green may cause some anxiety. At the next you have a 366-yard par four, and after carrying the rough of gorse and heather from the tee, you can come in with a not too difficult pitch. The thirteenth, 396 yards, and usually into the eye of the wind, I find much harder, with bunkers, and quite deep ones, biting into the green's edge. Far too often I seem to end up with a six here.

After another short hole, to a plateau green backed again by Wigton Cover, we turn for home with a splendid 405-yard hole. You hug the cover to your right as close as you dare, as the hole is curved to the right all the way, and then from a humpy fairway, hit home to a plateau green, with a bunker protecting it on either wing, and over a big cross bunker eighty yards or so from the centre of the green. If you go too far you can find a pond at the back. Frank

	Alwoodley Golf Club: Medal Card				
	YARDS	PAR		YARDS	PAR
1	405	4	10	478	5
2	305	4	11	168	3
3	510	5	12	366	4
4	481	5	13	396	4
5	371	4	14	207	3
6	420	4	15	405	4
7	142	3	16	417	4
8	546	5	17	437	4
9	193	3	18	439	4
Out	3373	37	In	3313	35
			Out	3373	37
		Total 6686 yards: par 72			

Pennink calls this hole the pride of Alwoodley, 'one of the best and most attractive dog legs to be found anywhere'.

This pond – and a fellow – with a great deal of gorse and scrub, confronts you on the sixteenth tee, after which your spoon or big iron to the sixteenth green has to miss a minefield of bunkers. At the seventeenth, you drive over the road between out of bounds to the left and traps to the right; to get home easily you must hug the left side. The green which needs a good full-blooded hit to reach is down a little slope from fairway level.

The last, 439 yards, is on flat ground, and rather pedestrian, although there are plenty of bunkers to come between you and your four.

Moortown

Moortown is not quite so blessed as Alwoodley, with which it is invariably compared, as it lacks the crisp dryness of the turf, the widespread heather and gorse and the sense of aloof seclusion. Nevertheless, the peaty moorland soil has produced some excellent fairways at Moor-

town, and Dr Alister Mackenzie has given us a fine, testing game of golf. Recently major changes have been made to the course.

As we go down the first fairway, a 492-yard par five, with some hopes of a birdie, the big birch wood which is such an attractive feature of the early holes is conspicuous on your left. At the third hole we are running close to it, and at the short fourth we play into the heart of it.

At the fifth, a 374-yard par four, we drive out of the wood into the open country, but the wood dominates the play, for we must cling to it as much as we can. Two new holes in this same woodland now follow, the sixth and seventh, after which comes the long par-three eighth uphill into meadowland.

Down again with a stiff par four and we are ready for the famous tenth, formerly the eighth. This is a short hole, built on a rock, known as 'Gibraltar', 176 yards to a well bunkered gently sloping plateau green. It is a handsome hole with its back drop of birch wood, and it needs a fine shot; what more can you want? A blind tee shot at eleven and an attractive shot to the green on a hill and you are at the end of the course. Here the land changes more to moorland style and you play on Blackmoor two tough holes before descending via a new fourteenth made out of the old thirteenth and fourteenth together, down to the richer green lands.

I remember clearly catching up with George Duncan and Walter Hagen at the turn in their Ryder Cup single in 1929. I can see George now, dormy nine, striding down the long tenth fairway to play a short pitch as his third to what was then the tenth green. He lifted his head, the ball never left the ground and finished stone dead; so he beat his opposing captain 10 and 8, as part of a famous British victory.

The finish is now ahead of us and I must confess the last four holes, all of a good par-four

Moortown Golf Club: New Medal Card					
	YARDS	PAR		YARDS	PAR
1	492	5	10	176	3
2	457	4	11	369	4
3	448	3	12	559	5
4	176	3	13	443	4
5	374	4	*14	425	4
*6	430	4	15	396	4
*7	510	5	16	423	4
8	221	3	*17	190	3
9	450	4	18	442	4
	3558	36		3423	35

Total 6981 (SSS 73): par 71

*Subject to measuring

length, were not outstandingly memorable, but all the books tell us of Sam King's Bridge, a stout affair of three railway sleepers over a stream at the sixteenth. These he had removed in order to play out of the ditch in the *Yorkshire Evening News* Tournament in 1949, which he subsequently won. Things have improved now as the seventeenth has been shortened to par three.

Playing in the Brabazon Trophy in 1974, Yorkshire county player Nigel Denham hit too strong an approach to the eighteenth, the ball bounding over the green and through the clubhouse door and into the bar; from there he chipped the ball back through an open window on to the green.

Lindrick

Lindrick is historic turf, for here in 1957 the British Ryder Cup team, starting 3–1 down to the USA on the second day, won six of the eight singles, and scattered their enemies in confusion and dismay. And not for another 29 years did our team win again and then only with reinforcements from Europe.

The match was not without its incidents, and the top single between Eric Brown and the irascible Tommy Bolt produced a few sparks,

Royal Birkdale: at the 13th hole

Royal St George's, Sandwich: the new 3rd hole

Rye: the President's Putter defies the weather

Royal Cinque Ports, Deal: links land at its best

Right: Wentworth: Des Smyth at the 17th on the 'Burma Road'

Royal Porthcawl: the first Welsh Championship course

Berkshire: the 11th
green and 12th hole,
Red Course

The Belfry: the famous
10th hole with its
Water Legend

Ganton: the 13th hole
from the tee

while on our side the late Harry Weetman expressed displeasure at being left out of the singles. At the end of a memorable day though, it was Dai Rees, our captain, who took the honours. Not only did he play well, but his infectious enthusiasm fired his whole team. In this he was grandly supported by Max Faulkner who, far from showing rancour at being displaced after the foursomes, did splendid service in all quarters spreading news and encouragement.

It has often been remarked how strange it is, in an individual game like golf, that a whole side, scattered all over the course, can suddenly become dismayed and finally lose from a winning position. Usually, it follows some spectacular reversal of fate in one key match, as when Ed Tutwiler, on the last day at Five Farms in Baltimore in the Walker Cup in 1965, won seven holes in a row from Ronnie Shade, and so, almost singlehanded, destroyed us. In the end, only a desperate putt on the last green by Clive Clark earned us a halved match, when at midday we seemed to have the game in the bag.

So it was at Lindrick and so it was again at the Belfry in 1986; our men started well, kept the pressure on, the crowd roared, the captain won by 7 and 6 and the US for once – and I emphasise, this is a most rare happening – fell apart. Only Hawkins won his single, and that most elegant of swingers in an age of bashers, Dick Mayer, got a half. How does one explain this? My view is that the Americans never felt at home on the Lindrick greens, though they seemed to me as we walked round to be perfect in texture and pace, but with many small folds and slopes that the Americans never managed to read as well as our men. In consequence, the Americans didn't putt nearly as forcefully as they usually do.

So now to the course. Lindrick serves Sheffield and has a venerable history going back now ninety-six years. It is on dry heathland with gorse and birch trees. The fairways and greens are excellent. Frank Pennink quotes Jackie Burke, the defeated American captain of

1957, as saying 'the course is a golfing paradise, the turf is perfect, the greens flawless'.

The hole that everyone remembers is the 480-yard fourth, where even after a long drive you have a long blind second to a green just in front of a river. John Jacobs reports that Bernard Darwin called this the worst hole of the course, adding that it must never, on any account, be altered. It is, I believe, at this green that in days gone by Yorkshire, Derbyshire and Nottinghamshire all joined. The area was therefore used for cock fights and prize fights in the past which could be hastily removed from one county to another.

My own recollections also put the second hole of 359 yards as a beauty, with a pitch up to a rising, heavily beset green. Here the British and American pros gave us some lovely shots.

But it is the finish at Lindrick which gives a real stretch. 464, 438 and 557 yards take you to the fourteenth green; the fifteenth 362 yards up to the far end of the course is some respite, but then you have a long one home at sixteen, 486 yards, downhill it's true, but usually into the wind, with a big quarry on the left, and then after a shorter par four you end with a stirring

	YARDS	PAR		YARDS	PAR
	Lindrick Golf Club: Medal Card				
1	401	4	10	368	4
2	359	4	11	173	3
3	163	3	12	464	4
4	480	5	13	438	4
5	433	4	14	557	5
6	141	3	15	362	4
7	434	4	16	486	5
8	318	4	17	397	4
9	435	4	18	206	3
	3164	35		3451	36

Total 6615 yards: par 71

finish, a solid bang of 206 yards over cross bunkers to an elevated green, itself trapped, under the clubhouse windows. The seven-teenth hole has the distinction of having cost Greg Norman 17 strokes in the Martini International tournament in 1982.

Sandiway

Sandiway lies in a delightful patch of rolling sandy heathland, rising out of the Cheshire clay, with attendant birches, beech trees, pines, gorse, bracken and heather. It is on the main road into Chester and North Wales from Manchester, about four miles west of North-wich. It has for years been a place of relaxation for the ICI staff and workers who abound in the area.

It dates from just after World War I, and although Ted Ray is named as the first designer, it bears the stamp of H. S. Colt most clearly. The original second, third and fourth holes have been lost through road widening and in many ways this is a pity, for the old second was a fiendishly difficult hole off the back tee, with a pitch up to a high plateau green, often off a hanging lie. Three was a difficult par five, but this has been taken care of by making two par fives among the new holes, the second seeming to run interminably into the sunset, while the new fourth runs back past a sinister little black wood for over 500 yards.

Meanwhile, we have missed out one and three, so we had better go back and start properly.

You lead off with an exhilarating drive from a high place alongside the pro's shop, clearing some of Mr Colt's big bunkers, and then hit a mid-iron of some sort up to a much bunkered armchair green which can gather your ball nicely. No. 2, as I said, runs 523 yards far out to the end of the course. The new short third hole runs across the end of the course, a pretty hole, amid the birch trees, and then after four back to the old terrain.

The fifth tee, close to a fine stand of beech trees, shows you little of the hole unless you are playing from the back tee, a high platform, known as 'Nicholson's Folly', after a former president of the club who became a director of ICI. This hole is a beauty with a small, tightly-bunkered green, hard to find and hard to hold.

The sixth is a pleasant, short hole with a great row of beech trees as a backdrop. Long, long ago I had the supreme pleasure here of my first hole in one. Then you drive across a patch of rough which used to be a cottage garden, which put all too many of us out of bounds, to a ridge across the fairway and hope to get home to a green, part masked by a slope on the left. I don't doubt that the hole is easier now that the out of bounds has gone. The eighth is a drive uphill and a pitch much uphill to a green in front of the clubhouse.

At the ninth you need a long drive to get a sight of the cross bunkers in the dip guarding the green, a fine two-shot hole this.

The tenth I always found one of the hardest holes on the course. Fine trees and rough catch a shot only slightly pulled; the fairway slopes from left to right, so all too often you end in the rough on the right. So you thrash it out and find you still have a pretty long third to get home to the green at the top of the hill.

Eleven is a dull, long par three down to the edge of Pettypool, the local mere, but twelve, running along its shores, is a very pretty hole. The green is on a shelf with rough and a track to the left and big bunkers eating into the right-hand edge, and thick, damp rough further right. This hole, I think, has not been improved by lengthening; it was a much better hole at about 410 yards than it is now at 446. I do think, though, that the trees which the greens committee ordered to be planted, in my day as a member, from the back of the tenth and running all along the left side of the twelfth, have grown into a great improvement.

After the short thirteenth, with its minefield of bunkers and drop down to a lane on the right, the fourteenth has a carry over an out of bounds field, a sore trial from the back tee with the prevailing wind across, and then needs a long poke with wood or a big iron to get up to the high green perched on its hilltop.

At fifteen, you strike back but need a big carry over a ridge to the right if you want the easiest line for your pitch in to the green.

At the sixteenth it all depends on your drive staying on a narrow fairway which slopes across the line towards the left, so that you can then bang the ball over the sharp ridge which confronts you, and be left with only a pitch shot to the sloping, difficult green.

The seventeenth is grand fun, as it is completely dominated by a huge oak tree in the centre of the fairway, about 200 yards out on the other side of a deep valley in front of the tee. There it is, and you have got to avoid it one side or the other, preferably on the left; after that you pitch to a small green entirely surrounded by bunkers, with a nice clump of beeches on the knoll above the green looking on.

The last hole is the fifth par three, and very

Sandiway Golf Club: Medal Card					
	YARDS	PAR		YARDS	PAR
1	405	4	10	467	4
2	523	5	11	219	3
3	193	3	12	446	4
4	502	5	13	138	3
5	416	4	14	441	4
6	151	3	15	362	4
7	413	4	16	519	5
8	357	4	17	305	4
9	396	4	18	182	3
	3356	36		3079	34
				3356	36
				6435	70

tight indeed, with bunkers on the ridge to the left, bunkers in front and behind and out of bounds right along the green's edge on the right. With a heavy cross wind, it is a wickedly hard shot. So ends one of the most attractive inland courses, and one which I had the pleasure of playing, but never mastering, for fourteen happy years.

Silloth-on-Solway

The special journey to Silloth, on the estuary of the Solway about twenty miles from Carlisle, was well worth while, for this is an admirable golf links with the added hazard of heather in the rough. On a warm September day with a minimum of breeze coming in with the tide, it looked and was a fine enough test for anyone; with a gale off the Irish Sea it could offer the full rigour of the game. While the layout is roughly out and home there are enough changes of direction to avoid the feeling of a monotonous beat out and a roller-coaster ride home.

There is great charm here, the course offering beautiful turf and some old-style blind shots –

and why not once in a while – and great natural beauty. On a fine day you have a grand view, north over the Solway to the lighthouse and links of Southernness with Criffel behind; to the west on a very clear day there is a view to the Isle of Man and southwards to the mountains of the Lake District, whence 'the red glare on Skiddaw roused the burghers of Carlisle' at the time of the Armada. Only eastwards towards the home of the famous Cumberland turf on the flat land by the shore is the view unkind, for it is dominated by a huge and hideous flour mill.

No great events had been held here until the

British Ladies' Stroke Play Championship in 1972 when the links was at its superb best and some fine scores were turned in. There were some of the other sort, too, as the short sixteenth claimed two nines, one from Mary Everard in the last round which destroyed her and let Belle Robertson in to win. It was noteworthy that the prizes for this competition were handed over by Miss Cecil Leitch, one of the very great lady players then at the good sound age of eighty-one. The Leitch Sisters although Scots by ancestry were the pride of Silloth for many years.

The ladies were back in 1976 and 1983 for the British Amateur Championship, which led to popular wins by Cathy Panton and Jill Thornhill.

The first hole gives you a slightly-blinded second shot, as the green is in a shallow saucer, so, too, is the second, but at the third the green is on a natural plateau. At five we are running all along the shore of the Solway and can slice on to the beach all too easily. The sixth is the first short hole, down from a high tee in the sandhills towards the interior. Then we have a beauty of 408 yards, with a blind second shot over a ridge to a small green in a dell, which is also shared with some rough humpy ground, a real charmer this.

Eight is all up a valley and the short ninth runs towards the sea again. At the tenth we cross the 'T' as it were, and then start in on the landward side. The eleventh is another pretty hole in its valley and twelve is a slightly downhill short hole where you can easily get shrugged off to the bunkers on the right.

Then comes the thirteenth, a great slashing hole with the green high on a ridge above you, 482 yards off, usually into the eye of the wind. The next hole, back towards home, is much the same length, with a fine second needed to get you over the big ridge which masks the green. Fifteen seems to get narrower as you get nearer and you end with a small green for a 417-yard hole.

Then comes sixteen, the killer hole, 179 yards off our tee with a plateau green well raised with sand on each flank, grass bunkers and heather beyond. The entrance looked painfully narrow,

---

Silloth-on-Solway Golf Club: Medal Card

NAME	YARDS	PAR	NAME	YARDS	PAR
1 Horse Shoe	380	4	10 Blooming Heather	308	4
2 The Close	325	4	11 Spire	389	4
3 Criffel	362	4	12 Heather Bank	192	3
4 The Mill	377	4	13 Hogs Back	482	5
5 Solway	486	5	14 Milecastle	484	5
6 Natterjack	184	3	15 Heather Lonning	417	4
7 Battery	408	4	16 The Mount	179	3
8 Valley	370	4	17 Duffers	486	5
9 The Manx	127	3	18 Home	387	4
Out	3019	35	In	3324	37
			Out	3019	35
			Gross	6343	72

I thought, and the green seems small, a feature of Silloth all round.

The seventeenth of 486 yards has a fearsome carry off the tee over a hollow full of heather with some sand to the right, the 'Duffers' Bunker' in full measure. The last is less fierce, but again the green is narrow and the wing bunkers therefore close at hand.

So ends a splendid links, not on any account to be missed, and one which, like Dornoch, used to be one everyone has heard of but few have succeeded in playing.

Ganton

This northern tour ends at Ganton nine miles inland from Scarborough. On the way out of York to Ganton we will probably pass Fulford, a good parkland course which hosts a big tournament every year. One feat long to be remembered there was Bernhard Langer climbing a tree to play his ball, which had lodged in the branches several feet above the ground.

The Amateur Championship was played at Ganton in 1964, the first time it had been held away from the seaside. The final, by the way, was won by Gordon Clark at the 39th hole. The Amateur came here again in 1977 when Peter McEvoy won for the first time. One of the finest performances of recent years was the winning of the British Youths Championship by the brilliant young Spaniard, J. M. Olazabal in his last tournament as an amateur in August 1985. On a blustery day he holed the course in 70 and 69. The Ryder Cup match was played here in 1949.

Ganton is on the lightest of sandy soil and resembles a seaside links as much as any inland course can; only the trees, which are sparse, and the surroundings reveal the truth.

You start out with a couple of par fours of no great length, though you can, of course, bunker yourself if you wish. The third was reachable wth a big hit from the tee, but a new back tee for the Ryder Cup has put the championship length up to 334 yards.

The fourth is a beautiful par four with the second shot across a gully and a sharp rise to a plateau green. Then comes a short hole with water hazards, which somehow seems to exact a four much more often than it should. There follow three big holes over 400 yards, of which the sixth is normally outside my reach, while the seventh, with its curvature and bunkering and the green on the crest of the rise, is just at the limit of my strength.

The half closes with the long ninth, nearly 500 yards, parallel with the main road. This is followed by an excellent short hole, always rather further away than it looks and well bunkered. Then the eleventh with some deep bunkers and a keen green and after that a decidedly 'inland' dog-leg hole round the end of a row of trees.

The par-five thirteenth shouldn't bother you unless you top your drive into a sea of gorse.

			Ganton Golf Club: Medal and Championship Cards			
	M	PAR	C		M	PAR	C
1	375	4	375	10	169	3	169
2	416	4	416	11	402	4	421
3	334	4	334	12	364	4	364
4	406	4	406	13	498	5	532
5	157	3	157	14	283	4	283
6	447	4	447	15	437	4	457
7	430	4	430	16	448	4	448
8	392	4	414	17	251	4	251
9	494	5	494	18	389	4	424
	3451	36	3473		3242	36	3347

Total 6693 and 6820 yards: par 72

Then comes the second of three big one-thump holes – if you include the third – a 283-yard beat downwind to a small green infested with bunkers with a choice of a drive-and-pitch by going to the right. Two excellent holes around 450 yards follow, reachable in two in the right conditions, the sixteenth with a big cross bunker to carry from the tee and a line of pines on the right, a particularly attractive hole.

The seventeenth is a 251-yard shot across a road to a much elevated green with all too many bunkers to evade, which yields more fours and fives than threes. Finally, you have a splendid testing last hole with a big diagonal carry off the tee over a huge sand dune – for no other word describes it – and the need to get well across to the right so that you can get a clear shot home through the aforesaid line of pine trees and over the road to the long, deep trapped green.

Ganton has had its long line of famous players, notably Harry Vardon, who was pro here in his early days and a stout performer in goal for the local football club. Also that great pipe smoker and champion of Britain – and the USA – Ted Ray. Ray the genial giant, was once pestered by an importunate member to impart the secret of his great length from the tee; removing his pipe for a moment, Ray replied 'Hit a bloody sight harder, mate.' And while we are on quotations, here is one from Harry Vardon himself, who, when approached by a 'Temperance' worker, replied 'Moderation is essential in all things, madam, but never in my whole life have I been beaten by a teetotaller.'

Chapter 7

LANCASHIRE COAST

Royal Liverpool, Hoylake

I suppose there is no famous links which offers less encouragement to the first glance of the visitor than Hoylake, except perhaps St Andrews, where the view from the clubhouse of the R & A is seemingly the ultimate manifestation of non-golf.

The view from the smoking room at the Royal Liverpool Golf Club on the first floor of that supremely plain Victorian clubhouse in red Ruabon brick shows a vast flat space, apparently without character or guile, bounded by some uninspired examples of later Victorian and Edwardian domestic architecture to the west; it is no longer relieved by that four-square Georgian barracks built in 1792, the Royal Hotel, now that it has been destroyed. Only far away on the horizon to the south and south-west is a distant range of sandhills to remind you that this is a links, after all.

Don't be put off: the reality is greatly different. First of all this is a long, tough, supremely competent golf course, one of the toughest and most searching of the great links. You don't get away with anything; what's more, the great long pros don't make a fool of it either. The 1967 Open was played here under almost unbelievably easy conditions. The

ground was hard and the ball ran; then just as this looked like making it all ridiculously short there was a storm in the night and two inches of rain, so that a decent respect for length was reimposed while the greens lost any risk of becoming fiery; there was never any wind and yet the course passed the test; it emerged in charge of affairs. True, twelve players averaged less than par for the four rounds but there were only nineteen rounds under seventy out of 370 played. The great Nicklaus, who had slaughtered the vastly long Baltusrol course in New Jersey a few weeks before, did not slaughter Hoylake.

When the European Open was here in 1981, the course did take rather a shellacking with over twenty players beating par and a 64 scored by Waites to top the 66's and 67's which were around. Even the famous back nine came in for some rough treatment when Marsh, the winner, holed it in 30 in one round and Ballesteros in another had four birdies in the last five holes.

Well, what does this rather dull field, with incongruous knee-high banks of turf called cops, really do to you? First of all these knee-high banks define out of bounds and already some unseemly clamour against this fierce ruling has been heard. The severe out of bounds between the first fairway, seemingly almost a right-angle dog leg, and the practice ground was under fire from the Levellers who succeeded in abolishing another severe out of bounds, over the cop to the left of the third, and totally destroying for the duration of the last Open Championship there the terrifying nature of the short seventh where the out of bounds cop is the boundary of the left-hand edge of the green. I am glad to report that these man-made difficulties at Hoylake are still in force at the first, seventh and sixteenth, although the green at seven has been eased.

But there's length at Hoylake and plenty of it, 7000 yards for the Open, plenty of bunkers too, though fewer than there were fifty and sixty years ago. The greens are beautiful and the fairways less uneven than on most links; the rough on the other hand, with dwarf rose and low-growing blackberry in places, is formidable. The fairways are often narrow and require the drive to be exactly placed or else the hole remains inexorably difficult.

For example, if you drive down the left side of the second fairway, the hole is not too tough, but drive down the right side and you never seem to get on terms. At Hoylake if you put your drive in the right place, the green, while not quite welcoming the second shot, does not seem unbearably hostile as it does to a misplaced drive. The greens are often tucked away at an angle, as at the tenth, twelfth and seventeenth, to make an entry difficult.

The genius of Hoylake is not one of these things separately but just the stringing together of hazards and penalties with good tees and lovely greens, the rewards for excellence and the penalties for incompetence which makes this such a great and such a just links, the Final Honour School, together with Muirfield perhaps, of British golf, where luck enters into it to the minimum and justice is not only done but manifestly seen to be done.

The Royal Liverpool club has not been afraid of change, and alterations have been made several times at Hoylake since golf started there in 1869. After World War I H. S. Colt was brought in to make momentous changes, a new green at the eighth and entirely new holes at the eleventh, twelfth and thirteenth, and playing them today it's a wonder that these excellent holes were ever criticised and disliked.

After World War II many bunkers were got rid of, such as those across the fairway at the eighth and the little pots to the right of the seventh green, no doubt to reduce maintenance, for assuredly these changes didn't make the golf any easier. Some 'modernisation' took place too, with the cross bunkers at the sixth and eighteenth done away with. This I rather deplore, for a good cross bunker here and there makes an essential uncompromising demand on the player which you can't easily argue is bad for him. The cross bunker in front of the eighteenth on the Old Course at Walton Heath is just such a one, and so was the bunker at the last at Hoylake.

In time for the championship of 1967 the third hole was considerably altered from a straight par five right into the eye of the wind to a slightly longer dog-leg hole to the left to the old fourth green, better and more elegant. Then the new short fourth up into the flanking sandhills to a plateau green is a great improvement on its dull flat predecessor.

So now let's set our minds on our game. The first hole can be a horror, for you can go out of bounds from the tee and even after a good drive at any point between your lie and the green. As a first hole it's a beast and as a nineteenth or thirty-seventh terrifying; the sharpness of the angle of the dog leg is most unusual and the closeness of the out-of-bounds cop and its sandy ditch to the entire fairway and green severe in the extreme. Robert Hunter, the American who wrote that excellent book *The Links* sixty years ago, says:

At the very first hole one is taught not to treat Hoylake with contempt. It is without doubt the most uninviting first hole on any first-rate course in Europe, but one has only to play that hole once to approach it ever afterward with profound respect. The sailing appears smooth enough but something always seems to be a bit wrong and after one has holed out one suspects there has been treachery somewhere – no obvious treachery but some subtle influence that makes what seems quite easy a very difficult performance.

Dire disasters have happened here, one of the classics being Bernard Darwin's loss of his match in the fifth round of the Amateur Championship of 1910 by running out of ammunition. On a minor scale, a friend of mine, George Cottam, reported only a few years ago that he had started out in a stroke competition with a fourteen and that on top of returning from holiday the night before to find that his house had been burgled.

The second requires an accurate drive or you're in trouble all the way, as the green is infested with bunkers and runs away from you. The new third is a long hole into the wind, rather longer than the old third, at which I once remember, in the days when I could hit the ball, playing the hole into the gale with a drive and four cleek shots – and who has a cleek today – the last of which pitched on the green and was blown back off it. But the Hoylake wind is a subject in itself, suffice it to say that after that game we calculated the par for the day in the bar and it came to 86.

Next is the new short fourth, a better-looking and more exacting hole than the old 'Cop'. Five is a straightforward and fairly undemanding par four, needing no superhuman placing or length and usually downwind. The sixth, the 'Briars', with the drive needing to avoid a corner of the playing fields of the Leas School, is a fine and famous hole guarded in the old days by a cross bunker and now by two close lying pot bunkers. Against the wind this hole is really testing. It was halved in nine during the final of the Amateur Championship of 1906. Bernard Darwin's description of J. H. Taylor slashing his second shot up to the hole side here with a cleek into the teeth of the gale and rain which ravaged the last day of the 1913 Championship

is famous. As Arthur Croome wrote 'his shot seemed to make a hole in the wind as it bored its way along'.

Then comes the short seventh, the 'Dowie', to my mind one of the greatest holes of golf, one which absolutely fits the test that you begin to worry about it before you get to it. The shot is a level one of 200 yards; it is rare for the wind to be against you – or with you – though it is often totally unhelpful. The green was originally pear shaped, the bulbous end the nearer – perhaps triangular is a better description, with an out-of-bounds cop all along the hypotenuse – so the chances of being blown or racing over it were painfully easy. The green has since been enlarged to hold the tee shot more securely but I'm thankful to say the out of bounds remains. In front of the green were a few small patches of wild rushes, now removed. The outer edges of the green all run down into a narrow shallow valley the outside of which is semi-rough. To pitch on and stay on requires a fine shot, not perhaps as fine as it once did, while to kick in from the safe region to the right needs a degree of luck allied with skill which is often absent, so you are left with a putt out of the little shallow valley or an approach across it out of the semi-rough.

The eighth takes you out to the far end of the links with a good hummocky par five without a single bunker except for a small pot under the right-hand side of the green. Here at this most straightforward hole Bobby Jones's pursuit of the Grand Slam in 1930 almost came to grief. After nearly reaching the green in two fine shots he contrived with all the ineptitude of you and me to take a calamitous seven, fluffing two chips and taking three putts – and he then had to wait a full ten minutes on the ninth tee while the rampaging mob was brought under control. A friend of mine, Tom Dobell, was watching through glasses and said that it was one of the most painful things he had ever witnessed on a golf course. Bob pacing up and down the tee, lifting and replacing his cap, lighting a cigarette and throwing it down and fighting the appalling possibilities of the situation. Then he was off, technique and courage in command, with a smacking drive down the humpy fairway of the ninth towards the green in its dell, a par scored and then home in triumph with hardly an error in the back nine.

So here we are on the tenth, a splendid two-shot hole, bearing left all the while, with a plateau green up in the sandhills. It was at this point in the championship of 1924 that Hagen, not on the green in two nor dead in three, learned that he had to come home in 36 to win, which he did in spite of having to recover thrice from bunkers.

Eleven is a fine one-shot hole with a long green, down by the shore and the sands of Dee and twelve, the 'Hilbre', is one of those excellent Hoylake bending two-shotters where the entrance to the green only accommodates a really well-placed drive, this time long and well out to the right. Thirteen is another attractive par-three hole, not very long but heavily trapped and usually played downwind as well as downhill.

Now comes the gruelling finish, the last five holes measuring 516, 460, 509, 391 and 395 yards for us and a bit more for championship play, the 'Field', the 'Lake', the 'Dun', the 'Royal' and the 'Stand'. Well, at least they don't all run the same way – fourteen, sixteen and eighteen run more or less east and the other two in the opposite direction. Depending on how you view it, this can be the most demanding finish in golf or a dreary slog up and down a vast flat field, up and down the old racecourse, in fact. To be fair, I think it's a bit of both. The first two holes of these five, I think, are really rather a weariness of the flesh, but the sixteenth, with the out of bounds eating into the fairway on the right, just where you don't want it, is a splendid hole – and who will forget who saw it, Roberto de Vicenzo's spanking great spoon shot over the lot and home to the heart of the green to clinch the 1967 Championship, or Jones's first serious shot with a sand wedge from the bunker on the left of the green to get

his third close to the hole for a vital four in the last stages in 1930.

The seventeenth, too, is a beauty, with traps to the right threatening the area where you need to put your drive, so as best to avoid the traps on the left of the green and the hard high road to the right and beyond it. The last hole is the mildest of the five and well it might be after the beating the others have given you.

As on all great courses, great things have been done at Hoylake, many of them by John Ball, whose championship experience spanned the period from Willie Park and Bob Ferguson to Bobby Jones and Walter Hagen. Here in 1902 the rubber-cored ball came into its own, both championships being won at Hoylake that year with a Haskell for the first time. Here the first foreign golfer, Arnaud Massy of France, won the Open in 1907.

The first men's amateur international match against the United States was played here, in 1921, leading to the Walker Cup series in 1922. The US side at Hoylake was one of the strongest ever fielded and they beat us hollow. Among our players was T. D. Armour who later went to the United States and prospered. On the US side appears the name of J. Wood Platt which enables me to introduce one of my favourite golf stories. Woodie Platt was playing in a friendly game at Pine Valley, near Philadelphia, perhaps the most severe inland course in the world. He did the first hole of 415 yards in three; at the 350-yard second he holed an iron shot for two. He did the third in one stroke and at the long par four back to the clubhouse he had a three. After such a start there was only one thing to do; Wood Platt, six under par, and the party all went into the clubhouse and remained there.

In the Amateur Championship of 1921 at Hoylake which followed, Bobby Jones had his first introduction to a bone-dry seaside links and found the ordeal trying. After narrowly beating a Mr Hamlet, for ever after known as 'the Florist of Wrexham', with a score of 86, he

Royal Liverpool Golf Club, Hoylake: Medal and Championship Cards

NAME	M	C	PAR	NAME	M	C	PAR
1 Course	428	428	4	10 Dee	409	409	4
2 Road	369	429	4	11 Alps	200	200	3
3 Long	505	505	5	12 Hilbre	395	454	4
4 New	184	195	3	13 Rushes	157	157	3
5 Telegraph	407	449	4	14 Field	516	516	5
6 Briars	383	423	4	15 Lake	460	460	4
7 Dowie	200	200	3	16 Dun	509	533	5
8 Far	479	519	5	17 Royal	391	418	4
9 Punch Bowl	393	393	4	18 Stand	395	395	4
	3348	3541	36		3432	3542	36

Total 6780 and 7083 yards: par 72

came to grief against Allan Graham. As Bob Jones said 'I came up against a genial sandy-haired gentleman who fairly beat me to death with a queer brass putter'. Graham went on to be runner-up to Willie Hunter that year. Later Hunter went to the United States and put Jones out of the US Amateur Championship. Then in the family tradition he turned pro and went to California and prospered there at the Riviera Club in Los Angeles, where Hogan won his first US Open in 1948. Willie Hunter, who was the son of the professional at Deal and the grand-son of a professional, lived to a ripe age; so did his son, Mac Hunter, and now Mac's son reigns as pro at Riviera.

Well, after those interruptions let us return to Hoylake, an examination paper, and 'A' level at that; not my favourite links, for many others would precede it as a place to play my last round, but if you do manage to play a good game there and score tolerably well you have earned some warm feelings of self-satisfaction.

It is a pity that the space required for modern stadium golf, huge stands and off-course areas for car parks and the tented village rule out Hoylake for future Open Championships.

Let Bernard Darwin have the last word: 'And whatever anyone may say Hoylake can look lovely when you are out practising all by your-self somewhere near the sandhills when the summer dusk is coming on and the lights are beginning to twinkle in the houses.'

Wallasey

Wallasey in Cheshire, near the mouth of the Mersey, where the qualifying rounds for the Open at Hoylake have often been played, is another fine links with some huge and splendid sandhills. It was reconstructed and improved some time ago; formerly it began and ended nobly in the dunes but had a flat sector in the middle which was not in keeping with

Wallasey Golf Club: Medal Card

NAME	YARDS	PAR	NAME	YARDS	PAR
1 Estuary	382	4	10 Mound	311	4
2 Willows	463	4	11 Saddleback	371	4
3 Valley	381	4	12 Old Glory	147	3
4 Seaway	504	5	13 Cop	498	5
5 Westway	173	3	14 Crookway	493	5
6 Boundry	343	4	15 Plateau	369	4
7 Lane	520	5	16 Bank	200	3
8 Hummocks	393	4	17 Gully	464	4
9 Stableford	154	3	18 Duncan Taylor	441	4
Out	3313	36	In	3294	36
			Out	3313	36
			Total	6607	72

the rest. The new layout was a big improvement.

The most famous member here, I suppose, was Dr Stableford whose name is used for a form of scoring in competitive golf which has spread throughout the world.

All along the coast north of Liverpool from Crosby to the other side of Southport is a rich belt of linksland with a fine diverse crop of golf courses: West Lancashire at Blundellsands, Formby, Hillside, Southport and Ainsdale, Birkdale and three more on the other side of Southport itself.

Formby

Formby, along the Lancashire coast, north of Liverpool is much less severe than Hoylake, but in the opinion of many a more enjoyable place at which to play golf. True the railway runs all along the eastern edge of the course but it is well screened by pine trees on all except the first hole. Apart from that you are in unspoiled linksland, with big sandhills and some fine sea-woods to give you some shelter occasionally.

The first four holes are on relatively flat ground on that fine sandy soil which all round here produces good links turf and also the asparagus for which the area is famous. From the short fifth onwards the course moves out into the big hills including the new tree-lined seventh, eighth and ninth holes and a new 214-yard par-three tenth, introduced by coastal erosion. These new holes provide a tough test of golf, as well as some spectacular scenery through the Formby pines.

Holes eleven thru' fifteen, as the Americans say, are all fine two-shotters, the eleventh, with its plateau green sandwiched between two higher mounds, a great favourite of mine, but all five on broken difficult terrain. Then all at once it's over; sixteen is a short hole of no great difficulty, judging by the number of twos scored there in recent Amateur Championships. There is a flat finish, a long seventeenth and a well-bunkered 412-yard eighteenth with a big green, where Marty Fleckman of the US Walker Cup team of 1967 had an outrageous two to take out one of Britain's last hopes for the championship who was lying close to the hole for a possible birdie three.

Formby came into the championship rota by accident in 1957. That year the Amateur was due to be held at Sandwich but because of petrol rationing, brought about by the Suez crisis, it was transferred to Formby, while the Open was transferred from Muirfield to St Andrews. Formby remains a favourite venue for the best amateur events, the amateur Championship having been last played there in 1984, the club's Centenary Year, when the brilliant young Spaniard José-Maria Olazabal won.

In the qualifying rounds for the Birkdale Open of 1976, played here, Maurice Flitcroft, a crane driver, who entered as a professional, went round in 121, the first time he had ever played 18 holes. He withdrew at this point

Formby Golf Club: Medal Card					
	YARDS	PAR		YARDS	PAR
1	415	4	10	214	3
2	381	4	11	384	4
3	518	5	12	405	4
4	312	4	13	434	4
5	162	3	14	420	4
6	402	4	15	403	4
7	377	4	16	127	3
8	493	5	17	494	5
9	450	4	18	390	4
	3510	37		3271	35

Total 6781 yards: par 72

but tried to enter again later. This time the R & A intervened and his entry was not accepted.

According to its handbook, Formby is the club where the original clubhouse was a small thatched hut and the bar consisted of a loose floorboard concealing a bottle of whisky and a collection box on which was written: 'A moderate go, 3d'; prices have unhappily increased since those great days.

Royal Birkdale

Of the courses near Southport, Birkdale has the most illustrious place in modern golf, having housed the Open Championship in 1954, 1961, 1965 and the 100th Championship in 1971, also in 1976 and 1983, the Amateur was here in 1946, the Walker Cup in 1951, the Ryder Cup in 1965 and 1969, also the Ladies Open in 1982 and 1986.

It is a great and justly famous links, 6711 yards off the medal tees and stretchable to nearly 7000 for the championships. Moreover, it lies in the heart of a great belt of linksland,

and towering sandhills are to be seen on every hand. However, in practice the sandhills are much more an ornament than a hazard, for rarely do we play over them, certainly not in the Sandwich sense; much more often we play along valleys with the great dunes flanking us, and valleys being what they are, of course, they gather what moisture there is, so that some of them are almost lush in their greenness.

These valleys are the Birkdale scene, then, and if all the big dunes were miraculously removed, the course, apart from exposure to the winds, would be hardly affected at all. The lies here are flatter than is usual on linksland, so bunkering and sheer length have to play a greater part, these and tougher than usual rough, creeping blackberry – whose fruit carry a matt blue bloom like an American blueberry – and utterly tenacious willow scrub amid the seaside grasses illumined in the season by yellow evening primroses.

From this gluelike rough Arnold Palmer played an almost miraculous six-iron shot to the present sixteenth green (then the fifteenth) in the 1961 Open after an errant drive and saved at least a shot at a critical moment. This notable stroke is today commemorated by a marker planted on the spot. The rough was criticised for its harshness at the '83 Open but so was the relative softness of the fairways and greens, this so-called Americanisation of the links, so that scores in the 60s abounded.

The first hole of 450 yards is mildly double dog legged, a sort of shallow 'S' in shape, as a sandy ridge comes in from the left to influence your drive away from the ideal position and another comes in from the right to protect the front of the green.

The second hole, a good stiff par four, is away out towards the sea and into the prevailing wind; there are plenty of bunkers round the green and a little sea-wood behind it, a very pretty hole. On the third you reverse direction and fire down a valley between the highest sandhills on the course and play to a green in a shallow depression. Number four is the first short hole, a good thump down from a tee up in the hills to a newly-formed undulating green with wing bunkers, tight enough in all conscience for a hole of 206 yards.

Next we have a drive and pitch of 343 yards parallel to numbers two and three out towards the sea; the green, as you would expect, at this length is very heavily bunkered. I remember seeing Stranahan in his Walker Cup foursome in 1951 – when he and Bill Campbell were playing Ronnie White and Joe Carr in the top match – hit his pitch off the socket, almost at right angles into a bunker. I'm glad to report that Stranahan, who was inclined to take things rather grimly, threw his head back and roared with laughter; so did the other three – and the gallery.

The sixth is a really big two-shotter, the hardest hole on the course with a ridge of low sandhills across the fairway for once, and a five is good enough for you and me. Then comes the second short hole, again down from the tee to a very well-bunkered green.

Eight and nine at 424 and 410 yards are two dog-leg holes, the first swinging to the left up a valley in the sandhills and the second to the right. The ninth in fact is a very attractive hole, a good drive over a stiff carry putting you on a level piece of fairway overlooking a big hollow in the fairway across which you hit your second shot to a markedly steep plateau green.

The tenth is a sharp dog leg to the left, the green being tucked away almost in a corner, amid surrounding hills; unless you hit a good drive out to the right you have a hellishly difficult second.

Eleven is a most pleasing hole, for you can see it all from the tee and you have the pleasure of hitting down from a rise. The green is small and set across the line, which is fair enough for a 374-yarder; there are cross bunkers too on your way to the green.

The twelfth is a comparatively new one shotter of 175 yards from a tee in the hills across a shallow valley to a green up in the next range; the green is narrow and looks very small, especially as it is framed by four deep and hungry bunkers and flanked by sandhills. It reminded me of one of my American books on golf architecture which has a photograph of the tenth at Pine Valley with the caption, 'There is no welcome here'; well, there's no welcome here, either.

Thirteen at 436 yards I think rather dull, a flat hole with a flat fairway; though the surroundings are agreeable they don't affect the hole; it's not easy, of course.

The short fourteenth is rather longer and

rather easier than the twelfth, which it somewhat resembles. The shot is more down-hill and the green is larger. I found it a good hole for my five-wood from a forward tee.

Now you have to gird yourself for a big finish, as tough as that at Hoylake, for the last four holes measure 542, 348, 502 and 476 yards. The fifteenth is on flat ground again, but three little traps *en échelon* threaten your drive on the left and it is heavily bunkered across the course where your second and mine want to go as well as at the green itself, a pretty tough par five, this one, but I would have liked a few more undulations in the fairway. At sixteen you have a blind tee shot over a sea of rough and little humps to a flat green fairway; then you have a really tight shot on to a high plateau green with half a dozen guardian bunkers; the green is not large and does nothing to gather the ball; how Arnold Palmer made it out of thick willow scrub defeats me.

For ordinary players the tee shot at the seventeenth is dominated by two big sandhills between which you drive; they give you a very narrow gap of less than thirty yards, at 230 yards from the medal tee. The rest of the hole I found too flat to be inspiring – flat and difficult. If you can get up in two shots, which I can't, it's a different matter. All the same Lee Trevino in the last round of the Open Championship of 1971 found real trouble from a hooked drive here and took a seven which nearly sank him.

The same arguments apply to the 476-yard eighteenth. I can't get it in two and so have a not very tough pitch to the small green, but if you can get up in two then what a splendid hole it becomes; bunkers to skirt from the tee, others en route, two small ridges on either side of the fairway on the way along and then three small traps, two on the left and one on the right on the very edge of the green itself. What a hole to

| | | *Royal Birkdale Golf Club:* | | | | | |
| | | *Medal Championship Cards* | | | | | |
	M	C	PAR		M	C	PAR
1	450	450	4	10	368	384	4
2	423	423	4	11	374	411	4
3	410	410	4	12	175	184	3
4	206	206	3	13	436	505	4/5
5	343	343	4	14	198	198	3
6	476	468	5/4	15	542	542	5
7	150	150	3	16	348	415	4
8	424	470	4	17	502	526	5
9	410	410	4	18	476	473	5/4
	3292	3330	35/34		3419	3638	37

Total 6711 and 6968 yards: par 71/71

have to be sure of getting a four at to win the championship!

So ends a big golf course, but to me it leaves a tinge of disappointment; the valley fairways are just a little too green and grassy and too flat for this old Tory.

The 1976 and 1983 Championships produced the usual quota of surprises and great happenings. In '76, Johnny Miller's year, the young Ballesteros showed what he might become. In '83 we had an opening round of 64 by Craig Stadler when all the putts flew into the hole, after which, his ration used up, he holed nothing more. Then Faldo led for Britain until the last nine holes but it was Tom Watson who won, beating Hale Irwin by a stroke. Watson's last shot, a superbly hit two-iron was a classic, which tied down his fifth win in only nine years. Irwin had missed a two-inch putt by carelessness, otherwise he might or might not have tied.

Southport and Ainsdale

Southport and Ainsdale, also in the famous belt of linksland near Southport, lies on one side of the electric railway and the fine Hillside links, on the other. S & A, as it is always called, has twice been host to the Ryder Cup match, in 1933 and 1937, and is a full-length circuit in real seaside country. It has its quota of big sandhills and these come into play quite a lot, notably at the third tee where you drive from a great height and at the 520-yard sixteenth, called 'Gumbley's', where you have to hit a second shot with wood over a vast hill fortified with a wall of black sleepers with two bunkers below them into which you bounce if you hit your second too low.

As at Birkdale, the fairways here are rather too flat for my taste and the seventeenth hole is flat indeed. However, the narrow humpy eighteenth fairway makes up for it with an attractive shot to a new plateau green, no longer the one where Syd Easterbrook in 1937 holed the last putt of the game, on which the entire Ryder Cup match depended. An attrac-tive links, this, and as much as anything, I like the unorthodox opening of a 200-yard shot to a very narrow-looking heavily bunkered green.

The secretary, David Wood, reports:

In the old days before the handicapping system had joined the computer age, we had a member, Sam Robinson, who played off plus 5. Sam, a quiet, unassuming chap, was donning his cloth cap and turning his trouser bottoms up in readiness for a round when he was invited by a lone visitor to have a game. Sam accepted and enquired of his opponent's handicap. 'Scratch' said the visitor proudly. 'Thank goodness' replied Sam, 'I only have to give you four shots.'

And this:

On the morning of a recent pro/am/celebrity, the steward received a telephone call from an obviously very affluent gentleman, anxious to impress, who enquired as to where he might land his helicopter. The steward very politely pointed out to him that 'most of the members landed theirs on the practice ground'.

Southport and Ainsdale Golf Club: Medal Card

NAME	YARDS	PAR	NAME	YARDS	PAR
1 Trial	200	3	10 Chair	160	3
2 Terrace	520	5	11 Regent	447	4
3 Braid's	418	4	12 Warren	401	4
4 Ridge	316	4	13 Firs	145	3
5 Hen-Pen	447	4	14 Gorse	383	4
6 Gap	386	4	15 Railway	352	4
7 Steeple	480	5	16 Gumbley's	520	5
8 Plateau	157	3	17 Heather	443	4
9 Old Dog-Leg	482	5	18 Home	355	4
	3406	37		3197	35

Total 6603 yards: par 72

Blundellsands

The West Lancashire club with its course at Blundellsands is one of the oldest in England dating back to 1873, and was the first course on the Lancashire coast, preceding Formby, Birkdale and the rest. The first course was all on the landward side of the railway but in 1960 an entirely new links was constructed with all the holes on the seaward side, together with a startling new clubhouse. The links is in flatter land than its neighbours to the north, but is of the real stuff and hard by the shore at that, with the shipping channel out of Liverpool close at this point. The course is 6756 yards long off the medal tees and has no fewer than six par fours over 400 yards.

The club has had many famous members and professionals such as John Ball, Harold Hilton, Ronnie White, Sandy Herd and Arthur Havers, Open champion in 1923, who was described in the Centenary booklet as looking in retirement as 'more like a retired bishop than the doyen of British Open champions'.

West Lancashire Golf Club, Blundellsands: Medal Card

NAME	YARDS	PAR	NAME	YARDS	PAR
1 Beacon	433	4	10 New	355	4
2 Shore	490	5	11 Railway	557	5
3 Bowl	158	3	12 Valley	178	3
4 Alt	412	4	13 Bar	363	4
5 Crosby	478	5	14 Bell	440	4
6 Hillside	156	3	15 Sniggery	391	4
7 Folly	370	4	16 Blundell	520	5
8 Mersey	448	4	17 Ince	175	3
9 Ridge	403	4	18 Cuckoo Hill	429	4
Out	3348	36	In	3408	36
			Out	3348	36
			Total	6756	72

Royal Lytham and St Annes

The most northerly of this great chain of famous golf links along the coast of the Irish Sea is at Lytham and St Annes, near Blackpool, on whose links golf has been played now for one hundred years. In this period the area has suffered major changes and what was once a piece of mixed agricultural and linksland, bounded by the railway and blown over by wild breezes and flying sand from the dunes along the shore, is now an oasis in a wilderness of modern housing, of rather unprepossessing style, in the great and growing conurbation of Blackpool and St Annes.

Inevitably, the character of the course has

changed in this process, as has that of so many of the great seaside links, and it has become more 'inland', softer, fatter and lusher. With a desire for better lies and softer greens, water and fertiliser have been applied and much of the bone hardness once so characteristic of St Andrews, Hoylake and here have gone for ever. With all this, Royal Lytham and St Annes remains a great course and it is now firmly established in the championship rota, with the Open here in 1926, 1952, 1958, 1963 and again in 1969 when Tony Jacklin won his famous victory – the first win by a British player since 1951. The Open came here again in 1974 when Gary Player, the winner, played a left-handed shot from the side of the clubhouse, and 1979 and is due in 1988. The Amateur was here in 1935, 1955 and 1986, and the Ryder Cup in 1961 and 1977.

Here, in the mists of the past, the first Ladies Championship was played; here Bobby Jones won his first British Open in 1926 in a dramatic finish after a day-long struggle with Al Watrous and here the first left-hander to win a major championship, Bob Charles of New Zealand, triumphed in 1963 after a tie. The first win for Spain came in 1979 when young Ballesteros beat off the Americans with his brilliant recovery shots and beautiful putting touch. At the last hole, when he had got his four after a wild drive, it was a happy new sight to see the Spanish brothers wrapped in a vast fraternal hug.

The links is approximately out-and-home in that the first nine run south-east with one diversion and the inward nine work back with rather more holes across the general line of play. The result of this is that the outgoing half, if the prevailing wind is blowing, is where you must build your score and the inward half, which is also longer, where you must strive desperately to defend it.

The course is rather flat, especially at the clubhouse end, and many of the 'seaside' hill-ocks and dunes are in fact the work of man not nature, fashioned by countless spades and cart-loads long before the days of the bulldozer but done with a skill which matches the folds and humps and hollows of the natural linksland across the railway nearer the shore. The far end of the course out by Ansdell railway station is in natural linksland with some notable sandhills and plateaux.

The round opens with a par three, which is a start disliked by many on principle, but it has its advantages and often makes for a freer start than, say, a 450-yard par four, where every novice waits swinging an inadequate brassie for the unreachable green to clear. The first at St Annes is tough enough at 206 yards to be respected.

Two and three run out along the railway and at 420 and 458 yards are a formidable pair; you can slice on to the line or if you pull away you can be bunkered or get yourself a harder second shot. At the fourth you reverse direction with a carry over shallow hills and a shot to a tightly bunkered green. Then the fifth is another par three, difficult enough in all conscience at 188 yards off the medal tee, and off the far back championship tee, whence I would need a driver, just horribly long. Two par fives in succession put you back along the railway again and then you play the splendid eighth hole from right up by the boundary fence to a high plateau green with a big swale in front which is not visible as you line up your second shot; you've got to hit right up to this perched up green and risk going over the back or you will inevitably run off to the bunkers guarding the front of the green; at 394 yards a grand hole.

So, too, is number nine, a short hole of 162 yards, tightly and grievously bunkered so that only a full carry to the green will do any good. A good hole indeed, but originally spoiled by its ugly urban surroundings, though now trees are making cover.

The tenth, 334 yards, has been recently leng-thened and in consequence a gap has had to be cut in the range of sandhills which you pre-viously had to carry off the tee. I don't think this spoils the hole; the green is an attractive cocked-up plateau, with deep guardian bunkers especially on the right. The eleventh has stretched for the championship play from 485 yards to over 550 and this into the prevailing wind.

From the twelfth to the seventeenth, the course beats to and fro with a par three at twelve and two huge par fours at fourteen and fifteen, too long for my taste. The sixteenth at 356 yards, with a bunkered hill to carry off the tee, is more merciful.

So we come to the historic seventeenth, where in 1926 Bobby Jones played the famous shot out of a rough sandy scrape – not, I think, a formal bunker, as there is there now. Looking today from where this shot was played it seems a fantastically difficult stroke, even from a good lie. The hole is a flat strong dog leg to the left with a flat green and on the corner where the drama was enacted was a wilderness of rough, sandy spots, and today bunkers, while the line to the flag is guarded by a trap in front of the pin.

Al Watrous, who was destroyed by Jones's shot, taking three putts from the front of the not very big green, had driven right up the centre of the fairway and played a seemingly safe suitable shot in; Jones in trouble took out his 'Old Equaliser', a mashie-iron, about the loft of a No. 4 today, hit the perfect shot out of a good lie in the scrubby scrape, drawing the ball in from the right to lie plumb in the middle of the green, and the championship was his; as Watrous said, seeing the shot, 'There goes a hundred thousand dollars.' A plaque in the bunker of today marks the spot from which Jones played.

The club with which the deed was done is in the big upstairs lounge, which has such a fine view over the links. It is by no means the clumsy iron monster which is often implied. The thick hickory shaft looks coarse to our eyes today, but the head is in my view a beautifully shaped deep-faced iron characteristic of the 'Pipe' brand clubs of Stewart of St Andrews. I must say that in the old days I always found a mashie-iron an indispensable club for shots out of short rough.

So, like Jones and Jacklin, we are 'only' left with the eighteenth hole of a modest 386 yards to do in four – but what with bunkers to carry and others threatening the tee shot to the left, a spinney to the right and greedy bunkers guarding the pear-shaped green – three each side – and a narrow entrance to it, a four is all too often missed; ask Eric Brown, O'Connor and Ruiz, each of whom had to do it in four to win or tie the 1958 Open and failed, leaving a tie to Peter Thomson and Dave Thomas. Jack Nicklaus met the same fate in 1963.

So possibly a little chastened in spirit let us repair to the big hospitable clubhouse for some of those delicious local shrimps for our lunch, or, if we are staying the night, to the admirable Dormy house after a hearty dinner.

The Amateur Championship has been thrice at Lytham and St Annes. The first time in 1935, when Lawson Little beat Dr William Tweddell in the final after a brave fight which went to the last green, for the doctor at one early stage had been five down. Of Tweddell when he won the

Royal Lytham and St Annes Golf Club:
Medal and Championship Cards

	M	C	PAR		M	C	PAR
1	206	206	3	10	334	334	4
2	420	439	4	11	485	540	5
3	458	458	4	12	189	200	3
4	393	393	4	13	339	339	4
5	188	212	3	14	445	445	4
6	486	486	5	15	468	468	4
7	551	551	5	16	356	356	4
8	394	394	4	17	413	462	4
9	162	162	3	18	386	386	4
	3258	3301	35		3415	3530	36

Total 6673 and 6831 yards: par 71
The eighteenth will be lenghened by 25 yards
for the 1988 Open

Amateur at Hoylake in 1927 this immortal verse was created:

> At Worplesdon and Leatherhead
> they speak of Jones and Wethered

but Stourbridge, happy Stourbridge
is going to strike a medal
to celebrate the victory of
Dr William Tweddell

Hillside

Hillside is next door to Royal Birkdale in that wonderful stretch of dune country on the Lancashire coast north of Liverpool.

Although the course has been used for a number of big-money professional events, it only recently came on to the championship rota when it was host to the Amateur Championship in 1979, a year which gave us an all-American final won by Jay Sigel.

Unfortunately Hillside became a championship course too late for me to add it to my complete set; by 1979 my legs had given out and my golfing days were over.

The first half of the course is the older and the holes selected for comment, I have learned, are close along that Liverpool–Southport railway which we have seen so much of, the fourth and fifth and the short seventh. The hillier second half was built comparatively recently out of sandhills adjoining the Birkdale links. Here praise goes to the short tenth and the sixteenth with a 50-yard long sloping green, and warning of care needed among great dunes at seventeen and eighteen.

It was at Hillside that Tony Jacklin virtually closed his distinguished career as a player, although his abilities as a team leader and captain are in full flower. In the PGA Championship here in 1982 he beat Bernhard Langer, the German, with a birdie three in a play-off. Although Jacklin was cruelly deflected from his second British Open win, from Britain only he, Vardon and Ray have won both the US and British Open Championships. If Jacklin can be

said to have closed his career here, Jack Nicklaus in a sense opened his, playing his first professional tournament outside the USA at Hillside in 1962.

In the qualifying rounds here for the 1965 Open at Birkdale an American telephone engineer, Walter Danecki, inveigled himself into the play and recorded 221 strokes for the 36 holes. His first round was 108 followed by 113. The *Golfer's Handbook* records that he said he felt 'a little discouraged and sad' and that he had entered because 'he was after the money'. This record play was later displaced by Flitcroft's performance at Formby in 1976.

Hillside Golf Club: Medal Card

	YARDS	PAR		YARDS	PAR
1	399	4	10	147	3
2	525	5	11	508	5
3	402	4	12	368	4
4	195	3	13	398	4
5	504	5	14	400	4
6	413	4	15	398	4
7	176	3	16	199	3
8	405	4	17	548	5
9	425	4	18	440	4
	3444	36		3406	36

Total 6850 yards: par 72

Chapter 8

CHANNEL COAST

Prince's

Nowhere in England will you find better seaside golf than on the coasts of Kent and Sussex, from Sandwich Bay to Chichester Harbour, especially if we include that Hampshire coastal links on Hayling Island.

Starting at the Kentish end, let us kick off, or rather tee off, at the Prince's at Sandwich. I wish I could like Prince's as much as my first loves on this stretch of wonderful linksland, Sandwich and Deal, but I fear I cannot. What's more, I can't feel that the new courses here, good as they are, are as attractive as the old one which was blasted out of existence in World War II.

Before the war, this championship links, on which Sarazen won with a record total in 1932, had a great deal of charm with its shallow valleys and dog-leg holes and the range of sandhills, the Himalayas, at the far end near the coastguard cottages, over which you had to whack twice, once as a second shot to the eighth and once as a drive to the eleventh.

The war altered all this; first the needs of coastal defence, then the use of the area for battle training, removed the landmarks and created a wilderness from which, with the best will in the world, the old links could not have

been revived. So an entirely new layout of twenty-seven holes was ordained by the new patron of the links, the late Sir Aynsley Bridgland, an eighteen-hole course of championship calibre, the Blue, and the nine-hole circuit, the Red.

The Red nine was not inferior in length and difficulty to the Blue and a combination of holes from each course was used in the Curtis Cup matches in 1956 against the ladies of America, which incidentally Britain won. This was the last win by the British ladies until their triumph in America in 1986, the first time that any British golf team has won an international match in the United States.

After the death of Sir Aynsley Bridgland in 1966, Prince's passed through other hands and it is sad to say that at times its condition rather deteriorated, but now a great revival has come about with the complete restoration of the quality of the golf courses and the building of a new clubhouse a mile or so away from the original, so creating a new layout of the holes which now radiate from the new clubhouse in three circuits of nine holes each. This is a great improvement as it brings into play much more easily the Red nine, now called the 'Himalayas',

Prince's Golf Club: Medal Cards

	HIMALAYAS MENS MEDAL	PAR		SHORE MENS MEDAL	PAR		DUNES MENS MEDAL	PAR
1	377	4	1	420	4	1	440	4
2	376	4	2	485	5	2	147	3
3	172	3	3	161	3	3	484	5
4	319	4	4	385	4	4	400	4
5	380	4	5	377	4	5	406	4
6	570	5	6	393	4	6	487	5
7	183	3	7	538	5	7	363	4
8	407	4	8	176	3	8	200	3
9	379	4	9	412	4	9	416	4
Total	3163	35	Total	3347	36	Total	3343	36

which was originally too far away from the old clubhouse to encourage its proper use. The holes of the Blue course now make two circuits, one known as the 'Shore' and the other the 'Dunes'.

For those who would like to follow the changes of layout, the 'Himalayas' makes no changes from what was known as the 'Red' circuit, the first and subsequent holes following the original plan. The 'Shore' nine starts with what was the fourteenth of the old 'Blue' eighteen and carries on from that point, ending therefore at the old fourth of its parent. The 'Dunes' circuit starts at what was originally the fifth hole of the 'Blue' and follows through in the sequence to finish at the thirteenth. These three courses are approximately of equal length and quality and combinations can be used for tournament play or indeed for the players' pleasure. For big events such as the qualifying round of the Open Championship, the 'Himalayas' and the 'Shore' circuits have been used.

Having played and much enjoyed the old pre-war course I had only just got more or less acquainted with the 'Blue' and 'Red' circuits, so

I am not quite certain of identifying the present holes correctly. Use has been made of some old greens and fairways from the original circuit, often approached from a different direction. Thus the present fourth green on the 'Shore' was the first green on the old original course; the old sixth, seventh and eighteenth greens were also used. One hole which seems to have survived from the old days is the famous old seventeenth which became the tenth of the 'Blue' and is now the sixth on the 'Dunes' nine. Apart from these there are, of course, all the new holes, many of them on a previously unused area near the beach, of which the short eleventh on the first 'Blue' layout, which I think is now the eighth on the 'Dunes', was notable for a small island green perched in the sand hills above a wasteland valley and then needing no bunkers to help or distract you. Then I recall the resolute hitting which was needed at the thirteenth, fourteenth, fifteenth, seventeenth and eighteenth to get home on the 'Blue'. These splendid holes still survive but not in such an important position in the round as they were. What were the last two are now the fourth and fifth on the 'Shore', as attractive a pair as you would find anywhere, the present fourth, 385 yards long, much beset by bunkers round the green, including a real live cross bunker in front and the 377-yard fifth without a bunker at all, but a crown green to throw off any but the straightest shot.

It is very hard to say why these great courses, and great they are all right, should fail to exercise the charm of Sandwich and Deal. The linksland, though lacking any large sandhills like those at Sandwich next door, is of the true quality, the shallow valleys are still there and full of folded and testing lies, the holes have been laid out with the greatest care to provide pleasure and pain depending on the needs of the day, by many alternative teeing grounds. There are many plateau greens of great charm and all the bunkers you need. True, the ground from the clubhouse looks uninspiring, but that's true in many another place; it is rather flat and somehow seems flatter than it used to be; it is treeless, but Deal and Sandwich are treeless too.

None the less, you do somehow get the impression that this is the less attractive end of the wonderful stretch of golfing country which runs for five miles from the outskirts of Deal

town due north to Pegwell Bay and the mouth of the Stour. Pegwell Bay is its wonderful blue, the cliffs of Ramsgate are shining white and the larks rise singing from the rough, as Bernard Darwin has often reminded us, but a hideous power station defaces the northern horizon.

The most famous son of Prince's – and this is literally true, for he was born in the clubhouse – is the Walker Cup player and captain, Wing Commander Laddie Lucas, who became a famous pilot in the Battle of Britain. Once when the fight was hottest and he was in dire trouble with a disabled plane he was able to make use of his local knowledge and land his damaged Spitfire at the far end of the course after first attempting to get down on the first fairway.

Important events have recently tended to pass Prince's by, but the qualifying rounds for the 1985 Open at St George's next door showed that the courses could hold their own with the professionals, as there was only one score under seventy and that by Massimo Manelli with a 69.

For important events such as this the courses can be stretched to 3321 yards for the 'Himalayas'; 3492 yards for the 'Shore' and 3455 yards for the 'Dunes'.

Royal St George's, Sandwich

The links of the Royal St George's Golf Club at Sandwich differs markedly from that of Prince's, its neighbour to the north, and of the Royal Cinque Ports at Deal to the south. Sandwich has a lumpier, hillier terrain than either neighbour, the sandhills are bigger, the valleys deeper and in places the waves in the fairways more pronounced.

Sandwich in its early days was known essentially as a driver's course and in truth it is so today, for the carries, especially off the back tees, and for me now from the ordinary tees, make you think. Long driving, if it be straight, pays everywhere and nowhere more than here.

Until recently, there was a more than ordinary carry at the short third, a big brute of a sandhill in front of the tee at the fourth, something similar at seven and the need to get well along from the ninth. The tee shots at the new eighth and the twelfth each require you to carry a substantial ridge and also at the 'Suez Canal' hole, the fourteenth. So if you are not hitting your drives or have a tendency to top or hit 'thin' you are in dire trouble, indeed you won't get round at all. But if you are driving well, then the game falls into place and the course is not monumentally long or harsh. True, some holes are very plentifully supplied with bunkers, notably the short holes other than number three, and in places the bunkering is very severe in its closeness to the greens.

Everybody remarks on the attractive solitude of Sandwich, where each hole seems to be cut off from all the others in its own valley or piece of empty links, so that however crowded the green may be, you are hardly ever aware of more than one game beside your own. There is a pleasant conservative air about the place, and the clubhouse, save for the elimination of sand boxes and earth closets, is as it always has been. A relaxed peaceful leather-furnished smoking-room persists and you can still get a tankard of ale from the wood. I wrote in 1972 that I had detected only one change for the worse: you had to pay for matches. It used to impress me enormously as a young man in the 'twenties when the steward said, while ignoring the proffered penny, 'There is no charge for matches in this club, sir'. I am delighted to learn that as a result of my earlier comment the civil practice of giving matches has been restored.

But changes to the course and surrounds were necessary and considerable modifications were made so as to make it and the approach roads fit once more after a lapse of years for the Open Championship.

There is a mild-enough drive from the first tee, but it should be well hit or you will end up in a hollow on the fairway called the 'Kitchen', from which it's a very long shot to get home. Even with a good drive the shot to the green is tight because of a big bunker right in front and right up close, a tough shot for a hole of 400 yards from the medal tee.

The second is shorter, with attractive humps and hollows in front of the green, which is on a little saddle of land with a fall on each side: nevertheless, this is one of the less difficult fours.

The old third, which was the 'Sahara', came next, a completely blind full belt of 228 yards, from the back tee, over a big sandhill to a big generous green. I always thought that this was a very poor hole, but it has been a famous hole

in its early days and was imitated, but not copied, at the National Golf Links of America, when Charles B. Macdonald was laying out that famous course on Long Island.

The new third is a hole of the same length as the old with the green up in the sandhills nearer the sea. All is in view now and a very pretty hole it is. It has already been modified slightly; the green now has a distinct step in it and there are no bunkers now on this hole.

The fourth out to the end of the links is a beauty. The medal player has an alarming drive right over a huge sandhill with two deep gaping bunkers in it. As Ian Fleming describes it in *Goldfinger*: 'you drive over one of the tallest and deepest bunkers in the United Kingdom.' If you surmount that you get a nice flat lie from which to play just about a full shot to a beautifully-sited green on a little plateau beyond some deep undulations of the fairway. For the championship players, the tee is nearer the third green and gives a less menacing prospect.

At the fifth you hit towards the sea and an invisible fairway with sandhills apparently everywhere, the great bulk of the tallest of all, the 'Maiden', away on the left. If your drive is to the right spot you can turn half left and hit a good stiff iron shot through a gap in the sandhills from which you can see the flat green beyond, out by the shore road. If your drive wasn't quite correct you will have to clear a sandhill, perhaps with a spoon or four-wood to make the green. Some think this hole too blind; I disagree.

At number six you play a short hole to a green under the shadow of the 'Maiden' to which you once had to come over the mountains. Into the prevailing west wind, if it is not too strong, it is about a four- or five-iron, I suppose, or even a six – not too exacting.

The seventh, out toward the sea again, needs a good carrying drive over the confronting hill, and there is a difficult bunker to avoid on the right, but then the play up a shallow valley offers no terrors if you are content with a par five.

The new par-four eighth replaces a short hole known as 'Hades' which was of no great distinction. The new tee is back by the beach and the drive once more has to clear a ridge; length is essential here to get a view of the green. Short of the green, which is in a shallow hollow, is a belt of rough grass and sandy scrub. Against any wind this is a truly formidable hole.

The ninth, the 'Corsets' – named after a pair of constricting bunkers now disappeared – is a beautiful hole. You play from a high tee down into a much folded valley; bunkers confuse the issue for you somewhat and then you have to play a high pitch, perhaps a six-iron to a narrow but long plateau green protected by a hump and trap on the left and a sharp fall-off to the right.

By the end of the first half you should have quite a good score if your driving has been sound; 36 or 37 is not too great a feat. The second half is a much tougher affair and for me anything under 40 is a real achievement.

You start with a splendid hole up a shallow valley and culminating in, say, a five- or six-iron shot to a small green the shape of a mushroom perched at the top of a sharp rise with cavernous bunkers guarding the entry on either hand. An insufficiently hit shot sometimes seems to run off cruelly and one hit 'thin' or too strong goes down a precipice at the back. Here in the last round of the 1985 Championship, Tom Kite, running well, came to grief; he was not quite up with his second, slid into the left-hand bunker, got too far out with his third and that was a six and the end of him.

The eleventh is now a par three played from the ridge we used to drive over, to the original plateau green with a protecting wall behind it and new bunkers on the left. This new hole, though not of great distinction, makes a better balance for the par threes with the shot in the opposite direction from that at the superseded eighth. The twelfth, with its diagonal carry, is a great favourite of mine; it is a short par four of 343 yards, but the tee shot is most testing. If you bite off too much you don't make the fairway, too little, and you have a hard shot to a green protected by deep bunkers right close to its edge.

The thirteenth is a really excellent hole, 438 yards off the medal tee, with a diagonal carry from the tee of no great severity. The second shot is one of the great ones in golf, for three bunkers *en échelon* eat into the fairway sixty to ninety yards short of the green and dominate your thinking – I've been in all of them – and then there are wing bunkers at the front of the green. The green is beautifully moulded, with a flanking hill to the right.

At fourteen you leave the big hills after another drive over the last range and get to the flat; your drive had better be a good one or you'll have to think about the out of bounds all the way along the right side and then the ditch called the 'Suez Canal', 328 yards from the tee, if there's any wind. Otherwise, as a par five, the hole offers no particular terrors, though it ruined Sarazen's chances in the Open in 1928 and it gave surprising trouble in both the 1981 and 1985 Championships. Here Sandy Lyle, getting a hard-won four followed by a three at the next, shook off the pursuit of the rest of the field in the 1985 Open.

The fifteenth, though quite flat, is a great hole 439 yards from the regular tee. Driving over some cross bunkers which shouldn't bother you, you are confronted with the need to hit to a narrow humpy green with a deep cross bunker only a yard or two short of it and another bunker to catch a shot ever so slightly hooked; even if you decide not to try for the carry the little pitch is no sitting duck; a four here is a joy, and to get home in two 'to carry the distant surf of the bunkers', as James Bond did against Goldfinger, is bliss.

Sixteen, 165 yards, has no fewer than eight bunkers round it, so you're on the green or in one of them for sure; I take leave not to admire it.

The seventeenth back among the humps is a fine two-shotter with a plateau green well set up, but with an 'armchair' back all round it –

save where bunkers eat into the edge of the green. Finally, there is another relatively flat raking two-shotter of 437 yards to end with, with the guarding bunkers just close enough to the prepared surface for comfort. All too often when a four has been needed to win or tie here a five has come on to the card, as happened to George Duncan in his great round in pursuit of Hagen in 1922.

Sandwich, like all great links, has some wonderful tales to tell. Possibly one of the most remarkable day's golf, at any rate in living memory, was in the Walker Cup match of 1930. J. A. Stout, 'the Bridlington Dentist', as the newspapers christened him, went round in the morning in 68 to be four up on Don Moe; what's more, he started 3 3 3 after lunch to be seven up and he was still seven up two holes later. Well, he lost. Moe went round in 67; he squared the match after seventeen holes and piled Pelion upon Ossa with a three at the eighteenth. Well might Stout say, 'That was not golf; that was a visitation from the Lord'.

Here the first foreigner took a British championship when Walter Travis, an Australian by birth and an American by nationality, won the Amateur Championship in 1904 and apparently got himself cordially disliked in the process; his uncanny skill with a centre-shafted putter resulted, it is widely believed, with what I hope is uncharacteristic British unsportsmanship, in this instrument being banned for forty years.

Tony Jacklin's hole in one at the sixteenth seen by millions on television and Harry Bradshaw's beer-bottle shot are also famous. In the second round of the Open of 1949, when leading the field, Bradshaw found his ball in a broken bottle at the back of the fifth green. Electing to play it, which authorities now believe he need not have done, he smashed the bottle and released the ball but took six to the hole. In the end he only tied for the championship and lost to Locke in the play-off.

Arnold Palmer made one of his rare appearances in England apart from Opens,

when he won the PGA Championship here in 1975. On the last day in a tearing easterly gale he did the lowest round of the day, a 71.

As you may infer from the quotations, one of the best accounts of Sandwich is in *Goldfinger* in which the captain-elect of the Royal St George's club describes the famous match between James Bond and the villain for $10,000 which reaches a surprising climax. Unfortunately, as the narrative reads, Goldfinger surrendered a match which he really had not lost; if he'd kept his head and known the rules, as he claimed, he could have maintained, quite rightly, that he'd holed out with the ball he'd driven from the tee and that was all he needed to have said.

The return of the Open Championship to Sandwich in 1981 was a great success and all the woeful prophecies about impossible access proving false and all the beliefs that the great pros would murder the course incorrect. In 1985 when we had the joy of a British win with Sandy Lyle some sour weather made scoring difficult and the winner's total was over par. These two championships show that Sandwich can well hold its own against the best players in the world.

Royal St George's Golf Club, Sandwich: Cards

	C	PAR	M		C	PAR	M
1	445	4	400	10	399	4	377
2	376	4	341	11	216	3	216
3	214	3	200	12	362	4	343
4	470	4	420	13	443	4	438
5	422	5	422	14	508	5	497
6	156	3	156	15	467	4	439
7	529	5	475	16	165	3	165
8	415	4	410	17	425	4	422
9	387	4	376	18	458	4	437
Out	3414	35	3200	In	3443	35	3334
				Out	3414	35	3200
				Total	6857	70	6534

Royal Cinque Ports, Deal

If I had one more round of golf to play on earth I would choose Deal as the links on which to play it. Sometimes I have thought that Sandwich would be the place for this mournful event, but after sixty years of golf the chopping and changing is past and I have decided now for Deal.

That this should be so arises partly from love and admiration for the golf, but as much from a sentimental attachment for the links formed years ago, then left neglected for decades and only recently revived in my old age.

For the Royal Cinque Ports Golf Club at Deal was the first championship links I played on, coming down here in 1925 as a rather fresh young man who was just beginning to put a game together and capable on such circuits as Southfield and West Byfleet of scores in the low eighties. We put up at the Royal Hotel, with the sea washing and sighing on the shingle under the windows, as it still does today; we were young and eager, playing thirty-six holes a day and sometimes nine 'after tea'; we drank a good deal of beer and danced every evening at the hotel to the gramophone; the receptionist had very pretty legs but I was far too shy to tell her so. Halcyon days.

The golf was an eye-opener; the sandhills, the humpy fairways, the awkward stances, the fierce rough, the cavernous bunkers full of soft fine sand, the shots to dells or plateau greens, and, above all, the wind, the perpetual, remorseless wind, combined to take all the starch out of this young man and leave a humiliated, chastened and wiser golfer. This process was repeated at Sandwich next door. A better and more experienced player might have realised that these famous links take some getting used to, that Bobby Jones had torn up his card in the 1921 Open at St Andrews in the third round after playing ten holes in 52 strokes and failing to reach the eleventh green at all, or that in the championship at Deal just a year before Hagen had taken 48 for the last nine holes,

while only two years before our descent on Deal, Sarazen had failed to qualify for the British Open at Troon.

Then at the end of this first visit came one shaft of sunlight through the racing cloudwrack; playing the rather short course at St Augustine's just north of Sandwich, as a reviver, I had a 76, my first round under 80 and so resolved to go on with the game. To round off these personalia, I might add that forty years later, on a sentimental journey, I had my first round under 70 with a 69 at St Augustine's and these were the only two rounds I have ever played there.

So, for Deal I have an abiding affection, one which could be uncritical if necessary, but luckily it need not be for this is one of the great golf links, great and difficult. Bernard Darwin says this:

Deal is a truly great course. I incline myself to think the most testing and severe of all the championship courses . . . yet it is not in these stern and almost sombre conditions that I best like to think of Deal or Sandwich. My day dreams are rather of them on a day of sunshine and light breeze – it is perhaps because it chances that here are the first really great courses that I ever saw, that this smiling corner of the earth's surface has for me something that no other spot, not even perhaps St Andrews, can quite equal. The larks seem to me to sing a little louder and more cheerfully there and the grass to have a more poignantly delicious taste of garlic. I am sure no other cliffs are so shining white as those beyond Pegwell Bay or that there is no view of shipping like that through the big plate-glass windows at Deal. Long may these things remain unchanged for future golfing generations to enjoy.' [And may I say hear hear to that.]

In spite of what Bernardo says, I must say I find the view from the clubhouse windows at Deal a little prosaic. To the right a new crop of council houses blocks out the hitherto uninterrupted view of the gasworks. To the left are the rolling sandhills of the links from which the players emerge after driving from the eighteenth tee, whose green on its shallow plateau is straight in front of you. Beyond lie the second fairway and the new sea wall protecting the links – all too necessary – from the pounding of the sea. In the foreground the first fairway, lush and flat and green, runs past the clubhouse, picked out by a few small clumps of rushes.

The course runs north and south at both start and finish, with four holes at the far end near the Sandwich links running at right angles to the general line of play. The prevailing wind, south-west, is off the land and has the maddening property of not helping you going out, for it comes over your left shoulder, and being a harsh enemy coming home. In high summer, with a gentle north-east breeze off the sea, the links plays easiest; then the terrible long beat home is a joy and not a supreme effort.

Now let's go round Deal from the short tee boxes, which take 335 yards off the championship length, for which I am truly grateful. The first hole of 325 yards, towards the town, past the clubhouse windows, should be no hardship; it is flat, verdant and unbunkered, the green is generous in size and a little ridge at the back protects you from going too far. There is just one snag; there is a ditch right across the fairway in front of the green. You have no business going into it, yet like the Swilcan Burn at the first hole at St Andrews many good men have done so, usually when the hole is played as a nineteenth.

At the second hole you turn north and at once you are in the real linksland with plenty of undulations on the fairway and the green half hidden by a low protecting ridge unless you can hug the right-hand edge of the fairway, a very attractive hole. Then to number three, a great favourite of mine. Off the tee you can see some very broken country in the distance along the fairway and only the top of the pin. Two big bunkers in a ridge across the fairway about 300 yards out are conspicuous, though you ought

not to get in them. Beyond them the fairway is almost excessively broken and folded and culminates in a deep punchbowl green, on two levels with a steep step, beyond the last of these folds. At 453 yards even with some help from the wind it takes two fine hits to get there and some luck from the run of the ball too. The lucky professionals are allowed a stroke more at the cost of 39 yards.

The fourth is a fine new short hole, replacing the old blind hole across 'Sandy Parlour'; you play from a tee high in the backbone ridge of dunes which bisects the course here, to a plateau green with severe falls on either hand; you need a good poke with a six or seven or sometimes a five-iron.

Five is a long hole, but not excessive for a par five, then comes the unorthodox and attractive number six, which has its plateau green close to the new sea wall; originally the green was right up to the shingle of the beach, but with the building of the wall a new green, nearer in but like the old, has had to be made. It is only 304 yards long from our tee, but the ground on the way is very bumpy and in front of the green is a really deep hollow out of which you usually have to pitch up sharply without lifting your head. There is a big protective sandhill to the right. In dry weather with a fair breeze astern you can get home with a good shot and what fun that is.

The seventh continues the run to the north with a drive-and-medium-iron hole, at which the green rather helps to gather the ball. The eighth is a heavily bunkered but not too difficult short hole towards the sea. Then come three holes of a duller and more prosaic texture, though the tenth is often selected for high, indeed I think extravagant praise. All three have a dog-leg element – the tenth very much so – with trouble at the joint, as it were. The ninth and eleventh both run away from the sea, though the new championship tee at the sea wall at the eleventh alters the configuration of this hole; they are too much alike and while not easy leave no memories and no scars.

At this stage, I hope you have got a good score on your card, fours perhaps or better, for if there is any west or south in the wind you are going to need it, for you are in for a straight beat in for the last seven holes. There are times, when, as Frank Pennink says, you would settle for a finish of five fives and a four, but it is really more fun to play them, at any rate for the first time or two, in milder conditions.

The twelfth is a 418-yard par four. The preliminaries are rather flat and dull, but the green, long and narrow, between two little ridges, is quite exceptionally attractive. The thirteenth, a dog leg of 400 yards, gives you a chance of an iron shot for your second perhaps, but the green beyond the row of bunkers across the fairway is always a little farther off on its up slope than it seems. Next comes a long tough par-three hole, 215 yards, with a hollow on the left of the green and two deep bunkers on the right of it, which catch a shot with any fade on it. A fair shot with a two-iron boring into the wind to fall lifeless on the green is a pretty sight here. It was here that that great Irish golfer Lionel Munn, who was walking round, was asked to demonstrate the hole, so he borrowed a club and ball and holed in one stroke while the feat was recorded in a bystander's camera. The picture hangs in the clubhouse.

The fifteenth at 420 yards is a splendid hole, where your second shot may be anything from a five-iron to a brassie, depending on the wind. There is a slight dog leg to the right here, with bunkers at the angle, about 190 yards from the tee. The hole is then dominated by a mild sandy hill beyond which lies the green; you can easily run too far if you pitch too far on to the down slope of this hill.

The sixteenth is to me the greatest hole on this great links – 456 yards from my tee and 506 from the championship tee-box. I am glad that this hole has been converted to a par five for the big events and indeed I don't see why you and I have to play it as a four. It really plays well as a five for the shot up to the pin is all carry and almost always against the wind. Indeed, for me

it is the greatest hole in golf. The green is lodged on a wonderfully moulded high plateau, rising, as Bernard Darwin says, sheer out of a lush green 'valley of inglorious security' with a protective knob and bunker on its right extremity. You drive past some fortifications of the last war over some bunkers on the fairway, then if you can't get up in two you make for the safe green vale rather left of the line; if you overdo this you are trapped deeply, if not you still have a good stiff pitch to play to this incomparable plateau. But if you can get up in two, as to my surprise I did not so long ago, to the angry resentment of two innocent women putting out, what a superlative joy it is to see the ball racing into the sunset to climb the ridge and give you a putt for an eagle against Colonel Bogey. A hole in a million.

The seventeenth is shorter, at 360 yards, but the fairway is very bumpy and there is a deep cross bunker about eighty yards short of the green, a tiny saucer set among humps and slopes. Finally to eighteen, where you drive out of the sandhills on to the flat ground in front of the clubhouse, cross a ditch and then fly up on to a shallow plateau. At 396 yards it takes two good shots to get home and if your second is less than fine the ball dies on the up-slopes of the plateau and you take five.

Great events have occurred at Deal. The amateur record stands to Michael Bonallack, who did a splendid 65 in the Brabazon Trophy in 1964, which he won, going out – with the help of two twos – in the astonishing score of 31, though his other three rounds did not destroy the course. A 63 was scored before the most recent changes by Gordon Manson in the qualifying rounds for the Open of 1981.

In the Open of 1920, George Duncan, whose first two rounds of 80 would not have survived the 'cut' in these days, came roaring in with 71 and 72 to snatch the prize from the unhappy Abe Mitchell. Abe, who led after two rounds with the aid of a one at the eighth hole, was a beautiful shot-maker, but could never quite do it in the pinch; he was unlucky enough to be

Royal Cinque Ports Golf Club, Deal: Medal and Championship Cards

	C	PAR	M	PAR	STROKE INDEX		C	PAR	M	PAR
1	361	4	325	4	14	10	362	4	362	4
2	399	4	364	4	8	11	398	4	382	4
3	492	5	453	4	4	12	437	4	418	4
4	153	3	153	3	18	13	420	4	400	4
5	502	5	494	5	2	14	222	3	215	3
6	315	4	304	4	12	15	455	4	420	4
7	385	4	370	4	6	16	506	5	456	4
8	154	3	154	3	16	17	372	4	360	4
9	404	4	383	4	10	18	407	4	396	4
Out	3165	36	3000	35		In	3579	36	3409	35
						Out	3165	36	3000	35
						Total	6744	72	6409	70

waiting on the first tee to begin his third round rather late in the morning and had to endure seeing the mercurial George with an enthusiastic crowd finishing the eighteenth; then his nerve gone, Mitchell started 5 5 6 4 8 and finished in 84, his whole lead of thirteen shots over Duncan gone with the wind. In that same championship Walter Hagen, later four times the winner, made his first appearance in the British Open and finished fifty-third out of fifty-four.

Many great things have happened, too, in the Halford Hewitt Cup games which are played by the public schools golfing societies each April, and are now so popular that some games even have to be played at Sandwich to relieve the pressure, while others start so early that, to quote Henry Longhurst, 'The lightship moored on the Goodwins was still flashing as we played the second hole.' This continues to be the biggest amateur event in the world with 640 players. Incidentally, the Royal Cinque Ports club has a very generous scheme of membership for all members of public school golfing societies.

Deal links has been severely punished by the sea breaking over the inadequate shingle bank protecting it. The last of these incursions was in 1978 and we can now hope that with the new sea wall these disasters will now end. The Open in modern conditions is unlikely to return, though the Amateur was played here in 1982.

Littlestone

Littlestone is a most pleasant and enjoyable links, with some considerable but not too emphatic sandhills. The lies on the fairway are less humpy than on the links farther north at Deal and Sandwich or farther south at Rye. Nevertheless, you have to hit your shots properly to score well. One of my favourite holes in the first nine was the second, where you had to beat your second shot over a hill, a blind stroke but fun, now made easier and duller by a cut in the hill to enable a straight driver to see his second shot. The third, where the green is on a saddle in the same range of hills, and the 'drive and iron' eighth out by the coast road are also enjoyable.

In the second half you come and go across the course until confronted with a splendid hilly sixteenth towards the water tower, where you can hope for a four but settle for a five. Originally, I think this hole had two vast bunkers to be carried from a tee in the face of a rise. The seventeenth is a splendid par three, a good hard iron or even a spoon or four-wood to a green on a ridge above the final plain of the last hole on which we have rather a dull eighteenth.

The club handbook says rather charmingly of the seventeenth: 'Pause a while on the tee (a) to allow players in front to move away, well clear of the green, (b) to discern, if you can, the coast of France on a clear day and (c) select the right club – it can be any one from a seven-iron to a driver.' The present layout at Littlestone is the work of Dr Alister Mackenzie, famous of course for Cypress Point and Augusta National in the USA.

The club dates back to 1888 and some early records survive. The second competition held on 1 September of that year was won with 105 net, while a professional competition on 1 November was won by Willie Fernie of Troon with 79 and 82, for which he got £12. At the Easter meeting in '89 the best score was 126–16

Littlestone Golf Club: Medal Card					
	YARDS	PAR		YARDS	PAR
1	297	4	10	413	4
2	410	4	11	356	4
3	392	4	12	393	4
4	370	4	13	401	4
5	491	5	14	183	3
6	157	3	15	359	4
7	507	5	16	468	4
8	385	4	17	179	3
9	185	3	18	488	5
	3184	36		3240	35
				3184	36
				6424	71

and the worst 220–36. This hardy member returned 225 next time out and 220 in the May medal. Littlestone is, I think, a rather underrated course and in my view, as *Guide Michelin* puts it, 'worth a detour'. Try it some time.

Littlestone is, I suppose, the driest spot in England. Its condition enabled it to offer to the Oxford and Cambridge Golfing Society the courtesy of the green for the playing of the President's Putter in January 1963 when Rye was under snow. In the qualifying rounds for the '85 Open Championship only four players beat 70.

There is an attractive nine hole course of 2000 yards as well.

Rye

Rye is a place for tradition. It is conservative, possibly even a little old-fashioned – and none the worse for that. Foursomes are played as a regular thing and it must be just about the only club in the world which puts up a notice saying: 'Three and four-ball matches are allowed, but they have no standing.' Tweedy plus-fours – knickers to Americans – are worn and small flat caps. There are no winter rules or improving your lie. The clubhouse is up to date now, though for years a most primitive corrugated-iron pavilion was sufficient until a German bomb destroyed it, and thank heaven the traditional scrambled eggs are still served at lunch.

The links is first-class, a little short for the big hitters but quite long enough for you and me.

There is a main ridge of sandhills running the whole length of the course which comes markedly into play and another subsidiary ridge parallel to it nearer the sea. There have been many alterations to the course since 1894, most of them made necessary by the increasing traffic along the road which runs all along the northern boundary. Major changes were made in 1913 and between the wars and new holes were built after World War II so that the whole of the first half, except for the present fifth, has replaced the old parts of the course closer to the road and beyond the coastguard cottages which now form the boundary at the end of the course.

The three opening holes on the flat to the north of the main ridge are difficult enough, if not spectacular, the short second being far from easy. Then comes the fourth, 410 yards long and surely one of the great holes in golf, with a painfully narrow hog's back to find and hold with your drive and trouble all the way to the green after the drive, sandy hills on the left and a plunge down to the plain on the right. Stay on the ridge and you're all right, but how difficult in a wind – and wind is something you have to expect at Rye.

The short fifth, once the eighth, is an attractive short hole of 168 yards across a wide gully to a shallow saucer of a green perched up high in the sandhills. The short seventh too, a new hole, is a splendid shot and so, too, is the short fourteenth.

The second half is full of very tough par fours and is less changed in recent years than the first nine though the tenth and eighteenth holes were remodelled. Now the eleventh hole is in the melting pot. The shingle waste land to the right of the eleventh fairway, the first you see of the course from the road from Rye, has vanished as the result of dredging for gravel, to be replaced by a lake stretching roughly from the tee to the green, a fearsome hazard if the wind is adverse; the final layout to take account of these changes has not yet been decided.

No longer at the last hole do you drive from below over a vast bunker fortified all the way round by a stockade of black sleepers, a hideous and horrifying hazard; instead you have a hard par four hole back to the clubhouse along the ridge. Sleepers in the bunkers which were once a feature of Rye can still be found, but not as widely as in the past, those in front of the seventh and to the right of the fourteenth green still come into play.

The second half has some fine holes; at the thirteenth, the 'Sea Hole' of 436 yards, you have to carry a great rampart of sandhills with your second, if you've hit a good drive, or your third if you have not, to a hidden green over the ridge.

The sixteenth is a grand hole with the ridge to be carried from the tee running across your line diagonally; and after you're over that, a good stiff iron shot is needed to get home or even a blow with 'the old man's friend', a five-wood. When Leonard Crawley was at the height of his powers he would play a long drive down the valley on the left parallel to the ridge; then, with a sight of the bottom of the pin through a gap, he would pitch on to the green, not a shot to be advised for you and me. Crawley, of course, was a great player and won many distinctions at the game, including the English Close Championship. He also hit and dented the Walker Cup by an over-strong pitch at the Country Club at Brookline in 1932. That year part of the play for the dented cup took place during a total eclipse of the sun.

Rye, then, is tough but perfectly fair, the fairways are of the old seaside quality, rather thin grass with plenty of run and dry at all seasons. The greens are also far from lush, and indeed can seem terrifyingly thin, even bare, in dry weather and some of the downhill putts can be alarming: but they are true and reward a properly-struck ball. And always there is the breeze, which never seems to help you but always to hinder, for the prevailing wind blows across the line of nearly all the holes.

Rye is the home of the Oxford and Cambridge Golfing Society which holds its annual

Woburn: Lee Trevino at the spectacular 2nd/3rd hole (1985 Dunhill British Masters)

Killarney: the famous 18th hole at Mahoney's Point

Right: Walton Heath: the 11th
hole on the Old Course

Newcastle: the
spectacular 9th hole
with Slieve Donard

Ballybunion: perhaps
the best of them all

Portmarnock: the
famous Irish links near
Dublin

tournament for the President's Putter in the improbable month of January. The first Putter competition was played in 1920 and in the intervening 66 years it has only once been called off because of weather; in 1979 heavy snow fell too close to the event to avoid its cancellation. Once frost intervened in the opening rounds and play was transferred to neighbouring Littlestone, which had escaped the frost.

The original putter, once owned by Hugh Kirkaldy and used by him when he won the championship in 1891, and used by the society's first president, John L. Low, when he reached the final of the Amateur, hangs in the clubhouse at Rye, replete with its row of balls commemorating the winners. A second putter, once the property of W. T. Linskill, who introduced golf to Cambridge University, now hangs below it, and it, too, is filling up with balls.

The most frequent winners of the Putter were Sir Ernest Holderness, one of Britain's best amateurs, with five wins, and Roger Wethered with four and a half, the half coming in 1926 when darkness prevented a finish. Not long ago a most discerning account of the Putter competition was written by the famous American writer Herbert Warren Wind for the *New Yorker* magazine.

Rye now has an additional nine-hole course, opened in 1977 and known as the Jubilee course, on land which was previously under water, and from which the sea has retreated. With a number of typical Rye holes, tightly-constructed greens and close-cropped undulating fairways, it is a tough test of golf and in no sense a poor relation of the old course. I had the pleasure of being driven round it by the secretary, Commander Bradley, on one of those fine winter days when Rye looks fresh and green and welcoming to the golfer.

Though essentially on flat ground compared with the old links, Donald Steel made full use of such ridges and hills as were available, an excellent example of this being the beautiful setting of the third green between two mounds which enfold it. By making use of alternative tees, the course can be varied somewhat if you wish to play a second nine. The journey out to the new course was especially pleasant for me as we drove along the old road-bed of the former Rye and Camber steam tramway. This

Rye Golf Club: Card

	YARDS	PAR		YARDS	PAR
1	483	5	10	425	4
2	182	3	11	335	4
3	437	4	12	420	4
4	410	4	13	436	4
5	168	3	14	179	3
6	469	4	15	429	4
7	161	3	16	418	4
8	393	4	17	224	3
9	294	4	18	438	4
	2997	34		3304	34
				2997	34
				6301	68

Rye Golf Club, Jubilee Course: Card

	YARDS	PAR		YARDS	PAR
1	232	3	10	492	5
2	350	4	11	350	4
3	381	4	12	381	4
4	323	4	13	154	3
5	317	4	14	317	4
6	142	3	15	142	3
7	385	4	16	385	4
8	401	4	17	401	4
9	494	5	18	494	4
	3025	35	In	3116	36
			Out	3025	35
			Total	6141	71

delightful little line, which was much used by golfers before World War I, did not survive the 1920s. If only it had been preserved in moth balls for sixty years it would have been a wonderful attraction today and probably highly profitable.

Cooden Beach

Very different from Rye, though as close, or closer, to the sea, is Cooden Beach, near Bexhill, but a pleasant and enjoyable place at which to play golf. Whereas Rye is on pure linksland, Cooden Beach, though only separated from Pevensey Bay by the railway and a bank of shingle, is on marshland soil and many drainage ditches from Pevensey Levels run through it. Indeed, the lower parts of the course almost give the impression of being below sea level, though doubtless they are not, and in all fairness, the course is very reasonably dry at all seasons.

While this may not be historic turf in the golf sense, the course is close to where William the Norman landed in 1066 to claim his kingdom. During the last war the course was restricted to six holes, so that the anti-aircraft batteries, which were the first line of defence against the flying bombs, could be deployed.

The earlier holes are on the flatter inland part of the course, which plays to a good length for its par scores. Once again, I will declare my interest in shorter par fours before saying that of these earlier flatter holes, I like the 352-yard fourth very much, with its dyke to carry in front of the built-up green, and the 304-yard fifth which follows it. The fine two-shot ninth takes us up to the higher ground by the railway and the shore, with a sharp rise on the second shot. However, we immediately come down to play the long tenth and the shorter eleventh all along Coles Stream to reach the far end of the course. The twelfth is an attractive par three across the end of the course to a slightly elevated green. We now run home with the wind at our backs, starting with a good two-shot hole to a high green near the tenth tee. Two dropping short holes help us on our way, and just as well, for the other three holes in are a par five and two long fours.

For many years, the pro here was Fred Robson, one of the greatest of teachers and a good player himself, for he was picked four times to play against America.

On a fine day with the sun sparkling on Pevensey Bay and a view out to the Royal Sovereign lightship – or rather the Royal Sovereign tower now – Beachy Head and the Downs behind, this is a pleasant place.

Cooden Beach Golf Club: Medal Card					
	YARDS	PAR		YARDS	PAR
1	429	4	10	448	4
2	445	4	11	394	4
3	150	3	12	173	3
4	352	4	13	374	4
5	304	4	14	154	3
6	406	4	15	443	4
7	159	3	16	164	3
8	476	5	17	422	4
9	330	4	18	476	5
	3051	35		3048	34

Total 6099 yards: par 69

Royal Eastbourne

On the lower slopes of the South Downs, two miles from their plunge into the sea at Beachy Head and just a mile from the centre of the town, lies the grassy downland course of the Royal Eastbourne Golf Club. Organised golf came to Sussex in 1887 and the first two clubs to be founded were Royal Eastbourne and Seaford, a few miles to the west.

The original nine holes at Eastbourne were laid out under the guidance of Horace Hutchinson, a founder member of the club and, at the same time, Amateur champion. These holes form an anti-clockwise loop round a spacious area of open grassland, known, long before golf came to the area, as the Links. They are, with only a few significant changes, still in use. A further nine holes were added in 1894 and extended in 1904 to the land now in use, which also includes a short, but by no means easy, nine-hole course derived from what was originally a ladies' course.

Royal Eastbourne offers good all-the-year-round golf on the fine downland turf with a rapidly draining chalk sub-soil. Tucked under the heights of the surrounding hills, it provides downland golf without the hard climbing over-exposed hilltops so often associated with that type of game. The lie of the land is parallel to the line of the downs, so its particular problems involve the mastery of side-hill lies and making

Royal Eastbourne Golf Club: Medal Card

	YARDS	PAR		YARDS	PAR
1	437	4	10	405	4
2	266	4	11	387	4
3	388	4	12	352	4
4	504	5	13	178	3
5	497	5	14	360	4
6	364	4	15	179	3
7	435	4	16	486	5
8	171	3	17	222	3
9	330	4	18	162	3
	3342	37		2742	33

Total 6084 yards: par 70

the best possible use of the slopes round the approaches to the greens. Although not over-long, this course offers the handicap golfer a good test of skill. The layout of the course also involves the minimum use of what one might call the 'gun platform' green.

In addition to Horace Hutchinson, notable members of the club have included several members of the Hambro family, former Prime Minister Arthur Balfour and C. J. H. Tolley, Amateur champion twice.

Littlehampton

Littlehampton is bounded on its eastern side by the estuary of the River Arun and its yacht harbour, and along its southern flank by a line of dunes which effectively shut off all view of the sea and the fine wide sands on the shore.

The first view of the links is as disappointing as that of Hoylake, a flat piece of grassland with its parallel mown fairways, grassy rough and a few greens, and away in the distance a line of

sandhills which hold out more promise. And, as at Hoylake, the holes in or near the sandhills are certainly the more attractive while the holes in the meadows are long and tough but not easy to distinguish.

The club is of a good age, going back to the '80s, but the course has been altered a good deal since its founding, first by the architects Hawtree and Taylor, whose trade marks, as at the

Royal Mid-Surrey, are there for all to see in numerous contrived humps along the fairways and around the greens, with or without sand at their base.

When World War II came, Littlehampton became very much the invasion coast – both ways – and a great many military relics had to be got rid of after the war at a cost of £10,000 to put the links in order again.

In my view, the first is such a good hole that it's a pity that it doesn't come at a more critical moment in the round; it would make an excellent sixteenth or seventeenth. You drive along a flat fairway with a possibility of out of bounds if you hook it, and then a big shot, I guess a spoon for me, up on to a plateau, with attendant bumps and bunkers on either side, which begins about 40 yards short of the green. A fine testing par-four hole with the added features of a ruined Victorian fort in the wall of dunes behind.

The second is a fine hole, too, played along the line of the dunes to a small plateau green surrounded by traps; the cross bunker in front of the green is all too near it for comfort and I suppose a wild hook might put you on the beach. It is pleasant at this hole to be able to hear the sea washing on the shore, even if you can't see it.

At the third, we play a par three down out of duneland, a new hole, and rather uninspired, I thought. After two par fives up and down on the meadowland, we play another short hole, this time up into the dune country, an improvement on the third, but a 'feature bunker' I had thought would add some picturesqueness, if not difficulty, to a straightforward three or four-iron shot. It is interesting to learn that recently this has been done. The seventh, with its tee up in the linksland, needs a good carry with a hump and some rough rough to cross, but after that you emerge on to the fairway and it is pretty plain sailing.

There is another short hole at eight, this had more character I thought; from the tee you see a little green saucer up in the grey-green links-

land rough, and it looks a small target. When you get there the green is quite long with a distinct hump in it which can give you some very trying putts when it is fast.

At the ninth we play along the sandhills again with an attractive and not too alarming short two-shot hole, once we have got the drive away over a big hump and some gravelly sand, which the literature describes as shingle.

The tenth continues on out to the far end of the course, still following the dunes, but then we turn inland for the run home on the flatter and less interesting terrain, bearing in mind that the holes are going to be difficult and also creek-beset from twelve right through to sixteen, the last short hole.

The par is 70, but if anyone thinks that this course will give you a flattering score, he should consult the honours board in the clubhouse. Incidentally, these honour boards are often interesting and useful sources of facts about a course and club. The clubhouse, which was destroyed by fire in 1985, has been replaced by a new building on a new site in 1986.

Littlehampton Golf Club: Medal Card					
	YARDS	PAR		YARDS	PAR
1	420	4	10	367	4
2	366	4	11	155	3
3	179	3	12	409	4
4	554	5	13	365	4
5	492	5	14	388	4
6	182	3	15	341	4
7	380	4	16	152	3
8	190	3	17	505	5
9	355	4	18	402	4
	3118	35		3084	35

Total 6202 yards: par 70

Hayling Island

The course on Hayling Island is a true links and a fine one. On a small island, between Langstone and Chichester harbours, close to Portsmouth, it lies on land once beneath the sea and today on the lightest of sandy soils. Even the rough, though it contains heather in places, is sparse. Until a year or so ago wild bush lupins grew extravagantly at the far end of the links. These, now, alas, largely removed, were perhaps too tough for proper rough and also harmed the many rare wild flowers which are found at Hayling, but they did form a most engaging bush with their honey-scented flowers.

The club was founded in 1883 by the Sandeman family and was brought up to date in 1933. The English Ladies' Championship has been played here several times but not the British Amateur, though I am sure the links is good enough.

In spite of the very dry soil and sparse turf there are some hazards where water can play a conspicuous part, notably the carry from the tee at the 405-yard fourth and the 423-yard fifteenth holes and dominating the splendid second shot to the 433-yard sixth. Nevertheless, in spite of this, the course in all weathers gives an impression of crisp dryness rare in these days. In total, the links measures 6489 yards, quite enough for a moderate player like myself. It can, of course, blow like the devil here and then it would be long indeed.

All this area was in the forefront of the battle in World War II and played a part in the vital defence of Portsmouth with guns and decoy fires; until recently, by a local rule, a ball could be lifted and dropped without penalty from a bomb crater.

I made my first acquaintance with Hayling Island very late in life, but was so pleased with this delightful links that although it was raining all the way round there was no thought of quitting. Yet in spite of this, and of heavy rain in the weeks before, the course played with a very reasonable amount of run and the seaside greens were quite fast enough.

The course is fairly evenly divided between the ten flatter holes at the beginning of the first half and the end of the second, and the eight holes starting with the par-five seventh which are among the sandhills and in the very best style of traditional seaside golf. This is not to say that the flatter holes at the beginning and end are not fine tests of golf – they are – with sometimes small and narrow greens with plenty of subtle slopes and borrows which require good shot-making. None the less, the holes out at the far end amongst the hills have the finest flavour.

Starting with the seventh, although a par five of moderate length, there is a small green well cocked up, with slopes carrying the ball away on either hand so that your third shot, even if a short one, has to be very straight.

The eighth is that rare thing, which is, I fear, disappearing fast from golf, a good short par four, only 352 yards. A line of sandhills across the fairway, though they make the pitch blind or half-blind, nevertheless prevents the big hitters from destroying the hole by their length, which indeed they will need in good measure at the next hole, which is a stiff par four and, alas, now barely within my reach. The drive over the sandhills at the ninth is attractive and reminded me of Sandwich.

The tenth is another short par four, indeed a very short par four (270 yards) though for some reason, probably the narrowness of its long green, it looks very much longer than it is. It is distinguished by the fact that the players in one four-ball once holed it in one, two, three and four strokes.

We then have an excellent short hole of 152 yards with a beautiful plateau green and attractive moulding of the protecting bunkers, a really lovely hole. Following this comes a great two-shotter running parallel with Langstone harbour, where, for my capabilities, two exceptional shots have to be hit to get home to the green, which is up a slope, 'defying you to reach it', as Bernard Darwin used to write, with a fall to destruction on the left. The drive is over wild rough, but the tree lupins no longer prevail here; a four at this hole, even with a rather scrambly little run-up, was a real pleasure.

The next hole, the thirteenth, is famous and justly so. You have to drive uphill over a long carry, possibly not as long as it looks but containing originally a monstrous bunker known as the 'Widow'. However, this famous hazard has now been allowed to grow grass on most of its surface which has made it less spectacular but at least as difficult. If you clear that with a good shot you then have a not too difficult pitch downhill to a green well below you: a less than good drive gives you a blind or half-blind second. Having managed to achieve a good drive here, the hole in retrospect looks absolutely splendid, though I suppose one of those drives, when, as the American pros say on TV, 'I come off it real baad', and so cutting the ball into some horrible sandy waste, would leave you with a rather different first impression.

The thirteenth green brings you to a unique feature at Hayling Island, and one I am not aware of anywhere else – namely, the secondary clubhouse. As the clubhouse proper is a long way round by road from Portsmouth and its neighbouring towns, which are the principal source of membership, and there is a passenger ferry across the island close to the thirteenth green, the club has built a small secondary clubhouse for those who come this way, and wish to start their round at the fourteenth hole. That hole, by the way, is a fine par five of 534 yards, with marshy ground on the left which can be water in bad weather to catch a pulled second shot, and a finely-moulded green just behind a protective ridge, rather in the St Andrews style.

Three of the four short holes at Hayling are in the flatter territory, one of them, indeed, the first hole of the course. This hole looks a rather dull number from the tee, but the nearer you get to it, the better it is, because you see more and more what an excellently shaped green it has. The fifth hole has its green on a very narrow plateau, which certainly doesn't invite the shot or gather the ball, while the sixteenth is also on a slight plateau where a shot off line will confront you with a most difficult pitch, one of which, to my intense pleasure, I managed to bring off more by luck than judgement.

So much for what was for me an intensely enjoyable round, rain or no rain. An added pleasure was my old caddie, who had been on and around the course for fifty-two years and was known by everybody as 'Sailor', now no longer with us. He was a caddie in the old tradition, who took an interest in the game, 'our' game, needless to say, and was an excellent judge of the shot and his partner's capabilities. He was also reputed never to lose a ball, even if it involved breaking the ice in winter to wade in and find errant balls. During the war his sloop was sunk off the Nab Tower, within sight of the links, by a bomb that went down the funnel and wounded him in the back. At the end of the game I gave him enough, I hope, to have a good drink, for he was as wet as I, saying: 'I hope you can get it without much difficulty', to which he replied: 'I always believe in having some in the house, sir'.

One final feature at Hayling is the names which the holes carry, though those are no longer on the card; as the captain of the club wrote in the centenary booklet 'Change is not always progress'. I am not usually much enamoured of named holes, especially if these have been all too artfully contrived, like those Scotticisms at Gleneagles. But here, if some of the names are simple like 'Plain' or 'Narrows' or 'Sea', others clearly commemorated some person or event which the little booklet issued by the course then ignored.

Hayling Island Golf Club: Medal Card

NAME	YARDS	PAR	NAME	YARDS	PAR
1 Trap	181	3	10 Pan-Ko-Chai	270	4
2 Sea	497	5	11 Woolseners	152	3
3 Broom	397	4	12 The Desert	444	4
4 Butts	405	4	13 Widow	341	4
5 Narrows	162	3	14 Farm	534	5
6 Cutting	433	4	15 Jacob's Ladder	423	4
7 Death or Glory	492	5	16 Wharram	179	3
8 Crater	352	4	17 Sailor's Grave	425	4
9 Plain	418	4	18 Sinah	384	4
	3337	36		3152	35

Total 6489 yards: par 71

However all was made clear in the centenary booklet in these words:

Although the modern tendency is to refer to holes by their numbers, the Hayling course, with its quaintly, and in some cases, strangely-named holes, has always intrigued visitors and members alike.

There is, however, one hole that is invariably referred to by name and that is the 'Widow', a hole that has seen the ruination of many and many a medal card. Yet the Widow, as constructed in the early days, had a horrendous sand dune bunker, much more fearsome than it is today. Hence the name and its meaning, 'Fall into the widow's clutches and it is difficult to escape!'

Of the other holes, some of the names are steeped in mystery and conjecture. But many are straightforward.

For example, the 16th – 'Wharram' – is named after Dr Wharram H. Lamplough who, it is believed, designed this hole.

The 10th, 'Pan-Ko-Chai' is Malaysian for 'Hell'. The name was originally given to the old 9th hole – a short 125 yarder over sandhills to the west of our present 8th green.

The 'Butts' was the title given to the old short 4th hole as it was on the site of a 1914–1918 rifle range. The name was kept when the present 4th was made, longer but near enough to the range . . . .

Mystery surrounds the name of the present 17th – 'Sailors Grave', as the lake was not there in those early days. There are two legends, one is that a body was found when the hole was constructed and secondly an old horse named Sailor lies buried under the first bunker.

There is no record to be found of the origin of the name 'Woolseners' given to the present 11th hole . . . .

And so the last hole, 'Sinah', which commemorates Sinah Common on which our forefathers had the sense to build a golf course, taking some years to complete, but on which we now enjoy our sport.

ISLANDS

Unhappily, my hope that we could perhaps have taken the ferry across to the Isle of Wight and played a round at Bembridge on the little nine-hole links which once was the home of the Royal Isle of Wight Golf Club did not work out, as the little links appears to have been abandoned, in spite of a venerable history. The course occupied a very small area near the village of St Helens, protected from the sea by a sea wall called the Duver, on which now repose some of the old coaches of the Isle of Wight Railway. The nine holes wove in and out amongst themselves and gave you some fine shots among the dunes on the seaward side. On the beach here Mr Horace Hutchinson many years ago reported finding his ball lying upon 'a dead and derelict dog'.

Well, if we can't play at Bembridge any more, we must certainly try to play in the Channel Islands which, while part of the British Isles, are not part of the United Kingdom, their relationship to the Crown being derived from having formed part of the Dukedom of Normandy in 1066. Be that as it may, they are pleasantly different from England and blessed by a rather better climate. Golf is well suited here and Jersey can be regarded as historic turf indeed. Golf in the Channel Islands goes back to 1878.

Harry Vardon, Britain's greatest golfer, six times Open champion, once US champion and twice runner-up, and his brother Tom, who was also a fine player, were born on the edge of the links near Gorey on the eastern shore of Jersey. Ted Ray, who won the British and US Open Championships, was a Jerseyman, so were the Boomers, Aubrey, a Ryder Cup player for Britain, and Percy, author of a book of instruction which was a classic; add to these numerous Gaudins, Renoufs and Le Chevaliers and the output of this small island, only some ten miles by five, appears prodigious.

The most recent Jerseyman to reach distinction has undoubtedly been Tommy Horton, a fine tournament player, now the resident professional at the Royal Jersey club. He was, in fact, born in Lancashire, as his mother had been evacuated from the Channel Islands before the German occupation in 1940.

There are two attractive courses in Jersey, both of the links type and a third shorter course. The La Moye course, at the western end of the island near the famous lighthouse of Corbière, is on top of the cliffs, overlooking the sea. The Royal Jersey course, at the opposite end of the island, is mostly on sandy low-lying links turf on Grouville Bay, though one or two holes in the inward half with protecting gorse are perhaps halfway between true links and downland golf.

Royal Jersey, Gorey

The Gorey links of the Royal Jersey club is the flatter and rather less exposed of the two and tightly compressed into a small area, so that there has been some interlacing of holes. A five-year plan has been started to reduce the risks and so improve safety on the links. A new green at the short eighth is the first step in this plan and a new green at the fifteenth has the same objective.

The course has a natural setting, with the greens where you find them. The first nine starts out right along the shore and the inward nine is more inland, with rather more bush in the rough to contend with. A hole that stands out in my memory – I suppose because I hit a fine shot at it – is the 395-yard twelfth, where a good spoon or four-wood may be needed to get your second right home over the bumps and guardian bunkers in front of the green.

This spot is historic turf indeed, for in this corner stood the cottage where Vardon was born, though it is there no longer. Other fine holes are the two-shot sixth and seventh, the long par-three sixteenth and the seventeenth up on its plateau green hard by Fort Henry. The last hole, a drive and pitch to an attractive little plateau green, was originally the first.

There are innumerable stories about Harry Vardon and the prodigies of golf that he performed in his prime – that he was never off the fairway in two years or that in an afternoon round he drove frequently into the divot marks he had made in the morning. Suffice it to say he had the unparalleled record of winning our Open Championship six times, interspersed with two attacks of tuberculosis, the US Open once and tying for the US Open in 1913, to lose in the famous play-off with Francis Ouimet and Ted Ray, and finishing second in it in 1920 at the age of fifty, beaten only by a sudden and furious gale in the last nine holes. Vardon played in the first international golf match between the professionals of Britain and the United States at Gleneagles in 1921 at the age of fifty-one and won both his matches.

Two stories of Vardon and Bobby Jones, the greatest British and the greatest player of all time, are favourites of mine. The first occurred at Inverness, Ohio, at the time of the US Open Championship of 1920. Young Jones, then eighteen years old, was impulsive and inclined to be talkative while playing; Vardon was quite the opposite. After a bad pitch shot which scuttled along the ground and over the green Bob turned to Vardon and said, 'Did you ever see a worse shot than that, Harry?' 'No', said Vardon and finished the round in silence.

The other, let Bob tell in his own words:

Looking back on the Grand Slam year [1930] I find that there is one little episode that was of absolutely no importance, yet it is one that I still have a great deal of pleasure in remembering.

During the Open Championship at Hoylake, Ted Ray, who won our Open in 1920, asked me if I would be willing to play a charity match at his golf club, Oxhey, sometime between the conclusion of the championship and my departure for home. There was something in Ted's manner of extending the invitation which led me to believe that he had not intended that he himself should take part in the match. To me, however, the proposition immediately suggested the possibility of having a most enjoyable game.

So I said, 'Sure, Ted, I'll be delighted to play, provided you'll play and that you'll get any two of Vardon, Braid or Taylor to complete the match.' These three, of course, comprised the Immortal Triumvirate, for which I had long had so much admiration and respect. Ray himself, with his boisterous good humour and slashing play, could not fail to make an attractive addition to any exhibition.

For my part, the occasion could not have had a happier result. Ted got Vardon and Braid to join us. I played one of those easy rounds which are possible only when every sort of thing is working smoothly and right.

My score for the round, with a bogey five at the last hole, was 68, which I understood at the time was the lowest eighteen-hole total ever returned for the golf course. It was not a record, though, because the British quite properly only recognise as records scores made in formal stroke-play competition.

Above all else, I like to recall an incident on the seventeenth tee. With my newly-acquired skill with the mashie-niblick, I had played a tee shot to within a yard of the hole. As Vardon stepped forward to play, I heard him say in his very quiet, soft voice, 'Ah, Master Bobby's 'ot today'. Since we had first played together in 1920, he had always addressed me as 'Master Bobby'. I liked it very much, and I liked also the combination of American slang and Channel Island accent. Old Harry was a very great player and fine gentleman. Every round I played with him was an event in my life.

I would also like to record Walter Hagen's first impressions of Vardon when he went to play in his first championship at the Country Club at Brookline, Massachusetts, in 1913, that famous championship which Francis Ouimet, who died only the day before I first wrote this, won against all the odds.

In the locker-room, a small fellow was pulling on a bright sweater. I recognised him immediately, for he was the defending champion and I'd read plenty about him.

'You're Johnny McDermott, aren't you?' I asked. 'Well, I'm glad to know you. I'm W. C. Hagen from Rochester and I've come over to help you boys take care of Vardon and Ray.'

That brought some laughter, of course, and a lot of kidding from the pros who were listening, but I didn't mind. I was meeting and seeing the greats of the game. I met Vardon and Ray, who'd both won the British Open Championship, and Vardon was touted as the best player in the world. As I expected to become the best, I decided to keep my eye on him. In fact, I stood around and gawked at him like any other greenhorn from the pastures.

Harry Vardon was a tall man with huge hands. My own was practically lost in his handshake. He was reserved, quiet, with almost nothing to say. But I learned plenty from watching him swing a golf club. He had a much more compact and precise swing than I'd ever seen. He had it in a groove and I tried it out in practice and it worked for me, too. I did not dare shift into the Vardon swing right then, but I did use it later in the tournament, when I had gone four over par for the first three holes in the final round.

O. B. Keeler, the chronicler of the Bobby Jones story, gives a wonderfully sympathetic, indeed affectionate, account of Vardon's sad ending to a great try for the US Open in 1920 when Ray beat him and three others by a single stroke.

My greatest regret in golf, I think, is that I never saw Vardon play, though I did see him in the flesh. When at last in 1936 I woke up and tried to arrange a game with him it was too late

and shortly afterwards he died, and, in the plain words of the *Golfer's Handbook*, 'He was buried in Totteridge Parish Churchyard in the presence of an assembly of his fellow golfers.'

Royal Jersey Golf Club, Gorey: Medal Card

	YARDS	PAR		YARDS	PAR
1	477	5	10	340	4
2	145	3	11	367	4
3	537	5	12	395	4
4	186	3	13	414	4
5	374	4	14	332	4
6	387	4	15	180	3
7	406	4	16	222	3
8	146	3	17	368	4
9	509	5	18	312	4
	3167	36		2930	34
				3167	36
				6097	70

La Moye, Jersey

La Moye Golf course is magnificently situated on high ground forming part of the south-west promontory of the island, overlooking St Ouen's Bay and Corbière lighthouse.

The scene from the clubhouse is fine – and indeed from most parts of the course – embracing the wide sweep of St Ouen's Bay with the sister isles, Guernsey, Sark, Herm and Jethou, beyond to the north.

The club was founded in 1902, largely through the influence of Mr George Boomer, a headmaster of La Moye School, who laid out a tentative course which was on the short side. Among enthusiastic early members were Mr Boomer's sons, Percy and Aubrey, both of whom subsequently became distinguished professionals.

The original course was reconstructed and

La Moye Golf Club: Medal Card

	YARDS	PAR		YARDS	PAR
1	364	4	10	159	3
2	497	5	11	505	5
3	166	3	12	188	3
4	395	4	13	424	4
5	190	3	14	449	4
6	342	4	15	478	5
7	479	5	16	372	4
8	428	4	17	412	4
9	390	4	18	435	4
	3251	36		3422	36

Total 6673 yards: par 72

considerably lengthened from plans prepared by James Braid, and has just been lengthened and strengthened once again to a full tournament length of 6700 yards. The reconstruction of the course has eliminated the old fourteenth and fifteenth holes across a ravine which were a weak feature. I have not played the new layout, but I don't doubt that it remains a delightful seaside course on its plateau 250 ft above the coast, with its greens in natural settings and at times, no doubt, fiercely windswept.

The par-three fifth, according to the club brochure, is 'without doubt the most difficult in the Channel Islands', the back of the green dropping sharply away. The seventeenth, they say, is the hardest hole on the course.

The first clubhouse was burnt down, and its successor, completed in 1932, was demolished by the Germans during their occupation of the island; a new clubhouse was completed in 1960.

A big tournament is played here every year and some big names have scored well here, including our two British champions, Jacklin and Lyle.

Royal Guernsey, L'Ancresse

There is one course in Guernsey, the links of the Royal Guernsey Golf Club on L'Ancresse Bay in the extreme north of the island, which is a testing course of 6200 yards with four short holes. It was all but destroyed during the German occupation and was rebuilt after the war to the designs of Mackenzie Ross. Standing out in memory are the short, tightly-bunkered third hole and the long two-shot second and fourth of over 400 yards each. The eighteenth, too, is a tester, a 153-yard belt home over a humpy entrance. A fine family of golfers, the Jollys, came from Guernsey.

Royal Guernsey Golf Club, L'Ancresse: Medal Card

	YARDS	PAR		YARDS	PAR
1	336	4	10	381	4
2	401	4	11	426	4
3	189	3	12	189	3
4	436	4	13	322	4
5	392	4	14	526	5
6	476	5	15	406	4
7	173	3	16	297	4
8	339	4	17	304	4
9	460	4	18	151	3
	3204	35		3002	35

Total 6206 yards: par 70

Isle of Man – Castletown

Golf here is as spectacular in its surroundings as anywhere in Britain, for this seaside course has the ocean on three sides of its layout, and the views are splendid.

The original horse race for the Derby was run here, the then Earl of Derby being resident in the island, with the site of the tenth hole the racecourse. Here long before that, battles were fought with the Viking invaders. Now the golfing battles are waged on a fine, challenging course, which features dunes, rock formations, gorse and the beach, hazards enough without winds which can change direction before the round is finished.

Castletown Golf Club: Medal and Championship Cards

NAME	M	C	PAR	NAME	M	C	PAR
1 First	251	251	4	10 Race Gourse	550	568	5
2 Watch Tower	390	390	4	11 Plateau	173	173	3
3 Long	516	558	5	12 Hogs Back	366	370	4
4 Butts	367	367	4	13 Dunes	345	345	4
5 Field	486	494	5	14 Bay	468	468	4
6 Short	135	135	3	15 Langness	375	375	4
7 Dog Leg	350	383	4	16 Cliffs	193	193	3
8 Road	410	428	4	17 Gully	414	432	4
9 Barn	368	378	4	18 Home	410	423	4
	3273	3384	37		3294	3347	35

Total 6567 and 6731 yards: par 72

When I first played the course several years ago, I did not take to it much, it seemed too rough and ready. Now, however, the whole course has been tidied up and brought to first-class standards, fit for tournament golf.

After not too tough a start, the third hole, 558 yards from the back tee, is a real test, and it is followed by a shorter par five two holes later, and then a short hole of 135 yards, played over a dip to a saucer green.

Castletown has its own 'Road' hole, the eighth of 410 yards from the medal tee, with a high tee, the beach not too far away, separated from the fairway by the road, so an accurate drive is all-important. The second shot is played over a cross bunker to a green on rising ground. A splendid hole, with many happy to settle for a five on the card.

The three finishing holes provide a challenge, especially the seventeenth, which follows a short hole of 193 yards. It is quite daunting to stand on the tee perched on the brink of a cliff, with a gorge in front and the sea on the right. The final two holes are both over 400 yards, with the eighteenth returning to the Links Hotel. To complete the round in par figures over this stretch is very satisfying.

Castletown owes its high reputation to Mackenzie Ross, whose post-war restoration of the terrain compares in achievement with his work at Turnberry. It is not the oldest of the island's seven courses – Ramsey, founded in 1890, is two years older.

Chapter 9

WEST OF ENGLAND AND WALES

Good things often come in threes, and this goes for golf courses, too – Woking, West Hill and Worplesdon; Pebble Beach, Cypress Point and Spyglass Hill; Prince's, St George's and Deal. In each trio, the courses lie close together, sometimes in sight of each other, sometimes even sharing an out-of-bounds fence.

Bournemouth has one of these trios in Parkstone, Ferndown and Broadstone, and a splendid group they are, fine examples of the pines and heather style of golf course. Which of these is the best and why, it is hard to say, and I don't think in layout, style or difficulty there is much to choose, all three have much in common and also wide differences. Parkstone and Ferndown are in residential areas, but well secluded in trees, while at Broadstone, parts of it are high on the open heath. None of them is backbreakingly difficult, but full of pleasant shots and lovely views over the Channel or the Purbeck Hills; what more can you want for a holiday?

Parkstone

I think I will come out for Parkstone as my favourite, for this was the first of the three that I played, back in the 1920s. The course was different then, with, I think, no fewer than six par threes – there are five now – and some very violent up and down climbing, and joyful shots down steep places. This was Willie Park's layout, and has now been superseded by the present course, which is the work of James Braid and Reggie Whitcombe, when he was the club professional.

The modifications were made in 1937, the year before Whitcombe won the Open Championship at Sandwich, which finished in a great gale which blew all but seven of the scores of the last round into the eighties.

Parkstone today is still one of those 'fives and threes' courses, like the Red course at Berkshire, for while there are five short holes, there are also five long ones, the two in the second half each well over 500 yards, so the scoring, if things go well, can be lively. Most critics agree that the par-five eleventh, with an uphill shot to the green, is the toughest, with a fall away to perdition on the right of the green itself.

Among the par fours, which on the whole are of medium length, some adventures can be had at 334-yard eighth, where a dog leg for the ordinary man can be hammered straight by the giant if he risks a drive over the trees, ditches and bogland which protect the left side of the fairway. With three short holes in the last five, although eighteen is a bit of a tiger, you have a chance to finish well, that is if you have survived the long valley hole up to the heather-girt green at seventeen.

Parkstone Golf Club: Medal Card					
	YARDS	PAR		YARDS	PAR
1	354	4	10	420	4
2	160	3	11	527	5
3	490	5	12	328	4
4	275	4	13	361	4
5	373	4	14	158	3
6	505	5	15	422	4
7	170	3	16	148	3
8	334	4	17	530	5
9	505	5	18	190	3
	3166	37		3084	35

Total 6250 yards: par 72

Broadstone

Coming next to Broadstone on the outskirts of Poole, you are again in heather country and a most attractive course is this one with not only the expected heather and gorse but pleasant trees, chestnuts, oaks, silver birch, pines and rhododendrons. The upper holes from the seventh to the fourteenth on the open heath give magnificent views of the Channel, Poole Harbour and the Purbeck Hills to the south and distant hills of Wiltshire near Shaftesbury to the north.

Streams of clear water cross each of the first four holes and at the ninth there is a fresh spring known as the 'Oakley Arms', named after a member who would on arrival there usually produce whisky for his companions. Originally the gone-but-not-forgotten Somerset & Dorset Joint Railway divided the course, a most attractive line with its own characteristic blue engines and coaches. In summer, till British Rail chose to close it, it seemed that innumerable trains passed on this line between the Midlands and the holiday coast, so the railway enthusiast had an added pleasure in playing here. I can't say that it improved the course, though.

The course was laid out by Willie Park in 1896; he was also the architect of the Old course at Sunningdale and two finer designs would be hard to find. Later H. S. Colt modernised the layout.

For my part, the seven holes up on the heath-land are the most enjoyable, especially to my taste the long, one-shot eleventh, backed into the hillside, and the beautiful two-shot thirteenth. Here is a 'Redan' hole, with none of the shortcomings of the 'Redan' itself, a fearful drop all along the left and there, perched up on the hill ahead, a green diagonally across the line with traps under the left flank; all along the right side are temptations of inglorious safety – and a certain five. I think the three I got here, beating home a full five-iron, all carry, to the holeside, is one I will remember when much else fails. Fourteen and sixteen are attractive finishes of this zone, both heavily and handsomely bunkered, and so is the short fifteenth, with a crater to cross and bunkers ahead and on each flank.

Then we cross over again into calmer waters,

Broadstone Golf Club: Card

	YARDS SUMMER	YARDS WINTER	PAR			YARDS SUMMER	YARDS WINTER	PAR
1	492	492	5		10	363	363	4
2	403	370	4		11	169	169	3
3	376	357	4		12	354	348	4
4	380	347	4		13	415	397	4
5	286	285	4		14	355	347	4
6	152	160	3		15	194	175	3
7	408	407	4		16	424	393	4
8	203	191	3		17	408	395	4
9	379	379	4		18	368	339	4
Total	3079	2988	35		Total	3050	2926	34
						3079	2988	35
						6129	5914	69

and play the seventeenth and eighteenth downhill towards home, matching the first and second going out. These rather pedestrian holes have been improved by tree planting and reshaping.

Ferndown

So we come to Ferndown, as the last, but by no means least, of the fine Bournemouth trio. Here we now have the famous original layout of seventy years ago, but also the New course of 5600 yards and par 70 to relieve the pressure and give you another attractive addition to your list.

I have only played the Old course, and that a few years ago now, but I remember well the attractive fairways, the purple heather, then in full bloom, and the sharp white sand of the hazards. Especially comes to mind the one-shot fifth, where after a shaky start, a round began to take shape, and two attractive short par fours, a type of hole which I like so much when it is good; these are the eighth of 304 yards, well bunkered, and the 305-yard sixteenth named Hilton's, after the designer Harold Hilton, where your blind tee shot over trouble leaves you with a short and difficult run in to a three-tier green.

Ferndown is famous as the home of the Alliss family, renowned as tournament golfers.

As well as these three famous courses there are two municipal courses of quite unusual quality, the rather short but attractive Meyrick Park in the heart of the town, and Queen's Park, rather farther out, which is good enough for professional competitions, where it by no means comes off second best. So, for a golf holiday, Bournemouth is very much in the picture.

The north coast of Cornwall, Devon and Somerset on the Bristol Channel has some fine links to offer, whereas the southern coasts have none; links, mind, not golf *courses*.

Ferndown Golf Club, Old Course: Medal Card					
	YARDS	PAR		YARDS	PAR
1	396	4	10	485	5
2	175	3	11	436	4
3	398	4	12	186	3
4	395	4	13	488	5
5	206	3	14	152	3
6	409	4	15	398	4
7	480	5	16	305	4
8	304	4	17	397	4
9	427	4	18	403	4
Out	3190	35	In	3252	36

Total 6442 yards: par 71

Ferndown Golf Club, New Course: Medal Card					
	YARDS	PAR		YARDS	PAR
1	355	4	10	360	4
2	162	3	11	179	3
3	327	4	12	300	4
4	492	5	13	480	5
5	173	3	14	112	3
6	344	4	15	406	4
7	316	4	16	342	4
8	485	5	17	477	5
9	143	3	18	151	3
Out	2797	35	In	2807	35

Total 5604 yards: par 70

St Mellion

This is an entirely new golf and country club development in the West of England, just over the border of Cornwall at Saltash ten miles from Plymouth. Nearby is the splendid monument to the great builder of the Great Western Railway, the Saltash Railway bridge which bears in great letters for all to see the words 'I. K. Brunel Engineer'.

The original course, which was opened here in 1976, has now been put entirely in the shade by the colossal, artificial American-style course designed by no less than Jack Nicklaus. Using the difficult terrain of a 200-acre piece of wooded parkland bought from the Duchy of Cornwall, Nicklaus has fashioned a 7000-yard layout, shaping and shifting great areas of land and water.

I must confess that I was dismayed rather than excited by the immensity of the facts and figures, a £250,000 design and supervision fee for the Nicklaus team and reputed costs of £100,000 per hole for the course itself. I am afraid that these huge numbers, and the news of artificial greens moulded from sand and peat, with the tanks of water guarding them,

streams which have been opened up and relocated and whole hillsides carved away with a total of 1,500,000 cubic metres of soil moved in the creation of the course, bewilders rather than encourages me. All this civil engineering is so far from the simple, almost primitive construction of say Liphook or Rye that it would almost seem to belong to a different game.

It is an interesting fact that these enormous courses laid out especially for tournament play and catering for masses of spectators with unobtrusive but positioned mounds do not daunt the great professionals who hit the ball so far that these giants are soon cut down to size and scores of 63 and 64 are achieved. I often feel that I would like to see what scores would be done on the old short but narrow links by the great players, scores not very much less I think.

The critics give high praise at St Mellion to the third hole of 356 yards from the ordinary tee where you drive from a high point down to a fairway carved out of the side of a hill which slopes abruptly up to the left and almost precipitously down to the right.

The fifth is also highly regarded; it needs a

water carry from the tee and water in the form of a ditch all the way to the green and around one side of it. Water is with us again at the tenth and at the short eleventh, where the green is protected by a pond under its left flank; water comes in also at the twelfth, where a pond has to be carried from the tee and a ditch in front of the green like it is claimed, that at the thirteenth hole at Augusta National. Water makes its last appearance at the eighteenth, where a pond originally on the right hand side of the green has been moved to the opposite side of the fairway. No expense was spared.

The full length of the big course is at present 7064 yards with tees for the ordinary player cutting the length to 6600 odd. The course has not been laid out specifically for buggy transport, though it is said that some of the distances between tee and green are considerable. The total development here with two courses, a hotel with all the facilities needed of bars, restaurants and other sporting facilities, indoors and out, together with 'Timeshare' cottages should as 'a piece of America in the heart of Cornwall' doubtless appeal to many.

	C	M	PAR		C	M	PAR
1	420	400	4	10	448	410	4
2	543	518	5	11	203	181	3
3	373	356	4	12	546	525	5
4	185	175	3	13	404	361	4
5	355	315	4	14	175	158	3
6	430	420	4	15	442	411	4
7	503	480	5	16	555	520	5
8	145	135	3	17	456	426	4
9	409	375	4	18	472	460	4
	3363	3174	36		3701	3452	36

St Mellion, Jack Nicklaus Course Championship and Medal Cards

Total 7064 and 6626 yards: par 72

Lelant

At at the far west of Cornwall, near St Ives and Penzance, there is the enjoyable links of the West Cornwall Golf Club at Lelant, near Hayle. Jim Barnes, who won both the British and American Open Championships in his day, was a 'Cousin Jack' from here. I met Jim Barnes at Baltusrol in New Jersey in the 1950s when he was sixty-seven years old, as spare and straight as a ramrod with a mop of silver hair. He was hitting some prodigious iron shots to instruct a young assistant pro from Johnny Farrell's shop.

Lelant is a good spot for a holiday, as you can stay at St Ives, a charming little town, where one of the hotels has an amusing little par-three course in the park.

The course at Lelant has real seaside turf and greens and many attractive and entertaining shots, even if there is not too much wooden-club play through the green. It is indeed rather

West Cornwall Golf Club, Lelant: Medal Card

	YARDS	PAR		YARDS	PAR
1	229	3	10	299	4
2	382	4	11	362	4
3	342	4	12	494	5
4	352	4	13	264	4
5	179	3	14	446	4
6	324	4	15	135	3
7	191	3	16	521	5
8	325	4	17	194	3
9	406	4	18	394	4
Out	2730	33	In	3109	36
			Out	2730	33

Total 5839 yards: par 69

short, being under 6000 yards, but there are five par threes which help to account for that. And once again remember short is often difficult.

You have a par three at the 229-yard first hole, where a four early in the day is likelier than not, and, as Frank Pennink says, 'hinting that the score of 70 net is a far from simple achievement'. You then voyage out towards the flanking dunes of the Hayle estuary, first up and then down, and then progress past St Uny's churchyard to investigate the bottom of the course – 'down in the reeds by the river' –

well, not that quite, but a lower level where there are two par threes and a short tricky par four; 'Calamity Corner' is good fun.

Returning to the upper level, we are in for much longer golf and the second nine has two par fives of the fullest potency, and though you have a long downhill stretch in the twelfth, the sixteenth is all uphill to the top of the links, on the landward side. Fine views out to sea and St Ives Bay are a delightful feature of the upper holes.

St Enodoc

Next stop is St Enodoc, near the village of Rock in north Cornwall, over the River Camel by ferry from Padstow, though you can go round by road.

St Enodoc is pure linksland, with some very considerable sandhills, and has all the irregularities of fairway and stance you can use. It is not long, just over 6200 yards, but as at Lelant, don't imagine that you are going to make hay here; there are five par threes and plenty of stout two-shotters in the 400-plus category. You open with three pretty stiff tests, the first a par five without sand trap, but there are awkward hollows confronting the drive and in front of the green and the fairway narrows at mid point by the encroaching of the sandhills; at the second you have a stiff second shot to a plateau green bearing right, and the third hole, though running downhill, and at 436 yards the shortest of the three, has a lowering hillside all down your left flank and an awkward angle of shot into the green.

At the fourth, 292 yards uphill, you can, of course, allow yourself four shots, and well you may, for if you want to avoid a horrible little pitch you must hold your ball well up to the right and go over the angle of an out-of-bounds fence and the green is up against this fence, too. Sir Ernest Holderness thought this hole good enough to get a place in his *Best 18 Holes in Golf*.

After a short hole we get the 378-yard 'Himalayas', a real old-fashioned linksland hole with a mountainous hill and bunker as a compulsory carry on the second shot; as Frank Pennink says, the 'Himalayas' dwarf the 'Alps' at Prestwick or the 'Maiden' hill at Royal St George's. Bernard Darwin also thought it was the highest sandhill he had ever seen on a golf course. It's no use trying to sneak by round the left flank, as three are pot bunkers and rough to defeat that very object. So over we go, or hang our heads in shame and get out our sand irons. I'm glad to say I 'made it', but taking no chances I laid on a four-wood.

This same hill and vast tract of sand confront you on the seventh tee as well, but after that shot you get out into more open territory, though not necessarily easier golf. The half closes with a short hole entirely beset by bunkers and a mild and rather innocuous par-four ninth.

At the tenth we appear to turn inland under the flank of Brea or Bray Hill, and the green is close to a brook which has been nagging at us all along the left of the fairway. We then play three rather more prosaic holes, a short one and two par fours round the little old ruined church of St Enodoc, which was at one time swallowed by sand blown in from the beach nearby.

Continuing home with the fourteenth, the

fairway sloping away from the hills on the left and the green in a hollow, we are ready for the run-in. First a par three with a mid-iron shot across a valley with ditch, fence and road in it, to a green on a bank beyond; then a good par five, the fairway cut across at about 300 yards by a belt of rough. Seventeen is another par three, a long one, across a vale of tears to a plateau green set among the sandhills, and the last a stiff two-shot – or to me two and a bit – to another plateau under the windows of the new clubhouse.

I think you will agree with Peter Ryde that the course plays longer than its length, even if you don't agree with his words that 'to a crooked driver it can feel like two rounds at Carnoustie'.

Since my last visit, an eighteen-hole course of 4165 yards has been added, which, while no doubt less exacting than the main links, is assuredly good fun, with ten stout par threes and eight short par fours to a total score of 62,

St Enodoc Golf Club: Medal Card					
	YARDS	PAR		YARDS	PAR
1	518	5	10	457	4
2	438	4	11	178	3
3	436	4	12	386	4
4	292	4	13	360	4
5	160	3	14	355	4
6	378	4	15	168	3
7	394	4	16	487	5
8	155	3	17	206	3
9	393	4	18	446	4
Out	3164	35	In	3043	34

Total 6207 yards: par 69

which I would guess takes a lot of doing; I wish I could try it.

Royal North Devon, Westward Ho!

Moving now into Devonshire, but still on the north shore, we come to historic turf indeed, the first English golf links and the first outside Scotland, at Westward Ho! named after Charles Kingsley's famous novel, which was written here. Golf was started here in a primitive way in 1853 by the family of the vicar of Northam, the Rev. I. H. Gosset. In 1860 old Tom Morris was brought down from Prestwick, where he was then stationed, to advise, and in 1864 the club was formed, with the vicar the first captain, as the North Devon and West of England Golf Club. It remains the oldest club in England playing on its original land.

Tom Morris came down again in 1864, and made two layouts, one of 17 and the other of 22 holes. The links, which has been altered several times since, lies on some low land called the Burrows, under the wing of the great Pebble Ridge, which protects it from the sea, and Barnstaple Bay. Sandhills march with the Peb-

ble Ridge and come into play in the first half. General Moncrieff, of St Andrews, on coming here to stay with the vicar in about 1860, said that 'Providence evidently intended this for a golf links'.

Westward Ho!, like Brancaster or Ballybunion, remains a supreme example of natural seaside golf, and it hasn't been altered since Herbert Fowler's reconstruction in 1908; in spite of that, its difficulties are almost as much with us as in the days of the founders like Captain Molesworth, 'Old Mole', and his three sons. The links is on common land and the commoners can and do graze horses, sheep and cattle on the Burrows, sometimes as many as 1000 sheep and 100 horses and ponies. These have at times rather soiled the course, but at present it is in good condition. The unique characteristic of Westward Ho! is the rushes which form the rough at many of the inland holes; up to six feet in height and 'as thick as a hedge', they end in iron-tipped spikes which can impale you with ridiculous ease, or spear a ball from cover to cover. You have to play over them or play along them and you pray that you won't get in them. There used to be no out of bounds, but inroads of blown sand in the late sixties has meant fencing part of the course to keep the animals from eating the protective grass which is now growing, so along from the fourth to the seventh there is out of bounds for the time being.

The Amateur Championship has been here three times, first in 1912, when John Ball won for the eighth and last time, beating Abe Mitchell, at the thirty-eighth hole; then again in 1925, when Robert Harris won, and for the last time in 1931, when a surprise winner – and none more surprised than he – was Eric Martin Smith, just down from Cambridge. But for its remoteness, there is no doubt that more use would have been made of this great course.

Two very great golfers were nurtured on this links: Horace Hutchinson, the graceful and gifted amateur, who twice won the Amateur Championship, and John Henry Taylor, five times Open Champion, who died in his ninety-third year. And what a splendid character he was, forthright, vehement and brave. I saw something of him in the late 'twenties, for I used to play golf with his son at Oxford. J.H. was fond of the Johnsonian 'sir' and used to say things thrice for emphasis. In his shop in Mid-Surrey was a picture of W. G. Grace, for once not attired for cricket; so I asked J.H. what sort of a game the Doctor played, and he said 'Like a boy, sir; like a boy, sir; like a boy.'

Just after he had captained the winning British Ryder Cup side at Southport and Ainsdale in 1933, I was in J.H.'s shop. He said, 'I had a terrible lot of trouble with that fellow Abraham Mitchell, Abraham Mitchell, Abe Mitchell, they call him. He came to me on the night after the foursomes and said, "It's no good, John, I can't play tomorrow; it's my back." So I said, "You'll play tomorrow, Abraham, back or no back, you can have Hagen or you can have Sarazen or you can have Dutra, but you'll play"; so he said, "All right, John, I guess I'll take the big bugger", and he murdered him, sir; he murdered him, sir; he murdered him.'

Apart from his distinction as a great golfer in the immortal Triumvirate, J.H. did much to raise the status of the professional, which in his early days was little above that of caddie and often miserably paid. When he retired, the profession was on the threshold of the million-dollar business it has now become. He could also be a speaker of rare charm and I will always remember his speech after the University Match dinner at Sandwich in 1928, when he thanked all present with a sincerity and emotion, which none could doubt, for being kind to his son, but in a way which showed that he had learned 'to distinguish between sentiment and sentimentality', so that no one was embarrassed, neither his son nor his son's friends. J.H. always said that his son's election to the presidency of the Junior Common Room at his college pleased him more than any championship he ever won.

In another way, surely 'Old Mole', another Westward Ho! character, must have been a great figure; always ready for a bet and a sharp match with one of his sons as partner. He lived to a ripe old age, until he was almost ninety in fact. On 5 September 1877, he set out to test the wager he'd made at Whitsun to walk the three miles to the links, play six rounds under 660 strokes carrying his own clubs, and walk home before dark. He started at 6.10 am and had a bad round of 120, followed by 105 and 122. The next three rounds were 108, 102 and 105, to a total of 662 for six rounds. Not put out by this, 'Old Mole' played a seventh round of 114 to make his total inside 660 by discarding the first round. On top of this, he was home by twenty minutes to seven. There was great argument over this result – some said the first six rounds constituted the bet, others that the seventh round was admissible. Who won the bet? History doesn't record, but I'd find for the captain.

Westward Ho! as a golf course has one misfortune: the clubhouse is on a mild slope above the links near the village of Northam, so that one has to open and finish the round with two holes across the flattest and dullest part of the Burrows. However, they must be played and they are long, and if dreary, hard enough, so if we start 5, 4, and end with the same we should be very well pleased.

Once at the third tee, we turn right and the first folds in the fairways appear. Again the hole is over 400 yards, with a hollow in mid fairway and well-bunkered green. Then at the fourth we are right in it; it is like going out of harbour in a ship when she puts her nose down into the first big wave and you hear somebody say, 'Now she's feeling it'. Across the horizon, stretching unbroken, it seems, as far as the eye can see, was, and I trust will be again, the huge 'Cape' bunker, looking a mile off; in fact, it is about 160–170 yards from the tee – 150 to the 'Duffers' Knob' – and fully 100 yards wide, but it shuts off the view and there is nothing but sandy waste and grassland between you and it, and its face is boarded with little scaling ladders at intervals to help you out. Once over, the hole is not too tough for the green is below fairway level and not very far off. Four or eight is often the alternative here. The reduction of the 'Cape' bunker to its present truncated size is the result of blown sand which indeed completely filled it up. It is, however, to be restored, I was assured, when the grass has grown in the dunes nearby to hold the sands in check.

Next a short hole, only 137 yards long but often into a hard wind off the sea, so you may on occasion want a much stiffer shot than you'd imagine; it is a pretty hole with a raised green and many bunkers, including a big one under the right flank.

Next come two superb two-shot holes, the first down from a high tee from which you can see the sea and Lundy Island for almost the only time; they are both two-shot par fours, running over broken seaside ground and take you nearly out to the estuary of the River Torridge. You can choose which you prefer, the sixth with its open plateau green, or the seventh, a mild dog leg with the green beyond a dip, containing some rushes and a bunker, partly shielded on the left by a hill.

Then you have another par three, the 197-yard eighth, the green slightly below you and plenty of trouble from a vale of rushes in front. You are now at the far end of the links and you start to beat in, against the wind probably, and here on the flatter ground the rushes start to intimidate you. The ninth with its green on a small natural plateau with a bunker in front is not too hard for it is 481 yards and you are allowed five, but the tenth is another cup of tea. The hole is a sharp dog leg to the left of 372 yards, and your drive is over a sea of rushes on your left and in front so that you bite off as much as possible, for it helps tremendously your shot into the small green; this may easily be another eight or four hole even though you are allowed a one-stroke drop for a lost ball. More rushes, too, at the 371-yard eleventh, to the left and again in front of the tee, and trouble to the right, so, to use J. H. Taylor's immortal phrase, 'What's the matter with the middle of the course?'

We emerge, hopefully unpunctured, after driving over rushes at the twelfth, for a longer par four with a flat green with the slope of a mound guarding it. Then at the thirteenth we can try for another four, for it is 440 yards long against the prevailing wind with a 'crown' green on a small plateau, exactly like pitching on to the proverbial bald man's head. Moreover there are three bunkers on the left and five on the right of the green. The short fourteenth is heavily bunkered and has a difficult green with a ridge in it. Then turning finally for home comes the attractive dog-leg fifteenth, in reach of two shots with a drive over rushes and bunkers on either side of the entrance. Sixteen is another short hole of only 145 yards; with bunkers left, right and behind the shot must be most accurate. As Patric Dickinson says, 'Deceptively easy and with a duck's back of a green off which your ball rolls like a waterbead.' Bernard Darwin, in the club's handbook, gave it high praise: 'The sixteenth has a more subtle devilry and is the more alarming as it comes so near the end of the round', and he goes on to quote from Mr Tom Simpson:

One of the most entertaining of all one-shot holes. The crowned plateau green, of a whaleback formation, exaggerates the effect of any unintentional spin on the ball which pitches on it. The tee is set at an angle to the plateau, so that the corner facing the tee turns a weak shot either way into a bunker. Visibility is poor; but the hole can never be left out of any eclectic list.

Darwin goes on,

When the wind is blowing, this is a hole where it almost seems necessary to pitch the ball on a particular square yard of green if it is not to kick inexorably one way or the other. It is one of those holes – and this is invariably high testimony to their terrors – at which it seems impossible to plant your feet in the right place on the teeing ground; try as you will, you cannot aim straight.

Visiting the course again recently I didn't think this hole was all that alarming; I would judge the fourteenth to be almost as difficult.

All that is left now is the distressing beat in along the immensely long, flat seventeenth, with the third shot having to cross a road and two ditches. Then up to the fence in front of the club runs the tough, flat 416-yard eighteenth, which presents you with a muddy ditch to cross quite close up to the green itself. So ends the round, and, as Frank Pennink writes, 'Westward Ho! is a historic club in historic surround-

Royal North Devon Golf Club, Westward Ho!: Medal Card					
	YARDS	PAR		YARDS	PAR
1	485	5	10	372	4
2	424	4	11	371	4
3	418	4	12	425	4
4	354	4	13	440	4
5	137	3	14	205	3
6	413	4	15	431	4
7	400	4	16	145	3
8	197	3	17	548	5
9	481	5	18	416	4
	3309	36		3353	35

Total 6662 yards: par 71

ings; it is worth every trouble, or any length of journey, to play golf there.'

Few people, indeed, have chewed up the course here. In the first 100 years of the club's history, only four scores under 70 were registered in the club's medal competitions. In another competition R. C. Champion has had a 65, a phenomenal score, but otherwise the honours boards until the last decade show almost as many scores in the 80s as in the 70s. After all there are 102 bunkers on the course and there used to be more, not to mention the rushes.

Let Bernard Darwin have the last word: 'If you have done anything near eighty, you may be thoroughly pleased with yourself, unless you are a very eminent person indeed.'

Saunton

The view from the windows of the Saunton Sands Hotel is superb. Below you is a huge strand fully a mile and a half long with successive rows of white-capped waves running on to the shore. Beyond lie the estuaries of the Taw and the Torridge with Northam Burrows, the Pebble Ridge and the links and village of West-

ward Ho! Half right is Barnstaple Bay with cliffs along its shore, ending with Hartland Point, and further right the open sea and Lundy Island.

To the left is one of the biggest accumulations of linksland I have ever seen, great sandhills, natural eroded pits like giant bunkers, coarse sea grass and little valleys and dells where the finer grasses grow, the whole a tumbling mass to make a golfer's dream. I think I only saw the like of it at Ballybunion in the west of Ireland. 3000 acres there are, so fifteen first-class golf courses could be built here, though only two at Saunton are there yet.

The new West course was opened in 1974–5 to the design finalised by the late Frank Pennink. The earlier links at Saunton, now the East course, is a big full-length course of championship calibre with three fine short holes and many splendid par fours. The original layout was to the design of Herbert Fowler and was lost in World War II when the links was taken over for battle training.

When the Schweppes Professional Championship was held here in 1966 in absolutely ideal windless conditions, there were only thirteen scores under 70 in six rounds, four of them 67s. Next year in the Brabazon, only one amateur beat 70 and that was the late Ronnie Shade; the next Brabazon here in 1976 produced no extraordinary scoring.

Saunton starts in a totally uncompromising manner with four holes which add up to thirty-two yards over a mile. The first of these at 470 yards is as severe a starting hole as you can find even if the drive is somewhat downhill; just at the waist of the fairway, where a good drive gets, the bunkers eat in from left and right. The second, if you drive clear of the sandhills, as you should, gives you a flat fairway and a second shot to a new green hillier and farther than the old. Three and four run out to the south, the third with a narrow tee shot and a mound which obscures the second shot and the fourth with a tight gut constricting the second. The fifth is a little beauty or a little fiend depending on how you fare, for it has a small green perched up on a hillock, with dire trouble under your nose and behind the green with a sheer drop and bunkers to the left and in front. This is a standing rebuttal of the idea of having to have short holes more than 190 yards long, even if Michael Bonallack did say,

and maybe he didn't, that 'if you can't play this hole with a wedge you ought not to be playing golf'.

Six and seven leave no great impressions, as the fairways are flat and unadventurous, but the eighth is the finest fun with a good old-fashioned drive over tall sandhills and a green in a bowl surrounded by hillocks. Against a strong wind the drive can be alarming and the second a wood shot. The ninth is not easy with a dog-leg line to the left and a new bunker in the hills on the left side of the slopes guarding the long narrow green.

The tenth is a pretty, shortish par four with a high plateau green up in the sandhills with two distinct tiers; in the face of the guardian slopes up to the green are two deep aggressive bunkers from which it would be difficult to be sure to get on with the next shot. I regard this as a hole with a lovely second shot even if there is nothing to stop too long a stroke going to perdition down the bank at the back.

Eleven and twelve on the flatter ground are less spectacular, but at the former you can give yourself a blind second shot over an out-of-bounds intrusion if your drive is too much right. The thirteenth, though, is a grand short hole in the best possible style. From a tee in the hills you play across a ravine of rushes and wild plants to a plateau green with flanking bunkers and fall to the right. The feature here is the very wide range of tees to choose from, which vary the aspect of the hole quite considerably.

The fourteenth is a long par four, a very testing difficult hole. About 230 yards out from the tee there are bunkers to steer between, then the long second has to be forced up a narrow spout, as it were, to a slightly-raised green; sandhills spreading in from the left mask the shot home if you have pulled your drive. Next we have a short par five which should not worry us too much unless we can get up in two which I can't – the green has a pronounced step.

The sixteenth is one of the great two-shot holes. You drive through a newly-made gap in the sandhills to a flat fairway, then turning half left hit a pretty big shot, a two-iron or a spoon, to a seemingly slightly sunken long green among the sandhills, protected by a ridge and a swale or valley in front with a bunker in the face of the little ridge. The green, in fact, is on its own little plateau in the dell. This hole grows on you as you progress along it.

The seventeenth is a 200-yard short hole downhill to a pear-shaped green among small sand humps. The last hole to the green in front of the clubhouse windows is not too strictly bunkered, but the fairway narrows at the point of maximum virtue so the four you need here has to be worked for.

The new, West course, was built approximately over the ground used by Herbert Fowler's pre-war New course which was also lost in World War II, but it does in one or two places creep into the high sandhills. The course is shorter and less severe than the East and with five par threes, gives a par of 70.

Saunton is renowned for its wild flowers and a visit at the end of June found the links bright with blue viper's bugloss, like small delphiniums, and pink orchis of several varieties; the hellebore orchis was not yet out, but there was a mild yellow variety that was. The rough contains willow scrub and sycamore and in remoter spots the violent thorny incorrigible buckthorn. Birds, too, and moths, congregate here, but for me it was enough to learn that three quarters of all the wild flowers of England are found on Braunton Burrows. Even so, we didn't see the wild yellow iris which we had seen at Westward Ho!

We can't leave Saunton without reference to the former secretary's dog. This spaniel has put up the almost incredible record of having found 25,000 golf balls over the years. According to John Goodban, not all of these were serviceable; the pro bought them for resale and the proceeds provided comfortable seats round the course for golfers to rest on.

Another feat is worth mentioning, that of the teams who took part in a foursomes competi-

Saunton Golf Club, East Course: Medal Card

	YARDS	PAR		YARDS	PAR
1	470	4	10	337	4
2	476	5	11	362	4
3	402	4	12	418	4
4	444	4	13	136	3
5	112	3	14	461	4
6	370	4	15	485	5
7	428	4	16	430	4
8	380	4	17	202	3
9	382	4	18	408	4
Out	3464	36	In	3239	35
			Out	3464	36
			Total	6703	71

Saunton Golf Club, West Course: Medal Card

	YARDS	PAR		YARDS	PAR
1	348	4	10	516	5
2	360	4	11	208	3
3	449	4	12	484	5
4	207	3	13	373	4
5	408	4	14	459	4
6	381	4	15	307	4
7	426	4	16	189	3
8	372	4	17	499	5
9	140	3	18	196	3
Out	3091	34	In	3231	36
			Out	3091	34
			Total	6322	70

tion to play from the first tee at Saunton to the last hole at Westward Ho! This involves beating through the thickest wastes of Braunton Burrows sandhills, along the shore of Braunton sands, over the River Torridge at the lowest ebb, a carry of 180 yards, over the Pebble Ridge and on to Westward Ho! links, in all a good 2½ miles. I was amazed to hear that the winners did it in 59 strokes. It is twenty two miles round by road.

Burnham and Berrow

So, then, into Somerset to draw up at Burnham and Berrow, near Bridgwater, where another prodigious waste of sandhills is also to be found. In this, an excellent golf course has been laid out for which I have a great regard, and not just because I played one or two good rounds there a few years ago.

We start with a couple of two-shot holes up characteristic valleys between the lowering dunes, the second with a plateau green. Then turning left we play a most attractive 384-yard par four, hitting home over knolls and a bunker to a green in a natural saucer. Now we are right on the coast of the Bristol Channel with South Wales away on the horizon.

After a modest par five near the shore, we have an excellent short hole of 160 yards very deeply bunkered in front. Next comes a new hole, par four, heading out towards the shore with a pond affecting the left flank. Then come two holes in succession, of which the eighth allows us five, rather flatter and duller than what we have had so far. I remember hitting a spoon-shot at the eighth which ran accurately under a Land Rover of the greenkeeping staff by the green without a touch and lay close enough to give an eagle putt. No doubt learning of this, the club has built a new and more difficult green. The half ends with a tremendous bunkered short hole, with a plateau green, fine stuff.

These hills we have to cross at the tenth and then turn half right to hit a five-iron or so up to the green. The short par five at twelve along the churchyard wall and across a road, which had to be shortened on Sundays, has been abandoned because of traffic, and a new par four built playing to a new plateau green on the other side of the church. A new thirteenth follows a par five, using part of the former sixth fairway and dog legging to a new long narrow green.

Then the fifteenth, another valley hole with a narrow green in a dell, is longer than it looks and plays all of 438 yards – a most attractive hole, I thought. Sixteen is a drive and pitch with little room on the green and then comes a par three which needs a full-blooded wood-shot uphill to the green high among the neighbouring sand dunes and fully bunkered in front. I remember needing a driver here against a stiff breeze and had the great joy of 'making it', so that I had a putt for two – which failed – just when I was protecting a good score. The sort of shot of which the pros say 'Get after *that* one'. The eighteenth is a comparatively mild hole if we are content with a five, but it crosses some

Burnham and Berrow Golf Club: Medal Card

	MEDAL TEES	PAR		MEDAL TEES	PAR
1	381	4	10	370	4
2	396(422)	4	11	422	4
3	384	4	12	388	4
4	480(501)	5	13	475	5
5	160	3	14	181(188)	3
6	397(435)	4	15	438(479)	4
7	450	4	16	329	4
8	483	5	17	201	3
9	163	3	18	449	4
Out	3294	36	In	3253	35
			Out	3294	36

Total 6547 yards: par 71

excessively broken ground and you can hit trouble.

The English Close Championship has been held here four times and also the Amateur Stroke Play Championship for the Brabazon Trophy.

A new full length nine-hole course has been added between the early holes and the sea.

Royal Porthcawl

I didn't get to Royal Porthcawl in South Wales until late in 1966, and more's the pity, for it is a mighty fine seaside golf course. However, I *did* get there in the end, and so completed my tally of all the championship courses of the British Isles, a pursuit which had begun at Deal forty-one years before. True, Porthcawl joined the select band rather late in the day in 1951 when the American Dick Chapman won the Amateur there, but it had its reputation made long before then. The Amateur came here again in 1965, which Michael Bonallack won, in 1973 when Dick Siderowf of the USA won, and again in 1980 when in wind and storm Duncan Evans won, the first Welsh win.

I have called it a seaside course advisedly, for it is indeed by the sea and the club's boast that you can see the sea from some part of every hole is true, but it is not all links golf, in the fullest sense, as there is a distinct hill which you climb at the fifth and on the upper levels from the fifth green to the ninth tee, and then again at the twelfth and seventeenth you are on something more like moorland turf with bracken and heather and thick gorse in the rough.

The course is not by any means abominably long, 6600 yards off the championship tees, and 6400 off the regular tees, so that several of the par fours are under 400 yards, that is until you get stuck into the second half, when the par fours lengthen out. Don't be deluded, however. The course is not easy, for on the whole the greens are small and the course is richly bunkered; the greens, moreover, have some heavy curvatures, steps and slopes, so that when the game needs to be tightened up some pretty difficult pin positions can be selected.

The location of the course is excellent, with a fine view over the Bristol Channel towards Minehead and Exmoor twenty miles or so away, and on down the coast to Ilfracombe. Inland are some attractive hills and across the bay the Gower Peninsula, with Swansea on its flank. Industry does not too much intrude, save for the emission at intervals of some pink smoke from below the sheltering hill to the west, which betrays the presence of the Port Talbot steel plant.

The Porthcawl club started its golf on a different site on a piece of common land to the east about ninety-five years ago, but it has been where it now is nearly as long, occupying a rough triangle of land, the best shape for a golf course according to Tom Simpson and especially if, as here, there is liable to be plenty of wind. Then the straight-out-and-home course is at a disadvantage and a layout on a triangle far better.

The first three holes run out to the west along the shore, the third, indeed, so close that you can drive on to the shingle without any trouble at all. Then you turn back and play inland to a short hole, well bunkered, with its green sitting up for you; then at number five with its long uphill pull to the green you are on the plateau. Here, as I have said, you are off the linksland, and indeed this part of the course reminded me a great deal of Ganton, but, after all, isn't Ganton a links inland or something very like it? Up here there is a very short hole, only 116 yards, but it is not easy, for it is heavily bunkered, the green is long and narrow and has some big slopes and borrows. The ninth, with a drive across a big dip, is a splendid hole, with a small much-beset green and with some good slopes on it, an excellent medium-length par

Royal Porthcawl Golf Club: Medal and Championship Card

	CHAMP. TEE	MEDAL TEE	PAR		CHAMP. TEE	MEDAL TEE	PAR
1	326	326	4	10	337	327	4
2	436	416	4	11	187	187	3
3	420	377	4	12	476	476	5
4	197	193	3	13	426	413	4
5	485	476	5	14	152	152	3
6	394	391	4	15	447	421	4
7	116	116	3	16	434	420	4
8	480	476	5	17	508	489	5
9	371	368	4	18	413	385	4
Out	3225	3139	36	In	3380	3270	36
				Out	3225	3139	36
				Total	6605	6409	72

four. My Welsh caddie, whose vast ginger moustache and whiskers extended from ear to ear, declared that it was the finest hole on the course, and I'm not disposed to disagree.

The longer holes in the second half really stretch you, holes like the thirteenth, fifteenth and seventeenth, which I couldn't reach on a soft November day, and there are two fine short holes in this half, the eleventh, which is longer than it looks – where I bolted a putt for a two – and the fourteenth, which is shorter, where I missed a much easier putt. Only the two long holes in the back nine seemed to me to be rather below standard, but the eighteenth is a beautiful finishing hole, with a downhill drive off the plateau straight towards the sea; there is a scrubby hollow across the fairway about 270 yards from the regular tee which no doubt bothers some, but keeping short of that was no trouble to me. The green is long and narrow and literally runs on to the shore, so a shot hit 'thin' can well end up on the shingle.

The greens throughout the whole layout are excellent.

Southerndown

Those in the know always couple Southerndown with its neighbour Porthcawl when South Wales comes into the discussion, and this is right, for it too is a fine big course in fine surroundings. From Ogmore Down, on which the course lies, are splendid views across the Bristol Channel to the shores of Devon and Somerset with the rivers of Ogmore and Ewenny at your feet.

The course is a strange one, in that it has sandy, seaside turf on what should be downland, but the explanation lies, I believe, in the prevailing wind which has carried the sand from the beaches below and made a cover over the native rock and soil. So we have what is almost a seaside texture 300 feet or so up. The course is not one I know, but judging from the scoring in a recent professional tournament it is tough, compelling and interesting.

Frank Pennink, who was such a good judge, gave it high praise, picking out the four par threes for merit, especially the fourteenth. Several well-known architects have been consulted here, notably Herbert Fowler in 1907, Willie Park in 1913 and finally H. S. Colt after World War II.

There are two short par fives on the card and four par threes, but don't let this lead you to suppose that nothing worse than a four is likely to be in your score.

Southerndown Golf Club: Medal Card

	YARDS	PAR		YARDS	PAR
1	373	4	10	181	3
2	448	4	11	427	4
3	412	4	12	411	4
4	401	4	13	478	5
5	172	3	14	160	3
6	484	5	15	377	4
7	231	3	16	412	4
8	428	4	17	428	4
9	367	4	18	437	4
Out	3316	35	In	3299	35

Total 6615 yards: par 70

Aberdovey

As Patric Dickinson writes: 'If one dares to write about Aberdovey at all, one must begin by letting Bernard Darwin through on the way to the first tee. For this links is his . . .' It is indeed, for the first holes, with their flower pots cut into the greens, were laid out in the early 1880s by his uncle and he played on it in boyhood and loved it with a passionate regard. He also won the first medal competition in 1893 with a score of 100.

Let us quote from his famous *Golf Courses of Great Britain*:

It is the course that my soul loves best of all the courses in the world. Every golfer has a course for which he feels some such blind and unreasoning affection. When he is going to his golfing home he packs up his clubs with a peculiar delight and care; he anxiously counts the diminishing number of stations that divide him from it, and finally steps out on the platform, as excited as a schoolboy home for the holidays, to be claimed by his own familiar caddie. A golfer can only have one course towards which he feels quite in this way, and my one is Aberdovey.

As on so many famous links, the land here is bounded by an estuary, that of the Dovey, and the sea, Cardigan Bay, and as usual there are sandhills and broken ground along the shore and flatter land on the inland side. The turf is crisp and many of the greens small.

Aberdovey Golf Club: Medal Card

	YARDS	PAR		YARDS	PAR
1	441	4	10	415	4
2	332	4	11	407	4
3	173	4	12	149	3
4	401	4	13	530	5
5	193	3	14	389	4
6	402	4	15	477	5
7	482	5	16	288	4
8	335	4	17	428	4
9	160	3	18	443	4
	2919	34		3526	37

Total 6445 yards: par 71

The course opens with a stiff four – most of us will be satisfied with five – and an uncomplicated four before reaching the famous short third 'Cader', once completely blind, with an almost blind shot of 173 yards over what was a huge sandhill, and bunker into a not unkindly gathering green. One used to watch the match in front through a periscope, now sadly defunct, but it is hoped this will soon be replaced by the grandson of the donor of the original instrument. Having played the hole your predecessors ring a bell to signal their departure. Then, grasping your four-iron or five-wood, you bend to it and hope to see the ball soaring over the mountain to the green. But if you are short or catch the top you can be in a very tough gravelly bunker with a sleepered face. The green is small, but gently gathers the ball. Next you have a cheerful drive down out of the hills to the plain and a punch home with an iron.

After the short fifth come three rather flat holes along the curve of the railway to the far end of the course, where wild iris appear in the rough, a rare attraction on any golf course. You play a short hole across and then come home on the sandhills side of the links. Coming in, I remember especially the odd-length sixteenth, 288 yards, but fiendishly difficult driving, with the railway on your left hand, a curving fairway with trouble on the right, and an evil pitch to a small humpy shelf of green with the hills near 'Cader' protecting the right, and a sharp fall off to the left; somehow the ball ran for me here, for I had a fluky three in an undistinguished round. Two fairly lengthy fours bring you in.

This is the permanent home of Welsh Seniors Championships for men and beloved of the Welsh Ladies Golfing Union for many championships.

Royal St David's, Harlech

To end our visit to Wales, we should call in at the Royal St David's Club at Harlech, with its superb views of Snowdonia and the castle, though I take leave not to care overmuch for the golf. This is, I am sure, my fault, and I certainly played vilely there, which always tends to make you take a grim view of the course.

Considering the territory, I found the course surprisingly flat and difficult – with less use of the big sandhills than I expected; they really only come into play at the last five holes and then the course becomes splendid, a notable great thump, all carry, over the vast 'Castle' bunker to get to the 218-yard fourteenth, then three stiff two-shotters and another but flatter three to finish.

The British Ladies Championship is to be played here in 1987.

Royal St David's Golf Club, Harlech: Medal Card

	YARDS	PAR		YARDS	PAR
1	436	4	10	430	4
2	346	4	11	144	3
3	463	4	12	427	4
4	188	3	13	451	4
5	393	4	14	218	3
6	371	4	15	427	4
7	476	5	16	354	4
8	491	5	17	427	4
9	173	3	18	202	3
	3337	36		3080	33

Total 6417 yards: par 69

For Championship play these extra lengths prevail:

No 2	373 yards	No 8	499 yards
No 7	481 yards	No 10	458 yards

Chapter 10

EAST ANGLIA

There is a wealth of good golf in East Anglia on heathland, on the cliffs or among the sand dunes along the shore. For instance, there are two heathery courses at Ipswich which I believe are very good, though I don't know either, I am sorry to say, and another such at Norwich where the Royal Norwich Club plays. Then there are two fine cliff-top courses at Sheringham and Cromer.

At Cromer the first international golf match of all was played, between the ladies of Great Britain and the United States, in 1905. We won the match handsomely. In the American side were the two Curtis sisters, each later to be US ladies' champion, who afterwards gave the Curtis Cup for the international match.

Felixstowe

The first course on our list is Felixstowe on the Suffolk coast, one of the oldest clubs outside Scotland, which was formed in 1880.

The course has been altered several times, for when the club has not been taken over because of war with the Germans – for this has always been a potential invasion beach – it has been continuously at war with the German ocean. A perpetual erosion of the coast has been going on for years and whole fairways have disappeared since the first layout. Two Martello towers grace the links, the nearer one is now on the edge of the sea, having originally had two fairways to the eastward of it and the battle is being continued with expensive protective works.

The first layout was a nine-hole links on sandy soil running both sides of the first Martello tower which once served as the clubhouse. The course was later extended to eighteen holes. Then after the military and marine damage of World War I had been made good an entirely new layout was devised by Dr Alister Mackenzie, embracing some flat estuarine land on the far side of the road to Felixstowe Ferry and some cliff-top land behind the clubhouse. World War II saw a complete shutdown and occupation by the soldiery, after which, again confined by the inroads of the sea, the present entirely new layout was made by Henry Cotton, abandoning the cliff-top holes, which had gone anyway, making the most of the sandy soil near the shore and extending the number of holes in the riverine plain. It could be said, therefore, that the last nine holes today are linksland, with thin turf, keen greens and some 'umps and 'ollows, while the outward nine are flatter, and inclined to be much softer. The original first six holes now make a finishing loop and come home to the clubhouse.

To start, the course runs right out to the second Martello tower, then across the road and then in again, but it is all so compact that agreeable variations can be played to give you almost any number of holes you like to play.

My knowledge of Felixstowe is confined to a bitter cold winter's day when I was afflicted by a weight-reducing regimen I was undergoing which left me ill-equipped to beat off the shrill wind or hit the ball at all well, but I enjoyed the few holes I played, notably the first, now the fourteenth, with its true seaside fairway and lightning green up by the Martello tower, the short par-four second, now fifteenth, on its plateau and the short eighteenth, the present twelfth, well guarded; most of brookside holes

are for another and warmer day, but it is a good and enjoyable-looking course and I want to go back.

Felixstowe Ferry Golf Club: Medal Card

	YARDS	PAR		YARDS	PAR
1	432	4	10	509	5
2	501	5	11	324	4
3	310	4	12	144	3
4	324	4	13	356	4
5	138	3	14	320	4
6	423	4	15	404	4
7	491	5	16	220	3
8	498	5	17	446	4
9	159	3	18	325	4
Out	3276	37	In	3048	35
			Out	3276	37
			Total	6324	72

Woodbridge

Next we come to one of those golfing trios, the courses at Aldeburgh, Thorpeness and Woodbridge on heathland near the Suffolk coast. I would not put these in any order of preference or merit, but we must start somewhere, so let us lead off with Woodbridge on the estuary of the River Deben near Ipswich, if only that about twenty years ago I had 'one of those days' there, when all the doubtful putts flew into the hole and I went round in 72 strokes and that with only eight clubs in a drainpipe bag.

Since I played the course first, a fine new clubhouse has been built which has meant rearrangements and the loss of the old downhill short second hole. The round now starts with the old third, played from a different angle; the second is the old fourth and good fun it is too, with a hearty beat downhill off the tee then a short pitch over a stream close up to the green; since I played here this green has been re-sited

Woodbridge Golf Club, Old Course: Medal Card

	YARDS	PAR		MEDAL	PAR
1	346	4	10	431	4
2	329	4	11	392	4
3	529	5	12	184	3
4	330	4	13	310	4
5	371	4	14	425	4
6	401	4	15	188	3
7	149	3	16	460	4
8	514	5	17	400	4
9	198	3	18	357	4
Out	3167	36	In	3147	34
			Out	3167	36

Total 6314 yards: par 70

with a pond waiting for mishits. The next four holes are unchanged and then comes a new short seventh to replace the missing old second. This new hole is one where it pays to be up, as it does at most short holes, but this has a nice bank at the back and left side to give a cushion.

The second half is less changed, except that the old short tenth is now the ninth and the old first hole is now the eighteenth. The whole layout is in typical heathland with gorse, bracken and heather in the rough and dry gravelly soil to give clean fairways and sharp greens, a thoroughly attractive course.

Recently a new relief nine has been built with a par of 31. There are lots of par threes, five in all, but there is a tough two-shot hole to start and another to finish with, with a small green, quite hard.

Thorpeness

Further up the Suffolk coast is Thorpeness, near the sea, but still heathland rather than linksland. The course was laid out by James Braid in 1922 since when several changes have been made. There is a tough selection of par fours over 400 yards each, though with three shorter ones to mitigate the sentence somewhat and four par threes. The course ends with a good dog-leg finishing hole; with the second shot you take aim at the fine old windmill which with the curious dwelling-cum water tower known as the 'House in the Clouds' dominates the skyline.

In reconstruction, two excellent holes, the fourteenth and fifteenth, were built out on the open heath; one a par five with rough to cross on the second shot and the other a stiff dog-leg four. The short seventh, once over marshy ground, has been converted to a formidable water hole over a pond.

Like Woodbridge, the course is on dry, sandy soil with heather and tree lupins as rough and silver birch trees for ornament. The course used to be divided in two by the now disused Sax-mundham–Aldeburgh branch railway whose station at the bottom of the course was the most primitive in my experience, two old carriages on stilts alongside the platform. Now just a road divides the holes on the open heath from those in grassier territory.

Although this is holiday golf, and nothing wrong with that, Thorpeness is not an easy course and plays to its full par value. It is on record that a 7-handicap member holed his second shot at the par five fourteenth and then finished 4 3 3 3.

Thorpeness Golf Club: Medal Card

	YARDS	PAR		YARDS	PAR
1	324	4	10	179	3
2	186	3	11	312	4
3	394	4	12	370	4
4	449	4	13	424	4
5	420	4	14	499	5
6	377	4	15	416	4
7	145	3	16	191	3
8	402	4	17	280	4
9	439	4	18	434	4
	3136	34		3105	35

Total 6241 yards: par 69

Aldeburgh

We now come to the near neighbour of Thorpe-ness at Aldeburgh. Once again this is a heath-land course, although almost in sight of the sea. The most conspicuous feature here is the brilliance of the yellow gorse which in its full flowering season almost dazzles the eyes with its golden masses of flowers. The brilliant yellow gorse of East Anglia was said to have been the inspiration of the colour scheme for the engines of the long gone Midland and Great Northern Joint Railway. The earliest recollection of my life is of being held up by my father to see a train go by, headed by a yellow engine, near Sheringham in 1907, and I now have a Hamilton Ellis painting commemorating this.

The golf at Aldeburgh is first-class, especially the second half, where some of the fairways are so folded as to be almost linksland. Several holes stand out in this nine: the severely bunkered tenth and eleventh, the drive-and-pitch twelfth with a huge bunker to cross close to the green and a very humpy fairway, and the excellent two-shot fourteenth to a high plateau green after an exacting drive between two huge trees, and a ridge to cross before striking up to the green. The short holes are good too; especially I like the fourth and eighth, the former with a huge sleeper-faced bunker which seems to envelop the entire green and the latter with a road to cross.

A new simple nine holes has been added at Aldeburgh, across the road from the clubhouse, a par-32 layout of 2140 yards and free of bunkers.

Aldeburgh Golf Club: Medal Card

	YARDS	PAR		YARDS	PAR
1	407	4	10	421	4
2	367	4	11	469	4
3	429	4	12	324	4
4	127	3	13	370	4
5	440	4	14	361	4
6	431	4	15	201	3
7	411	4	16	457	4
8	165	3	17	142	3
9	383	4	18	425	4
	3160	34		3170	34

Total 6330 yards: par 68

The north of Norfolk is a strange and remote place, and, except in a short holiday season, sparsely inhabited. It is flat and open and you get the impression of immense horizons and huge skies. Off the coast the sea is shallow and great sandy beaches stretch for miles; it is bracing, and, truth to tell, rather cold. The hinterland is often protected by marshes and saltings and there are many wild birds. You might be in Denmark, and that goes even for a lot of the domestic – but not ecclesiastical – architecture. You either take to these wide open spaces or you don't. I happen to like them, and not least because two very fine classical golf links lie on this coast.

Hunstanton

Hunstanton, a little resort town, lies on the Wash and on a clear day you can look across to Lincolnshire and the great church tower of Boston Stump. Last time I was there, checking my facts, was as far back as January 1968 when a

brisk north wind was blowing straight off the Pole with alternating sunshine and snow showers. I remember few colder days on any golf course, but I remember, too, warm holiday golf there in July when the weather was perfect and one day when the temperature reached 90°F.

Since its start in 1891, Hunstanton has had many alterations, the first from its original nine-hole layout. After extension to eighteen holes, James Braid had a hand in tightening things up and in 1925 James Sherlock made several improvements. More recently the seventeenth and eighteenth on the low land on the inland side have been replaced by two new holes among the folded ground on the seaward side. It is now a fine full-length links of 6670 yards off the back tees and its own brochure made the modest claim that it is 'said to be the finest test of golf between the Humber and the Thames'. One might go farther than that.

The links lies between the shore, with its huge beach, and the little River Hun and a straight irregular range of shaggy sandhills divides it into two parts, the flatter low-lying holes on the inland side and the exceedingly humpy holes nearer the sea. The ridge itself is used extensively for siting greens or afflicting tee shots.

Many tournaments of importance have been held here, except for the two major championships, and the ladies have often used it for the English and the British titles; the English Amateur has been here and the Amateur Stroke Play Championship. Oxford has met Cambridge here several times.

My only regret at the alterations has been that the old first tee is now occupied by the eighteenth green, with the first tee pushed over to the right. As a result, the great intimidating bunker which has demoralised so many over the years is now only a menace if you hit a pretty quick hook. The rest of the hole on the flat inland side is not exciting; nor is the long second in the same area. The third, a long par four, is much of the same, though you can cut your second into the Hun without much difficulty.

We then play a short fourth towards the sandy ridge and the sea, well beset by bunkers, fifteen, I think. Then back with a two-shotter on

to the plain again. Well, so far, not much, and you would be pardoned for thinking that there was nothing special to crow about. However, from now on things are on the up and up and the remaining thirteen holes are first-class.

The change starts with six, a drive-and-pitch hole towards the ridge, of 332 yards. The green is set on a high plateau guarded by bunkers on either hand and in front, and a deep pit of short rough to the right of the green which runs precipitously into it; it was once the old green but doesn't look like it today. The green is none too big and is well sloped; putting can be a problem. To my taste, a lovely hole.

The next is even better, a gem of a hole, 162 yards from plateau to plateau with a long deep trough of rough in between and a big bunker in front of the green. To the left are the sandhills of the main ridge and on the right some sandhills of a subsidiary ridge; these combine to give the perfect setting of what a true linksland hole should be.

You now have to prepare yourself for some pretty resolute hitting if you want to score, for No. 8 is 483 yards long out to the end of the links, then the ninth is 508 yards back to a green under the seventh tee. Two tough, uncompromising holes, these, and you can't have the wind helping you at both; indeed, with a norther blowing it won't help you at either. Ten is out towards the sea, and the eleventh runs back again along the shore; these are among the newer holes at Hunstanton. At the twelfth we are attacking the ridge again, this time from the sea, and cross it with a 356-yard par four. Then we immediately recross it with the unorthodox thirteenth, 387 yards long. You drive over the ridge and then run out of fairway, for the green is an island and the second shot in has to clear a belt of rough and some sandy hillocks round the green. Patric Dickinson regards it as 'one of the greatest two-shot holes in golf'. I'm sorry to say at this point that the whiff of change is in the air and already a new green has been built dogleg to the right instead of the left.

At fourteeen it's the ridge again, this time a

blind one-shot hole, once so fashionable, now so rare. I hope they don't change it. There are bunkers in the ridge face and round the green, so at 216 yards that's quite tough enough. Alas, change is lurking here with a new, and to be fair, good alternative short hole without blindly crossing the ridge. Then comes a short par five and then another short hole down from the ridge on the seaward side; a pretty good stiff iron shot is needed here. We finish with two more recent holes among the sandhills which were opened in 1951, the seventeenth a fierce two-shotter of 446 yards to a shelf green with a hillside to the left and a drop to the right. The last hole is shorter, 398 yards, but again the green is a plateau and a small one at that, protected in front about fifty yards short by a sandy road where you can get a distressing lie – but then you have no business to be there.

Perhaps Hunstanton's most famous character was the professional James Sherlock, who died in his ninety-second year and served the club for many years. He was near the top in professional golf and beat Vardon in the final of the *News of the World* Match Play Championship in 1910. More remarkable, perhaps, he won the over-seventies' Seniors' Cup in his eighty-second and eighty-third years. When a mere lad of sixty-one he did two holes in one in one round. He also played in the first match against

the American professionals at Gleneagles in 1921 and won both his matches. One of his great sorrows was the death of John Lyon, one of the promising young men of English golf, who used to play at Hunstanton; he was killed in World War II.

An outstanding feat was perpetrated by Bob Taylor, the Leicestershire player, who holed the sixteenth in one stroke in three consecutive rounds during the 1974 Eastern Counties Foursomes.

	YARDS	PAR		YARDS	PAR
	Hunstanton Golf Club: Medal Card				
1	343	4	10	372	4
2	532	5	11	439	4
3	443	4	12	356	4
4	165	3	13	387	4
5	424	4	14	216	3
6	332	4	15	476	5
7	162	3	16	188	3
8	483	5	17	446	4
9	508	5	18	398	4
	3392	37		3278	35
				3392	37
				6670	72

Royal West Norfolk, Brancaster

Moving east along the coast road a few miles to a still more remote spot, we come to the links of the Royal West Norfolk Golf Club at Brancaster.

Whereas Hunstanton has undergone many changes in seventy-five years or so, Brancaster has had few, although the sea stole two holes of the links in 1939 and 1940. As my friend Laddie Lucas wrote to the Yates family in Atlanta, Georgia, 'the links was laid out in 1891 and has been unchanged ever since'. Although this is not quite true, you do have here something of a museum piece, yet it is a most enjoyable and

testing links to play. I love it. A lot of it does look very old-fashioned, especially those huge wooden sleepers lining the faces of the bunkers. But they do put the wind up you, none the less; they are alarming to play over and terrifying to play out of, and even after fifty years I can remember starting out 4 10 4 on my first round here. Lucas, by the way, with it seems to me a totally uncalled for handicap of twelve, recently won the Summer Medal with a net 61.

Brancaster has much in common with Hunstanton, ten miles away, many similarities and many differences; the links lie between ridge and marsh, but the ridge this time is right along the edge of the shore and the marsh is wetter, indeed it may be flooded at very high tide, like the road leading to the clubhouse! The grass is uncompromisingly seaside, spare on the fairways and painfully thick in the rough; the greens are of a seaside keenness but true to the properly-struck putt. Wild sea-lavender and sea-holly grow in the marsh.

We start out prosaically enough with a drive over a chasm which was once a huge sand bunker and then turn half left to hit up into the hills, but it is 410 yards, so we'd better hit a good drive. Two is not too tough, either, in spite of Allen's ten, though we meet the sleepers here for the first time with a big boarded bunker to catch a pulled drive. At the third we really have a facer, a 407-yard hole with the green on a narrow plateau guarded about forty to fifty yards in front by a huge boarded cross bunker. If you don't hit a good drive you've got to go for it with wood – and there's no way round. Even if you get over, the green is not welcoming and may shrug you off into a bunker under the escarpment.

The fourth is a little terror; a pitch from a high tee over a vale to a very high plateau green, guarded in the face by a grass bank, revetted with sleepers below which is a single wide cross bunker. If you land on the bank you fall back into the trap; hitting the sleepers finishes anywhere. With a strong north wind you might even have to take wood here! Normally it is about a number seven, but there's no temptation to be short.

Keeping near the marsh, we play the next three in 4 3 5, we hope, but you can get into the saltings if you hook at the short sixth or slice at the long seventh.

At the eighth we have a celebrated hole, with two arms of the marsh to carry – it is not out of bounds – or two arms of the sea, as I have once seen it. The first carry is from the tee and diagonal, so the more you can bite off, the

better. If you've hit a good one you can bear down on the green with your second over the second inlet. However, par allows five here, so you can adjust your efforts to your drive and if need be poke one along the arm of a fairway and then pitch across to an open green.

You drive over the marsh again at the 404-yard ninth and then have to hit a firm second over a huge sleepered bunker to the green.

You now turn for home on the seaward side of the links, with a 151-yard short hole on a plateau green. There follow two more holes among the dunes, the 478-yard eleventh and 386-yard twelfth, with their greens in natural dells, then a new hole replacing the short thirteenth, a short par four with a green overlooking the sea, a rare treat. Then comes fourteenth, a famous old hole along the bumps and hollows of the linksland close to the shore; it is 432 yards long and that would be all right if there were not a big swale full of short rough and sand about fifty yards short of the green; so your second shot is all carry and that to a pretty small target area. The green here is cheek by jowl with that of the short fourth, and mishit shots at either can finish up on the other.

We then face another desperate shot at the fifteenth, or so it seems. The hole is 188 yards long and it looks – only looks, it is true – as if the green were immediately beyond a huge enormous pit of a bunker, deep, dark and cavernous with a boarded face. Reality is rather kinder, for the green is about fifty yards past the trap, so your carry is only about 140 yards instead of what you first guess; even so, it is not easy, for the green, on the inevitable plateau, is small and easily casts your ball aside.

The sixteenth is a nice short par four of 346 yards slightly dog leg up into the hills; the guardians here are only small pot bunkers! At seventeen you cross the play to the second and an exceptionally bad drive puts you into a bunker, sleepered, of course, but otherwise at 377 yards the seventeenth is not too tough. At the last, 384 yards, we do need a good drive, as we have to carry a boarded bunker about 150 yards in front of the green and yet stop on a keen surface, remembering there is grass hollow at the back. So ends Brancaster and if you think the inward nine at 3059 yards is going to be short, try it against a westerly wind.

Have I given an impression that Brancaster is impossibly severe, too harsh in its punishments and too brutal with its cross bunkering and ancient style? I hope not, for in fine weather it can be amazingly beautiful, the sea birds wheeling and crying overhead, the marsh with its own flowers and, perhaps, after a blow, the sea making a continuous roar on the sands out of sight beyond the rampart of dunes. Remote, serene and unspoilt, may it long continue. As the late Tom Scott, former editor of *Golf Illustrated*, said:

It has a quiet and restful beauty and when you leave the clubhouse and drive across the marsh to the main road in the dusk of a summer evening, look back for a minute and perhaps you will be rewarded, as I have frequently been, with a view of the red sun setting over the sea with a golden glow. You will see, too, the long shadows cast by the great sandhills, and you will hear the call of many birds across the marshes, a sound to my mind typical of Norfolk.

Royal West Norfolk Golf Club, Brancaster: Medal Card

	YARDS	PAR		YARDS	PAR
1	410	4	10	151	3
2	449	4	11	478	5
3	407	4	12	386	4
4	128	3	13	317	4
5	421	4	14	432	4
6	186	3	15	188	3
7	486	5	16	346	4
8	478	5	17	377	4
9	404	4	18	384	4
Out	3369	36	In	3059	35
			Out	3369	36
			Total	6428	71

Well said, and even on a bitter January day, with snow flurries, a walk out to the fourteenth green and back with a game leg was a rewarding experience.

Royal Worlington and Newmarket

Royal Worlington and Newmarket, in West Suffolk, is the home course of Cambridge University and a fine place for young men to learn to build up a strong game. It lies about seven miles north of Newmarket in a surprising belt of sand, when all around the land is East Anglian clay or chalk hills, and in consequence the course is always dry and is a splendid place for winter golf. The greens are keen and fast, too, at all seasons.

Worlington is a nine-hole course and astonishingly compact at that. It has often been described as the best nine-hole course in Britain and occasionally as being the best nine holes; by that, I judge the claimant to mean that they constitute the best consecutive nine-hole stretch anywhere in Britain.

Well, is it and are they? In my view the answer to the first is yes, though if an old favourite of mine, the little nine-hole links at Bembridge, the Royal Isle of Wight, had survived, I could have disputed the matter. As for the wider claim, fine course though it is, the Royal Worlington and Newmarket certainly isn't the best nine-hole stretch in the country – among courses of the same type I would put in claims for Liphook, Ganton, St George's Hill or Sunningdale – and most certainly its holes are not the nine finest individual holes in Britain.

Having said that, let no one deny that this is a

splendid golf course. You open with a 486-yard par five steering up a fairly wide fairway sign-posted with traps on either flank. The shot to the green is deceptive, as there is a hollow of dead ground in front of it. So there is at the second, which has an 'inverted saucer' green which pushes aside or over the back any shot that is not really well hit; a most difficult long one-shotter to find from the tee or to chip back to from the sides. Driving back across the second green and over a big cross bunker, you have a very narrow tee shot, the hogs-back fairway constricting just where you wish it wouldn't. The shot to the green which lies beyond a marshy valley is a light iron but quite tight owing to the traps on the left; a very attractive hole this.

Number four into the west wind is a 495-yarder, a short par five for the hitters, but the green is protected by a bank just in front of it, which makes it uncommonly hard to get a shot of any length close to the hole; moreover, the green is hard up to the boundary fence.

The fifth is a famous hole and so it should be. It is 157 yards long and it is without a single bunker or obstacle between the tee and the green; it is slightly uphill, with a pleasant line of pine trees behind the green, but the green is fiendishly narrow and contoured to take your ball off to the stream or rough on the right or to a large deep hollow on the left, which my caddie assured me was called 'Mugs Cottage', though I am assured that 'Mugs Hole' is the correct name. From either of these positions it is abominably difficult to get the ball to stay on the narrow green, let alone near the hole. On medal day I think most of us would settle for a four and walk to the sixth tee.

The sixth hole is a long two-shotter of 458 yards with the same row of pines which frame the fifth along the entire right-hand side of the fairway; the left side is trapped extensively, but that is the side to be on unless you can fade a long shot into the green past the last pine of the

row. This is a really splendid hole for someone who can hit the ball just a bit farther than I can.

Next comes a rather unmemorable short hole, though for some reason one often under-hits and gets stuck on the rise in front of the green. The eighth runs back along the pine trees parallel to the sixth and is a tough 460-yard hole, too long for me to regard as a par four. There is a cross bunker about 120 yards short of the green, but this is only troublesome if you've been in trouble already, and there is also a big bunker eating into the left side of the green. You end the round with a drive-and-pitch hole, the drive across the stream – and you can easily slice into it – and a pitch across the road with a tough deep bunker at the back of the green for the shot hit 'thin'. The green here is fiercely contoured, so that this 300-yarder is no pushover as a finishing hole.

So supposing you have holed in 37 or 38 strokes, which is not beyond the powers of many of us, you have to do it all over again, and that's not as easy as you might think, perhaps you make a new set of errors or even do the same ones once again.

Royal Worlington and Newmarket Golf Club:
Medal Card

	YARDS	PAR
1	486	5
2	224	3
3	361	4
4	495	5
5	157	3
6	458	4
7	165	3
8	460	4
9	299	4
	3105	35

Total 3105: par 35

Chapter 11

GOLF IN IRELAND, EAST AND NORTH

Poor tormented Ireland has a record of unhappiness and unrest second to none in the western world, yet it is also the home of gaiety and charm. Nowhere in the world are you made welcome with more genuine and spontaneous kindliness. It is still refreshingly different from the rest of the British Isles and a visit there makes a pleasant change.

That the Sabbath is made for man and not man for the Sabbath is devoutly believed in Ireland, so, provided that you are not pressed for time or trying to cram two days' work into one or something silly like that, you can relax and enjoy yourself. The towns are different and not always better than in Great Britain, though Dublin is a city of much charm. Much effort has been put into the tourist industry and many new hotels have been built to suit all purses; some are excellent, some less so. The food varies from superb to bloody awful; the country is lovely with mountains and coastal scenery without equal, and, when it does not rain, gives as fair a prospect as the heart can desire in blue, green and brown.

The Irish love all sports and have produced some splendid golfers – Joe Carr and son, Lionel Munn, Cecil Ewing, James Bruen, Harry Bradshaw, Christy O'Connor and nephew, Fred Daly, Max McCready, John Burke, Garth McGimpsey, Des Smyth and the whole Hezlet family.

Good golfers don't come without good golf courses, and these Ireland has in plenty. Henry Longhurst put it this way: 'Some of the Irish links, I was about to write, stand comparison with the greatest courses. They don't. They *are* the greatest courses in the world, not only in layout but in scenery and ''atmosphere'' and that indefinable something which makes you relive again and again the day you played there.'

For years, the best-known courses were on the east or north east coasts, Portrush, Newcastle and Portmarnock, which stand comparison with any on earth and make a magnificent trio; then Royal Dublin at Dollymount comes close to these and then there is also a splendid and relatively-unfrequented links at Baltray, about half way between Dublin and Belfast, and add that most enjoyable holiday links at Castlerock, near Portrush.

But recently there has been a great upsurge in the far west, with Ballybunion taking the lead with two great links courses as good or better than any in the world, together with Lahinch in County Clare and Rosses Point, near Sligo, wonderful links well exposed to the Atlantic weather, and new ventures at Waterville and Tralee. Nearly all these great courses have superb coastal scenery which adds greatly to the pleasure of the game. Then, in addition, all over Ireland there are many simple layouts quite unknown, which provide excellent sport.

Royal Dublin

We will take our tour of Ireland starting from Dublin, where there is first-class golf inside the city limits on the links of the Royal Dublin Golf Club at Dollymount. The club celebrated its centenary in 1985. The links lies on an island on the northern outskirts of the city, connected to the mainland by a bridge. One may ask why the Royal title is still maintained in an independent republic, but this is Ireland.

The links is narrow and exceedingly compact; like the Old course at St Andrews it must occupy one of the smallest acreages of any first-class course. The layout unfortunately is straight out, straight home, or very nearly, so that if the prevailing west wind is blowing you have a very fierce beat in, particularly as this is much the longer half. All the same, the links is of the true metal, the ground, though rather flat and without mountains of sand, is of the proper sandy soil and the grass and rough are 'up to test'.

I think one has to place Dollymount in a category rather below the Irish Big Three of Newcastle, Portmarnock and Portrush, not quite so tough, not quite so interesting, and not quite so beautiful, though the Hill of Howth is an attractive feature and the Wicklow Hills beyond the city make a good backdrop.

The best holes at Dollymount to my taste are the par-four third and seventh of 408 and 370 yards, the latter with a new, raised plateau green. The 179-yard ninth across the far end of the course is the best of the one-shotters, I think, though the 270-yard sixteenth makes for a big hit which may give good satisfaction if the wind is not too much against you. I remember seeing a local character, Bertie Briscoe, find the green in a round of the gone but not forgotten

---

Royal Dublin Club, Dollymount: Medal and Championship Cards

NAME	M	C	PAR	NAME	M	C	PAR
1 North Bull	386	397	4	10 Marne	400	416	4
2 Babington's	483	492	5	11 Colt's	525	538	5
3 Alps	366	408	4	12 Campbell's	187	207	3
4 Feather Bed	173	180	3	13 Dardanelles	421	468	4
5 Valley	408	460	4	14 Moran's	476	500	5
6 Pot	184	185	3	15 Hogan's	422	437	4
7 Ireland's Eye	332	370	4	16 Dolly	255	270	4
8 Ben Howth	476	509	5	17 Coastguards	367	380	4
9 Davidson's	177	179	3	18 Garden	476	463	5
	2985	3180	35		3529	3679	38

Total 6514 and 6859 yards: par 73

Irish Open Amateur Championship years ago. He was playing an unpopular Englishman and remarked audibly to his supporters in the crowd 'that's got the bugger sweating'. It had, too.

On the inward nine, the eleventh and thirteenth at 538 and 468 yards need big hitting into the wind, but have attractive greens in natural dells which I like, though not as a steady diet. You end the round with a right-angled dog-leg hole, a short par five, which allows you to take a dangerous short cut across a big out-of-bounds carry right up to the edge of the green, which, if you bring it off, yields you a birdie or even an eagle to go home with.

Christy O'Connor once finished the round eagle, birdie, eagle, but few of us can hope to follow that. Carrolls Irish Open has been played here for three years, with two wins for Ballesteros and one for Langer the German.

Dollymount is a bird sanctuary and 3000 specimens have been identified there, I was told, but what I liked were the hares. The far end of the links is full of hares, big ones, young ones, little ones, loping about on their long legs or stopping with their big ears cocked to look and listen. They are fairly tame and unafraid, as no guns are allowed on the island. I startled a young one which had been lying in the rough with its ears back; it sprang up from under my feet and ran off and you could see the little nest its body had made in the grass

Portmarnock

Moving north from Dublin along the coast we soon pass the promontory of the Hill of Howth and are in sight of Portmarnock, the club and links separated from the road by a stretch of water. You circle round and come on to the peninsula from the north and there you are. In the old days you could go by boat or at low tide by horse carriage.

Portmarnock is a great course, one of the greatest, and there are some who would say *the* greatest. Moreover, it is big golf, the links all of 7000 yards from the back tees, and yet off normal tees, and with some summer run on the ball, it is not too harsh, even for the elderly, provided that you don't get a wind. The greens are perfect – no other word is adequate – of the finest grass that only many years of care and the right climate can produce; keen, true and without weed or blemish.

It is such an attractive place, too, with water on three sides of it; as you stand in the middle of the course there lies the Hill of Howth to the south; to the east a line of sandhills marks the strand and ocean, and beyond the clubhouse to the westward you see the sheltered waters of an arm of the sea. Up in the sandhills by the shore you can get a splendid view on a fine day, the islands of Lambay and Ireland's Eye in front of you, Howth to the right, and far up the coast the Mountains of Mourne sweeping indeed down to the sea. I can remember vividly just such a day here on my twenty-third birthday, alas now nearly sixty years ago.

Another attractive thing about Portmarnock is that there are never more than two consecutive holes in the same direction, so that you can tack about all over the ground, constantly changing direction, and when there is a wind of any size – and of course it can blow like the devil here – you don't get battered to death for nine holes on end or blown forward all the way in or out like a leaf on the gale.

The links starts with three par-four holes of moderate length all under 400 yards just to get you going, as it were, but none of them is easy, as they have some nagging bunkers, so that it is all too simple to miss these fours which you are going to need so much later on when the going gets tougher. Four and five are par fours of fuller length, the fourth at 435 yards.

Then at six comes the first of three huge par-fives holes, this one of 569 yards. This is a completely new hole as the old hole was needed to become part of a new nine-hole course a few years ago. To reach this hole in two is beyond my imagining for there is a large bunker, and a pond, on the left approach and a very deep bunker to the right. Off the championship tee at 603 yards not even Ballesteros tried to make it in two. A short hole follows of no conspicuous merit, after which you turn for home with a par-four dog-leg eighth with a little narrow plateau green, all too easy to miss, and then a longer par-four ninth by the clubhouse also with a plateau green.

Indeed, plateau greens are a feature at Portmarnock, for the tenth has one – and it can look painfully small – and so has the short twelfth. The twelfth is a refutation of the now fashionable doctrine that all par threes must be something like 190–200 yards long. This one measures only 151 yards, with a small green cocked up in the sandhills by the shore, protected by a steep up-slope in front and a big hump on the right; there are also traps about. It is all too easy not to get on the green from the tee and all too difficult to chip near the hole from off it.

The thirteenth is another big par five, 549 yards this time, and this can very easily be dead into the wind as it runs north-west. The same goes for the 513-yard sixteenth. They can make a very tough pair of holes indeed, but in between comes the splendid 385-yard fourteenth hole, back towards the sea with a leftward curving fairway and a plateau green protected by two bunkers in the face of the rise and folds and slopes round the green, itself to take off a misplaced shot – a really superb hole and to my mind the best on the course. Henry Cotton, I believe, rates this as the best hole in all golf and I would not disagree. Fifteen is a short hole along the edge of the strand where the green notably fails to gather the ball for you. Arnold Palmer is reported as calling it the best short hole in the world, though I would not go that far.

Seventeen is a long and slightly dull par four, probably because at 431 yards I find it imposs-

ible to get up in two, but it is made up for by a superb finishing hole, the 399-yard eighteenth, where you have to beat home to a plateau green, the flag at the top of a slope defying you to reach it, as Bernard Darwin used to say. With bunkers on either side of the rise to the green, and the prevailing wind against you, or at least not helping you, you have to hit a fine shot to get home, and then what pleasure you get.

The general appearance of Portmarnock on a fine day in summer I have mentioned, but it is such an attractive spot that I willingly do it again, white water to the west, blue sea and sky, the rough a pale khaki colour, the fairways the light green of an olive, the watered greens the colour of emeralds, picked out by black and white posts topped by scarlet flags. What a wonderful place to play the best of games.

But don't forget the autumn gales and the soaking rain from the west, like on that famous day in 1927 in the old Irish Open Championship, when all the tents were blown out to sea. On the morning of that day only one player beat 80 and that was Jack Smith, who thereby led the field by eight strokes and George Duncan by

Portmarnock Golf Club: Championship and Medal Card

	C	PAR	M		C	PAR	M
1	394	4	378	10	370	4	372
2	378	4	352	11	434	4	429
3	385	4	380	12	151	3	147
4	444	4	435	13	565	5	549
5	389	4	388	14	390	4	385
6	603	5	569	15	187	3	183
7	185	3	167	16	525	5	513
8	401	4	384	17	474	4	431
9	440	4	422	18	423	4	399
Out	3628	36	3475	In	3519	36	3408
				Out	3628	36	3475
				Total	7147	72	6883

fourteen after three rounds. In the afternoon Jack Smith took 91, but George Duncan, well protected from the weather inside and out, had a marvellous round of 74, the only round under 80, and won by one shot from Henry Cotton, who had had 86 and 81 for the day.

There was a similar gale here at the Dunlop Masters in 1965 when the whole day's play was washed out like the tented field, destroyed by the gale; then later Bernard Hunt came from away back in the ruck with a tremendous 66 in the last round to beat out the leader, Peter Thomson, and win the competition.

Let us recall, too, 1949, the only time the British Amateur Championship was held in Eire, when Max McCready won for Ireland, albeit the North of Ireland, and recorded a fine victory in the final over an American, one of the great Turnesa family. With sour wisdom that famous commentator Henry Longhurst remarked that it was a sobering experience to have to go through customs and immigration to play in a British Championship on foreign soil.

The Irish Open disappeared in 1953. In 1975 the revived Irish Open, sponsored by Carrolls the cigarette makers, came to Portmarnock and produced fine winners, Ballesteros the most recent in 1986 after two wins elsewhere. Mark James of England has won twice here and it is pleasing to find Ben Crenshaw, a great supporter of links golf, also a winner.

The Island

Just along the coat from Portmarnock, at Malahide, twelve miles north of Dublin, you come to the Island links. Great changes have come here since I played it in the late sixties. First of all, it no longer *is*, so no more do you start out by taking a voyage in a small rowing boat with an outboard motor across the harbour from Malahide, the cost of which was included in your green fee.

The holes along the harbour marshes lay in some of the lumpiest dune country you could imagine; you could not always see where you were supposed to go and there were lots of blind shots. I suppose the eighth hole, 'The Andes', was the most spectacular, for there you propelled a three-iron or a five-wood shot over a towering sand hill absolutely blind, with wind-eroded bunkers on its summit; if you succeeded in this your ball landed on a furious down slope and rushed on to the green in a nice gathering hollow – or over it in dry weather, a splendidly old-fashioned hole. The bumps, humps and hollows round the greens of the ninth and short tenth holes are almost as pronounced. There was, too, a splendid par-three finishing hole which is now the fifth after the rearrangement made necessary by the new clubhouse. Here a slice or even a fade put you on the beach while a good straight shot could be held up by broken ground in front of the green; a very narrow and difficult hole.

Frank Pennink, whose book of reference is an absolute necessity for the writing of a book like

	YARDS	PAR		YARDS	PAR
	The Island Golf Club: Medal Card				
1	356	4	10	393	4
2	510	5	11	176	3
3	310	4	12	352	4
4	405	4	13	332	4
5	240	3	14	442	4
6	298	4	15	314	4
7	558	5	16	194	3
8	200	3	17	350	4
9	396	4	18	420	4
	3273	36		2973	34

Total 6246 yards: par 70

mine, gives the origin of the name of the 510-yard second, the 'Cricket Field'. W. G. Grace had brought over a team to play cricket in Ireland and on the Sunday they met the Island at golf and lost every match. At lunch the Doctor said it was a pity his side couldn't play the Island at cricket, whereupon the greenkeeper was sent for and told to roll out a pitch. This done, the players went to cricket and W.G. was bowled first ball by Harry Jackson.

It was wonderful to find an old layout preserved like this, for this is what golf was like in the time of W. G. Grace – narrow fairways, really rough rough, sometimes consisting of those tenacious dwarf wild roses, small greens, unwatered, and sand dunes of spectacular hugeness. Now and then, too, there is a grand view down the coast to the south to the island of Ireland's Eye and the promontory of Howth.

More changes are coming including five new holes.

Baltray

Pushing on up the Belfast road through Swords and Balbriggan, we start looking in Drogheda for signposts for our next stop, by which time we are thirty miles and more out of Dublin. This is the links of the County Louth Golf Club at Baltray on the coast three or four miles from Drogheda. It is a fine, big golf course, well spaced out among the sandhills along the strand and on lower ground further inland. The present layout has in it the revisions of Tom Simpson made in the thirties. As so often happens, the flat holes on the landward side, at the beginning and end of the round, are less exciting and amusing than the others, but probably day-in day-out play harder. For my choice, however, the holes in the humpy, full-bosomed linksland are the best and the most fun.

The course has recently been reshaped to give better access to both halves of the links from a new clubhouse. This has meant altering the numbering of the holes and the layout of the old seventh and eighteenth holes.

The short holes are good, five and seven especially, cocked-up in the sandhills and needing a good, hard punch with a four, or even a three-iron to get up. Many of the holes show us a characteristic feature of Baltray, the greens being protected in front by a small scattering of little humps, so that, while neither a plateau nor a dell, the green needs a lofted approach. We find this, or something like it at the fourth and several times again, a sort of vee in the hills, protecting the front of number eight for instance, giving a way in, and also at sixteen; guarding the plateau at the famous and delightful fourteenth are more humps and bumps.

You start with a new par four, followed by the old eighth, now a par five, where you play up into the threshold of the sandhills. The third, the old ninth, comes down and you then go on to the relatively mild drive-and-pitch hole, originally the first, now number four; then we have an excellent short hole with its small green up in the hills, traps to the right and a fall-off to the left. The sixth is a big long par five with a small plateau green, an excellent hole with a green of appropriate size for 521 yards.

The short seventh up into the sandhills is like the fifth in length and you have to clear a protecting bunker and play on to the width of the green, an exacting shot.

Eight is a grand two-shot hole, where a straight drive lets you go on through the gap to the green to get home. The course then gets on to the lower ground before at twelve you are back in the hills with two charming two-shot holes of 418 and 419 yards, taking you out to the far end of the links.

You turn home with the hole I like best on the

Baltray Links: Medal Card

	BLUE COURSE	WHITE COURSE	PAR		BLUE COURSE	WHITE COURSE	PAR
1	428	412	4	10	393	381	4
2	482	476	5	11	498	498	5
3	546	539	5	12	418	418	4
4	348	334	4	13	424	419	4
5	165	165	3	14	339	339	4
6	528	521	5	15	157	157	3
7	165	165	3	16	392	392	4
8	404	396	4	17	187	187	3
9	420	409	4	18	504	495	5
	3486	3407	37		3312	3286	36

Total 6798 and 6693 yards: par 73

course, the 339-yard fourteenth. Here you clamber up to a high tee which gives you a fine view up the coast to the Mountains of Mourne, thirty-five miles away to the north. You have the fun of an exhilarating drive down to the fairway below, and then a punch up over the protecting bunkers and hillocks to a small plateau green.

The fifteenth is a short hole toward the sea, 157 yards over a big bunker to a built-up green which slopes away from you. Next is a typical Baltray two-shotter in the linksland to a green, again protected near the entry, nestling among the dunes, a pretty hole.

At the seventeenth we are on the flat with rather a dull par three of 187 yards, and then followed by a plainer, flatter five hole of no great merit to end.

Royal County Down, Newcastle

Our next stop is over the border in Ulster at Newcastle, County Down, to visit the golf links of the Royal County Down Golf Club under the shadow of the Mountains of Mourne. This, to my mind, is the toughest course in the British Isles and second only to Pine Valley as the severest golf course in the world. I was interested to learn that no less a player than Dai Rees shared my opinion.

Newcastle is a superbly beautiful place in which to play golf. Behind, to the south-west, as a superlative backdrop, are the Mountains of Mourne, topped by the 2800-foot peak of Slieve Donard; out to sea to the east and south-east lies Dundrum Bay, with a great arc of strand, across which on a clear day you can see the mountains of the Isle of Man, forty miles away. On the opposite hand is a row of hills by Ballynahinch, while to the north-east along the shore is a tangled wilderness of huge wild sandhills which is a continuation of the links.

I have a great sentimental attachment to Newcastle, for I played there much in my youth with a family of Irish friends, the Mitchells. It is also the scene of my first and almost my last championship in 1927. In those days if you had a handicap of four (worth six today, I suppose) you were eligible for the Irish Open Amateur Championship and this gave an impecunious undergraduate the chance of ten days' first-class golf – for neighbouring courses gave you the courtesy of the green – for four guineas. A party of us from Oxford used to take advantage of this, and even those of us who failed to survive the first round had a splendid golf holiday for very little.

The course has two great virtues, first that it is laid out in two separate circuits of nine holes, very different from each other in character, and, secondly, that each hole is separate and private to itself, in its own valley. You can only see the hole you are playing – and not always all of that – so that the sense of solitude and quiet enjoyment is never destroyed, even when the course is busy. In this, it is like two other great favourites of mine – Sandwich and Pine Valley.

The claim for Newcastle's difficulty I would make on the grounds that the rough is really rough – seaside grass, heather and gorse on the landward nine, and wild roses, sandhills and dunes of uncompromising severity on the sea nine, coupled with heavy bunkering. Herbert Warren Wind, that discriminating writer, was particularly struck with the narrowness of the fairways, and thought it was the most difficult test of driving he had ever encountered. 'It was in fact the sternest examination in golf I had ever taken.' On top of this there is a carry off most of the tees – not one to terrify the experts, perhaps – but quite enough to give cause for care and thought to the moderately skilled if there is any wind, and there usually is, and sometimes enough to devastate the novice. The bunkering, allied to the fierce rough, is such that rarely does an indifferent shot escape severe trouble. Moreover, the placing of the drive makes a big difference. In consequence, I would rate Newcastle, off equivalent tees, to be two shots a round harder than Portmarnock or Portrush.

Many of the greens are small and, how shall I put it, unwelcoming, like the tiny second green

with two dominating pot bunkers to the left and a fall off the green to the right. I know that this is a short par four and should require a good tight shot, so all right and it certainly has to have it. The greens at the seventh, eighth and fifteenth, to pick three, all seem to be on a little summit with a fall-off in front, on either side and sometimes behind.

You start out along the coast with a friendly fairway and a comparatively easy par-five hole, yet many who have sought a birdie here have retired discomfited with a dull six, for the green is long and narrow and somehow fails to gather the ball as you hoped it would. Number two is the fine 374-yard par four, with a drive which has to carry over a range of sandhills and a pitch over another ridge to a minute green, easy to miss. The third was once a five and is now one of those par fours which only seem endurable downwind. Behind the green is a vast mountain range of sandhills, perhaps the biggest in captivity. On the next tee you can astonish the first-time visitor by suggesting that he tee up to carry this monstrous rampart and having had your laugh you turn him round to play a comparatively mild par three back towards the club-house and Slieve Donard.

The fifth is a fine right-bending dog leg with a carry over a ridge of rough, illuminated by a characteristic Irish white stone as a marker, a fine two-shot hole with a big hit needed to get home against the wind. The sixth, after a tough carrying drive, is a milder par four altogether. Then comes a minute par three with a greedy bunker just in front of the green, so that any shot which towers into the prevailing wind falls slap into it and any left-tending shot into the wind charges off downhill to two horrible bunkers on the left; behind the green the ground falls away too; it is like playing on to a very small dome.

Eight is a fine two-shot hole of 427 yards, with a small green falling off both left and right, just beyond the throat of a pass, as it were. Then comes the ninth, one of the most spectacular holes in all golf. You drive uphill towards a post on the summit of the fairway. If, as you should, you clear all this, you find a superb prospect below you: the hill over which you have driven falls in a precipice to the green fairway far below. From the flat ground below the hill you have to belt your ball hard into the eye of the wind, over two protecting bunkers on an up-slope to the plateau of the green beyond. Behind all this lie the demesne and Gothic brickwork of the hotel, with its dark fir woods, and behind again the whole mountain mass of the Slieve Donard.

Slieve Donard, of course, is the masterpiece of all Newcastle's scenery; now purple in the autumn light, now indigo, now dark bottle green, now half hidden in mist and rainstorm, now glittering with rocks wet after rain has gone by; it is a perpetual gazingstock.

So to the landward nine, quite different from the seaside half. Less spectacular, far fewer huge sand castles and monster dunes, flatter lies, less awful bent grass but more heather and gorse in the rough; but alike in maintaining solitude and privacy with each hole on its own.

After a short, overbunkered tenth hole you have a fearsome carry over a vast sandhill at the eleventh, after which the second to the flattish green is not too exacting. Similarly the twelfth, a short par five, which could perhaps be called the only easy hole on the course, is very much on the same lines, though here your drive by contrast has to carry a pit. The thirteenth, however, is a beauty, with a curling fairway, not really a dog leg but more truly a banana hole, up a valley with hills of heather on either hand, going always to the right, so that if you don't hit a good drive you have to bite off a deal of trouble in the rough to your right to get home.

A short hole comes next of fair merit but not one to be remembered on one's deathbed, followed by a splendid tough two-shotter uphill and back towards home with a small green which does nothing to gather your ball. This is almost as hard a four as the thirteenth at Pine Valley and I can't speak higher than that. After

Royal County Down Links, Newcastle:
Medal and Championship Cards

HOLE	CHAMP.	PAR	MEDAL	HOLE	CHAMP.	PAR	MEDAL
1	506	5	500	10	200	3	200
2	424	4	374	11	440	4	429
3	473	4	473	12	501	5	476
4	217	3	217	13	445	4	422
5	440	4	418	14	213	3	213
6	396	4	368	15	445	4	445
7	145	3	129	16	265	4	265
8	427	4	427	17	400	4	376
9	486	(5)4	431	18	545	5	528
Out	3514	35	3337	In	3454	36	3354
				Out	3514	35	3337
				Total	6968	71	6691

Total 6968 and 6691 yards: par 71/72

that you coast in with a short par four of 265 yards on a plateau which I wish I was still young enough to reach with one great blow from the hilltop tee, a modest seventeenth and a long tough par-five eighteenth into the wind again to get home.

As at all famous golf courses, great deeds have been done at Newcastle, notably, perhaps, Eric Fiddian's two 'aces' in the thirty-sixth hole final of the Irish Open Amateur Championship in 1933, in spite of which he had to give way to the late Jack Mclean, who so nearly won the US Amateur Championship in 1936.

The remoteness of Newcastle and the absence of facilities for players and spectators on a massive scale has kept from it so far the British Open Championship, and more's the pity, but the Amateur Championship came here in 1970 and Michael Bonallack made history by scoring his third victory in a row. Newcastle has been a great place for women's championship golf, however, and a course which for some reason has been particularly rewarding to French girls, three of whom have won the British Ladies' Championship here.

There is also an amusing short course with a par of 60.

Royal Portrush

Portrush, which comes next on our list, is in the extreme north of Ireland, with a superb view over the Atlantic across the Skerries to the Isles of Western Scotland and the Paps of Jura. Be assured that it can blow violently here. I first played here on the old course with my friend Charles Mitchell sixty years ago; we drove up from Belfast on a dark winter's day, lunched well, and then with all the careless rapture of youth and kummel hit two tremendous shots down the first fairway, followed by two scorching irons to give a putt for a three to each of us, after which, and out of sight of a mildly interested handful of members in the clubhouse, we disappeared into the sandhills and never hit another shot properly.

When we came back twenty-five years later to tempt Charles Hezlet out to play, the course had been rebuilt by H. S. Colt and I don't think much trace of the old links remained, certainly none that I could see. In place of the old historic turf is one of the grandest circuits you can name, laid out in stupendous tumbling dune country. After a quiet start and an attractive par three at the top of the duneland you play a long par four and then at number five comes one of the great spectaculars of golf.

You are on the tee, and there, surely much more than 386 yards away and below you, is the green on the edge of the Atlantic, with nothing but a sea of rolling dunes, rough and sandhills in between. Well, it's not as far as it looks and there is a fairway down there, so if you are not hypnotised by the scenery and don't try to cut off too much you can play it as a dog leg and a very fair and reasonable hole it becomes. A few winters ago the green and the sixth tee were damaged by storms and the sea, but I'm glad to say that the repairs were carried out to restore the full glory of the hole.

There are some great holes in the second nine, the uphill drive-and-pitch thirteenth, with its little plateau green, is one, to be followed immediately by the 205-yard 'Calamity' fourteenth, an appallingly narrow shot with utter disaster down a violent slope into a dell on the right and below the green and no help from the bumpy hillocks all along the hole on the left. Just about all that will do here is a perfect shot, straight to the green. Then comes a swooping downhill hole called 'Purgatory', after that you are more or less on the level, passing the clubhouse to go out to the seventeenth green and then turning back. Patric Dickinson takes special note of the very long tee, 65 yards, at the sixteenth; he says 'If one is

---

Royal Portrush Golf Club: Medal Card

NAME	YARDS	PAR	NAME	YARDS	PAR
1 Hughie's	381	4	10 Dhu Varren	477	5
2 Giant's Grave	493	5	11 Featherbed	166	3
3 Islay	150	3	12 Causeway	389	4
4 Primrose Dell	454	4	13 Skerries	366	4
5 White Rocks	386	4	14 Calamity	205	3
6 Harry Colt's	191	3	15 Purgatory	361	4
7 Tavern	420	4	16 Babington's	415	4
8 Himalayas	365	4	17 Glenarm	508	5
9 Warren	476	5	18 Greenaway	477	5
	3316	36		3364	37

Total 6680 yards: par 73

---

at the back end, it is rather like the runway of an aircraft carrier.'

The Open was played here in 1951, Max Faulkner getting home with an average of just over 71 per round. The course held the upper hand all the way that year and only two rounds in the whole tournament beat 70. The Amateur was here in 1960 and gave forth an Irish victory, as Joe Carr beat the tar out of Cochran, the American, in the final. In 1988, the centenary year, the Irish Close Championship will be here.

Castlerock

Castlerock lies a few miles west of Portrush on the northern coast of County Londonderry, and it, Portstewart and Portrush make a fine group of three for a golfing holiday. I spent a happy ten days in these parts some years back and played a good many rounds at Castlerock with congenial friends. I found the course excellent holiday golf – which is not in my language a pejorative term – not too harsh for pleasure and not so easy as to be boring. Moreover, the view down the coast each way is attractive, especially to the westward where the great headland of Irishowen in Donegal stands out to sea.

The golf is divided between some rather inland holes along the railway at the beginning and end of the round and true linksland holes in between on the shoreward side. These latter in my view are the better, though the third, fifth and fifteenth holes, all par five, in the grassier parts need plenty of stick.

Among the links holes, I liked the first, a fine drive-and-pitch hole too early in the round to be appreciated perhaps, the short ninth amongst the rumpled ground and the two-shot seventh called the 'Armchair', with its plateau green embedded in the surrounding sandhills. You finish with a fine resounding thump off the tee to get up on to the final plateau.

Castlerock Golf Club: Medal Card

NAME	YARDS	PAR	NAME	YARDS	PAR
1 Knocklayde	349	4	10 Fairy Dell	395	4
2 Sconce	347	4	11 Coastguards	506	5
3 The Whins	515	5	12 Spion Kop	429	4
4 Leg o' Mutton	200	3	13 Swallow Hill	376	4
5 Railway	480	5	14 Corner	192	3
6 Burn	349	4	15 Homewards	527	5
7 Armchair	408	4	16 Summit	152	3
8 Bulldozer	424	4	17 Inishowen	489	5
9 Quarry	201	3	18 Mussenden	355	4
	3273	36		3421	37

Total 6694 yards: par 73

Chapter 12
GOLF IN IRELAND THE WEST

Rosapenna

Leaving the north coast and continuing to tour Irish golf in an anti-clockwise direction, we will soon be through strife-torn Derry and into Donegal where we might turn aside for a look at Rosapenna on Sheephaven Bay, another well-known holiday place which used to be served by a vast wooden hotel built in Norway which ended up as you might expect – in ashes. Today a modern up-to-date hotel has replaced the terrifying old fire trap.

In my day the golf here was rather disappointing, with too many holes inland on the downs and too few in real links territory. Mr Frank Casey, who has been helpful with information, tells me that recently money has been spent on the course and it has been brought up to first-class standards, including the elimination of the horde of rabbits which once infested the course. The original layout was by Tom Morris and later alterations were made by that rare architect Harry Vardon with James Braid. The first ten holes are among the dunes and the others on the downland above. A hole to remember in the linksland is the short sixth with an attractive plateau green protected by a deep swale.

Rosapenna Golf Club: Medal Card

	YARDS	PAR		YARDS	PAR
1	281	4	10	543	5
2	428	4	11	427	4
3	446	4	12	342	4
4	386	4	13	455	4
5	255	4	14	128	3
6	167	3	15	418	4
7	367	4	16	216	3
8	485	5	17	358	4
9	185	3	18	367	4
	3000	35		3254	35

Total 6254 yards: par 70

Rosses Point

On then through the Barnesmore Gap in the Muckish Mountains down to Donegal Town and Ballyshannon, where once the cherry-red engines of the Donegal Railway used to haul vast excursion trains; we are soon in County Sligo and on the look-out to find the road to Rosses Point, where the County Sligo Club has its links.

The course is a mixture of high and low ground, the latter more linksland than the other, but throughout you have good crisp seaside turf and from the upper holes the most superb views of sea, estuary and coastline and inland the flat-topped Ox Mountains beyond Sligo Town with much of the course below. From the ninth tee it is reported that you can see five counties, Donegal, Sligo, Roscommon, Leitrim and Mayo.

Again, the most memorable holes are the lower ones on the truer linksland and I recall especially the long twelfth, out against the prevailing wind, and the strandside short thirteenth, though the two-shot fourteenth is reckoned the best on the course.

County Sligo Club, Rosses Point: Medal Card

	YARDS	PAR		YARDS	PAR
1	371	4	10	378	4
2	299	4	11	400	4
3	490	5	12	482	5
4	164	3	13	171	3
5	468	4	14	393	4
6	371	4	15	394	4
7	412	4	16	188	3
8	409	4	17	421	4
9	151	3	18	354	4
	3135	35		3181	35

Total 6316 yards: par 70

The record holder and chief character here for years was that tremendous figure, the late Cecil Ewing, Walker Cup player and runner-up in the British Amateur Championship in 1938 and winner of innumerable Irish championships.

Lahinch

Next we continue down the Atlantic coast of Ireland through Galway to Limerick, a fine fair town with some beautiful Georgian houses with ornamental fanlights. From here, we must make for Lahinch in County Clare, about 40 miles to the north west, past Shannon Airport, a little seaside town overlooking Liscannor Bay and the famous precipitous cliffs of Moher.

For years I had heard of the great golf links here and at last in 1987 I was lucky enough to see it, and in full detail, from the pick-up truck of Duncan Gray, the young Scottish links superintendent, who took me all the way round – at times into the wildest and most unlikely places – so that I should miss nothing. Better

still, his own game was just of the calibre of those this book is designed for, so that he could show me the right tees – the medal rather than the championship lengths – the distances to be carried with the drive, the landing areas on the fairways for a good tee shot and the right club to play to the green, always bearing in mind that the prevailing wind off the sea might require you to play anything from say a five-iron to a spoon for the same approach on different days. It was a most interesting and enjoyable morning in good company.

The links here dates from 1893 when Old Tom Morris did the first layout, so it is considerably more venerable than many of the great names further south. Old Tom remarked that 'the links is as fine a natural course as it has ever been my good fortune to play over.' The famous Dr Alister Mackenzie, of Dornoch and American fame, supervised its reconstruction in 1928 just after he had produced the masterly Cypress Point in California and before he tackled Augusta National.

Mackenzie, who was not one to think ill of his work, said: 'Lahinch will make the finest and most popular course that I, or I believe anyone else, ever constructed.' The links we play today is largely Mackenzie's layout except for some very recent and successful modifications to add length enough for the course to be host to the 1987 Home Internationals. Some of the doctor's greens have been flattened somewhat and three of Old Tom Morris's greens are still intact at numbers 5, 14 and 17.

The first two holes uphill from the clubhouse, and then down again parallel, are straightforward enough with room for your drive and no alarming hills to carry or hazards to avoid. The third is an attractive hole with big hills as a backdrop; it measures 153 yards from the medal tee and its platform green has a drop to the left from which a little pitch back looks uncommonly difficult.

The fourth is where you say 'this is the start of the big time', for you have a formidable hill in front of your drive and you need a good big hit to get to the top, without which you can't hope to get up in two. If you do get there, though, you see the rest of the dog leg down towards the sea over a lumpy undulating fairway and needing a pretty solid iron shot to a generous green; a less good shot will be drawn inevitably into a hidden bunker on the left. A hole of great quality I thought, three stars.

The fifth is the controversial par-five 'Klondyke', usually down wind, away from the sea, which is just as well as it is a tight tee shot up a valley and we need to get as far as we can for our second has to cross a huge towering sandhill, a wall of rough dune 25 ft high, which allows no way round. The carry, after a good

drive, may not be more than 120 or so yards but it *looks* more. The green is about 130 yards from the top of the hill, so downwind this can be a birdie hole. Then the sixth, 'The Dell', a hole of 150 yards, which you play back over another Himalaya of sand to a completely blind little green in a hollow set across the line immediately below the mountain. This is usually against the wind but in still air a five or a six-iron should do it, though again it *looks* more alarming than that, a great deal more alarming. I thought this a charming old survivor and although it and the fifth are regarded by many as hopelessly out of date, I'm all for allowing no tampering with them. Herb Wind said: 'These are really defective holes in this day and age but at Lahinch they are absolutely right: two living museum pieces, two perfect Irish holes.' Three stars for 'The Dell'.

A mighty fine par four follows out to the shore needing again a drive to a hilltop. It is here that you are beginning to think: 'This is a driver's course, like Royal St George's.' On the way to the new green on the edge of the sea are two huge grassy pits and the dell where the old green used to be, a fine hole. The eighth away from the shore at 339 yards is no great length, nor is the ninth at 352, but the second of these is far from easy. First you have to drive well to the left, keeping below the diagonal step in the fairway or you'll never get a proper angle for your second shot to the green. The green itself is a real Mackenzie special, too, 50 yards long and narrow with a fall away to the left and only accessible from the proper direction. Full marks here I thought.

At this point it was interesting to note that the club has provided a spare hole, number 9a, a par three, which can be put into use to rest any other hole on the course. I was assured that this was not just an alternative hole for those who disliked the blind sixth. I'd not met a true nineteenth before.

The tenth is a tough one; there is plenty of landing ground say 200 yards from the tee, but you need a long carry before you tackle the second up to a high plateau; it seems hard work to get up there, although the hole is only 421 yards and usually down wind. The eleventh, 133 yards, is an absolute beauty. Its green, in a dell with great towering sandhills round it, is not blind just totally secluded. Full marks here for its setting and the beautifully moulded, folded green with just one small bunker.

The twelfth is a new hole with the tee practically in the river Cullenagh; all along the left flank is the estuary, a lateral water hazard and your drive must carry 150 yards to reach dry land; a long par four even down wind. This exemplifies what we will also find at Tralee, Ballybunion and Waterville, that having the open sea on one flank of the course and an estuary on another is a most admirable combination for the design of golf courses.

Next comes a shortish par four and you must fade the second into the green to avoid the traps to the left. Fourteen, a par five of 478 yards, is not too tough, although the entrance is very narrow, and fifteen back again towards the high hills did not seize one.

The sixteenth, the last short hole, is all carry and no sort of fairway intervenes between tee and green. At 179 yards it can be a three-wood or a five-iron and the pot bunkers are deep. Then comes another big carry for your drive at seventeen and with a cross wind the road on your left is intimidating, and the second shot too with a tight entrance. The last hole, a par five of 498 yards, Duncan Gray thought the hardest five on the course though on the flatter, inland side it doesn't seem so. You drive across the sixth and fifth fairways and the green is, it seems, very difficult to hit even with a wedge, although it looks big and spacious enough.

So ended a memorable round on a memorable course with something to suit all tastes, greens in dells and hollows, greens on

Lahinch Golf Club: Medal Card

	YARDS	PAR		YARDS	PAR
1	377	4	10	421	4
2	505	5	11	133	3
3	153	3	12	453	4
4	410	4	13	374	4
5	491	5	14	478	5
6	150	3	15	433	4
7	384	4	16	179	3
8	339	4	17	408	4
9	352	4	18	498	5
	3161	36		3377	36

Total 6538 yards: par 72
From the Championship tees the course measures 6822 yards.

plateaux, tough drives, attractive short holes, *very* attractive short holes, great sandhills to carry or avoid, a mixture mostly of dune land and some flatter linksland.

The South of Ireland Championship has been played here from time immemorial and it will be interesting to see what the amateurs of the four Home Countries make of it.

Across the road there is an attractive holiday course of 5100 yards with a par of 67.

There is one sad loss to report here. The wild Lahinch goats which used to foretell the weather, migrating to the shelter of the clubhouse when storms were on the way, have disappeared, possibly from eating something poisonous.

Lahinch's most famous son was the late John Burke, a great Irish golfer and Walker Cup player.

Ballybunion

Next we move on from Limerick into County Kerry for some more grand linksland on the Atlantic coast. We first meet this at Ballybunion, a small resort town with a ruined castle, on the northern shore of the county near the mouth of the Shannon. Don't be put off by the unattractive name of the place – it means 'Town of the Sapling' – for here is great golf, great in every sense of the word. The links run as near to the sea as any I know and great towering sand dunes, miles of them, dominate the play. Among, on to, over and from these sandhills you must propel your ball and as the ridges of dunes run roughly at right angles to the shore, they are far more formidable in their influence on the golf than, say, the great hills of Birkdale.

And always there is the restless wind and the Atlantic ocean beating on the stony strand, which has had to be restrained by a special and costly protective wall. Herb Wind, the famous American writer on golf, who knows the game so well here, says just this: 'Very simply, Ballybunion revealed itself to be nothing less than the finest seaside course I have ever seen.' Tom Watson, five times Open Champion, who loves Ballybunion said: 'one could almost imagine golf began here'.

Indeed, Ballybunion, like Dornoch, has sprung to life and eminence in recent years after decades of quietly and peacefully minding its own business. In its earliest days, the honorary secretary was Patrick McCarthy, general manager of the fantastic Listowel & Ballybunion light railway, a mono-rail on the Lartigue system of almost incredible complexity and inconvenience. It is one of my life's regrets that it had disappeared before I had the chance to ride on it.

Until a few years ago Ballybunion was only known to a discerning few, now the great and famous pronounce upon its renowned splendours, and like Dornoch, all must go and visit the shrine. A new clubhouse has been built and a tremendous second course laid out by the famous American architect Trent Jones, who said that the new course would occupy 'the finest piece of linksland I have ever seen, and perhaps the finest piece of linksland in the world.'

I had missed this great course until late in life, until 1970 in fact, and as I dragged my arthritic legs round it, I wished with all my heart that I had met it twenty years earlier. Then, even on a quiet grey spring day, with no serious wind to contend with, it seemed a mighty long course, and as so often happens on a big links, the holes *looked* longer than their yards; some of the par-four greens looked immensely far away from the tee, though to be fair the holes *played* their true length.

Finally, to add to the fine scenery surrounding it and the splendid sandhills of the links is the possibility of seeing the spectre, the famous 'Vision of Killashee', of people walking on a bridge, which appears on rare days of calm in the sea near the Long Clare Peninsula, a phenomenon which, as the handbook said, 'lasts for about fifteen minutes before it fades into nothingness, leaving the sea clear and blank as it was before. "What is the vision?" Go to Ballybunion and you may even see it for yourself. Par total for course 71.' So let us now set out for our round of the Old course.

The building of a new clubhouse in 1971 made an alteration in the order of play of the holes, since I had been there the year before. The new first is the old fourteenth with a controversial fairway bunker impeding the drive, called 'Mrs Simpson', in honour of the architect who was advising on some changes in the links in 1936. It was said that he was given carte blanche to alter the course, but in the event he chose only to move three greens, the second, fourth and twelfth, and add one fairway bunker. On the right of the first fairway an old graveyard reminds you of how time flies.

You continue out at the second, the former fifteenth, where after a narrow tee shot tending uphill, you have a big carrying second to get home to a high green perched on top of a ridge, a formidable shot to cover the 445 yards from the back tee and a stiff enough one even if you have driven from the medal tee.

Three is a long, prosaic par three down to the inland boundary of the course by the road and then came the original finish of two rather dull par fives along the landward margin of the course, though the end of the fifth gives you a nice plateau green once more to pitch up to. While these two holes made a rather poor finish to the great links, now, early in the round, they are more easily digested.

The sixth, which was the original first hole still along the landward side of the links, is quiet going it seems, without a bunker to be seen and for its length, 364–344 yards, wide enough. It is not quite as innocent as you might suppose, for the green is long and narrow and on a small plateau, like a scalene triangle with its point towards you, so you may easily miss it with your second shot, especially if you come at it at the wrong angle. After the six opening holes, the full majesty of the links envelops you. As my friend Ike Grainger, of the USGA fame, said of the back nine at the National Golf Links of America, 'From now on you've got a real golf course.'

The seventh, back along the shore, is a charmer, 400 yards this time, and again with a beautiful plateau green right above the roaring Atlantic; a par four here is grand golf. Alas, there is the erosion problem from the battering of the sea, at its worst here, and a new reserve green has had to be built, but the old green is still available, I was glad to find. Then you clamber up to a high tee in the sandhills and have a superb little short hole, a gem of a hole, 134 yards long, in a fold in the dunes below; hit to the left or short and you are bunkered, to the right and you roll off. I'm glad to report that

Tom Watson shares my liking for this hole; so full marks or three stars here.

Next comes a big tough par four with a plateau green and after that, at number ten, a most attractive shorter par four of 336 yards somewhat dog legged back to the edge of the sea. Once more the green is on a plateau and separated from the fairway by a deep swale. This hole has earned great praise from the critics and it gets three stars from me, too, especially as I managed to do it in four, oh so long ago.

Eleven is a par four with successive falls in the fairway between the towering hills to your left and the very fringe of the ocean to your right, then up once more to an isolated green with no sand bunkers; this is one of the great holes of golf; and one of the most photographed.

The next hole at 179 yards with the green high, high up above the tee perched on a ridge of sandhills. Here I had to fall back on old man's play, and hit a brassie or two-wood, but oh, the joy of a sweetly-hit shot, carrying the whole way but for a foot or two, and so securing a three. Downhill then goes the drive at the thirteenth and up over a ditch goes the shot towards the green for a par five; once more the green, looking remote and distant, is perched up on a small plateau in the hills.

Then at fourteen you go up into the hills again with the green 125 yards away up in a saddle but with a fall off to the right and to the left to a shallow swale; so the tee shot has to be dead right to make the island green, a tight exacting shot.

And so my word it is at the next, back downhill 216 yards from the back tee to the green, which looks a tiny target with great ravines of rough to catch a topped tee shot, a big sandhill at the left and bunkering to catch a slice. This looks a desperately long and brutal hole, even if it is downhill, like a tremendously greater Hoylake 'Alps'; but again, if you hit your shot you can get home.

You work up into the hills to the south at

number sixteen with a dog-leg par five and home two with two par fours, including a waste of gravelly sand called the Sahara to cross on the eighteenth. According to Frank Pennink it is the remains of a 500-year-old Irish midden. The last shot is unique at Ballybunion, it is a blind one. This makes a fitting do-or-die finish to a great golf links.

On our visit in 1987 I had the great good fortune to be driven round the course by that famous local figure Sean Walsh, who not only enabled me to refresh my memory of the Old course but make acquaintance with the New, difficult as it was to get a car near to many of Trent Jones's hilly placements. However, we managed to see a lot, aided by what seemed to me a venturesome drive along the sandy estuarine shore of the River Cashen where it begins to become Atlantic water.

The New course is in no way, either consciously or unconsciously, the secondary circuit at Ballybunion; it is planned to be in everything as big a course and as fine a course as the famous Old. By the wise decision of the club, enough linksland of the same fine quality as supports the Old course was bought to the south of the new clubhouse in 1971, so permitting the new course to be laid out without interfering with or complicating what was already so good here. Opinions differ as to which is the better or the more difficult of the two rounds. Let it just be said that both are excellent with just at present, until the New course fully settles down, the edge I think going to the Old. One feature of Trent Jones's design which will help cater for the crowds that will come here is his fitting of the course into two halves, each ending at the clubhouse.

The first two holes on the New course follow out to the south without tackling the big hills, then at short three you hit into them with a small green protected by sand in front.

Four with its saddle and five hug the water, but in opposite directions, two lovely holes where Trent Jones is said to have conspicuously followed his usual liking for 'tough par, easy

bogey'. Six is another par three, a pretty shot across a valley, then comes seven, a real devil of a hole with a narrow shelf of a green up in the hills above a valley and needing a sharply uphill pitch to get home. Eight is a monster, a vast dog leg to the left, no less than 615 yards off the back

Ballybunion Golf Club, Old Course: Championship and Medal Card

	C	M	PAR		C	M	PAR
1	392	366	4	10	359	336	4
2	445	394	4	11	449	400	4
3	220	211	3	12	192	179	3
4	498	490	5	13	484	480	5
5	508	489	5	14	131	125	3
6	364	344	4	15	216	207	3
7	423	400	4	16	490	482	5
8	153	134	3	17	385	368	4
9	454	430	4	18	379	366	4
	3457	3258	36		3085	2943	35

Total 6542 and 6201 yards: par 71

Ballybunion Golf Club, New Course: Championship and Medal Card

	C	M	PAR		C	M	PAR
1	437	413	4	10	328	317	4
2	397	377	4	11	142	133	3
3	153	142	3	12	262	251	4
4	404	341	4	13	387	370	4
5	445	425	4	14	398	351	4
6	154	140	3	15	489	476	5
7	346	316	4	16	145	133	3
8	615	600	5	17	484	476	5
9	501	486	5	18	390	369	4
	3452	3240	36		3025	2876	36

Total 6477 and 6116 yards: par 72

tee and 600 yards off mine. Moreover, you have to hit a big drive up to a hill top to get on terms and then the hole seems to stretch interminably from you. Not content with that we have another narrower par five along a valley in the sandhills and crossing a big hollow in mid-stream, as it were, to get back to base.

The second half is distinctly shorter than the outward nine. Trent Jones had a great liking for the short par-four tenth. He said: 'there is no more natural hole in the world, an outrageously beautiful stretch of God-given terrain.' I would pick also on the twelfth hole, a very short par four, up to the summit of the links; with a fair wind this hole can be driven, across the dog leg, but a short pitch normally is needed. Next I liked the thirteenth down, down towards the sea; it also has a story. When the green was being constructed an old burial ground was discovered by Sean Walsh's daughter, no less. It dated from the fifth century and contained a fully-preserved skeleton. The plan had been to excavate this spot to build a green in a dell but meeting archaeological objections the plan was altered and the graveyard covered over, reverently I hope, by the thirteenth green on a little shelf which now protects it.

The fifteenth hole is an attractive par five driving down from the links again into the prevailing wind to a small level of fairway, then on down over rough hollows and up to a perched up green.

Sixteen is a par three with a kidney-shaped green, and seventeen a par four all along the shore before, to end, we turn away up to the clubhouse. Hillier, yes, tougher, I doubt it, less subtle, surely, but a splendid foil to the Old course.

Tralee

Also on the Kerry coast, we find a new links and a big one opened in 1985 and the first course outside America designed by Arnold Palmer and his colleague Ed Seay. The course is about ten miles from the rising town of Tralee and faces the open Atlantic on a treeless point where the Barrow Harbour issues into the sea.

The course is in two sharply different halves, the first nine being fairly flat downland and the second half set amid the most tumultuous sandhills and uneven, rolling duneland that you can imagine. In the accounts I had read, the first half of the course, I had thought, was perhaps praised too little and the second half perhaps too much. The view I formed after an extensive and detailed tour with the secretary/manager Mr John Kleynhans in his car, was that the first nine had some splendid and spectacu-lar holes, notably the second, third and eighth, while much of the back nine looked almost too tough to be manageable if there was any wind.

The course starts out from the present temporary clubhouse with a simple straight-forward par four towards the sea with a green on a slight rise. What follows is a spectacular mighty par five (593/566 yards) along the curve of the coast line and painfully close to the shore at times, ending with a hilltop green. No bunkers are in sight here and it might be remarked at this point that there are only twelve altogether on the whole course. And indeed with nature in such form few more are needed. Tough as it is, three stars to the second hole.

The third is par three and short at that but to see it tucked into a corner of the cliff scenery on the very edge of the beach with the round tower of the old fort behind and nowhere to go but to the green itself is to mix admiration with terror. This hole is said to resemble the seventh at Pebble Beach. This it only does in its closeness to the waves. In my view it is the harder and the better of the two. Three stars here. Four, five and six up and down the downland did not ring out either cries of joy or of pain but I did like the short seventh, a plain short hole towards the sea with a two-step, three-tier-level green.

The eighth is star quality again. You drive across an arm of the sea and you need to be on the forward edge of the tee to take in the full horror of the possibilities. The carry is about 170–180 yards from the medal tee, then turning a full dog leg to the left you hit about 150 yards up to the green close to the water's edge. After this you are glad the ninth back to base is ordinary and indeed the breather is welcome.

Now into battle, and you take off with no great difficulty at the tenth, with the green in a dell, nor indeed at the long, long uphill eleventh, a hole which makes few friends. The twelfth is in John Kleynhans's view the most difficult par four he has ever seen. The fairway is narrow and humpy with not much space to come and go. If you hit 240 yards dead straight, and the wind may well be against you, well and good. If not you have problems, for the green is a small shelf on the flank of a huge dune and if you are not up with your approach, heaven help you. For all its difficulty a star hole, I think.

So, too, is the short thirteenth, mercifully a not too long punch across a rough valley with no vestige of a fairway apparent, to a green in its own shelf in the sand mountains and a grassy pit in front. There seems nothing to play from with any confidence between tee and green.

Leaving fourteen and fifteen to look after themselves let us address ourselves to another death-or-glory short hole, the 197/161 yard sixteenth. The green is right on the cliff edge in a shallow bowl, with a huge grassy pit in front and again no fairway visible. You can slice onto the strand and not out of bounds either, but then at least you will have the satisfaction of seeing at close hand the location of part of the film 'Ryan's Daughter'. So once again, it's all carry like so many shots on the course; indeed I know few courses where the choices were so stark, hit it right or perdition, Pine Valley perhaps.

Then comes the famous seventeenth, only a short par four 332 yards off the medal tee. The curving fairway is narrow and beset with lumps, indeed from the tee it looks painfully narrow. If you drive well enough you then have a seven or nine or even a five-iron up to the hilltop green depending on the wind. Difficult but not impossible and I think a justified three-star mark.

	BLUE	WHITE	PAR		BLUE	WHITE	PAR

Tralee Golf Club: Blue and White tees

	BLUE	WHITE	PAR		BLUE	WHITE	PAR
1	403	388	4	10	421	405	4
2	593	566	5	11	580	564	5
3	154	140	3	12	456	437	4
4	424	401	4	13	158	147	3
5	457	410	4	14	402	389	4
6	425	412	4	15	299	287	4
7	156	140	3	16	197	161	3
8	387	370	4	17	353	332	4
9	493	484	5	18	461	437	4
	3462	3311	36		3327	3159	35

Total 6789 and 6470 yards: par 71

You cruise home on a mercifully simple eighteenth. A successful nine holes played here unquestionably earns a pint of good Guinness if ever one did, though it is not impossible to think that the plainer front nine plays harder against par than the spectacular inward half.

As I said to my charming and delightful hosts here, 'I'm glad I'm too old and infirm to try' for this is big-time golf.

Killarney

I must admit to writing rather a sour report of the golf at this famous place when I played here some years ago and I'm glad to be able to take a different view now after a visit in 1987.

The whole picture has been transformed by the splitting of the rather pedestrian old course into two, adding 18 new holes, so creating the first-rate Killeen course and the less exciting and indeed duller Mahoney's Point course for those who want an easier ride.

As a place to play golf, Killarney must be the most beautiful in the world; at any rate, I know no other course to match it, out of 400-odd visited in 60 years of golf. The combination of lake and mountain which is there at every hole is superb and if I had to name contenders for these honours I could only think of Banff Springs and Jasper Park in the Canadian Rockies and possibly Gleneagles.

The courses are on parkland and many of the fairways look like wide open spaces, though all of these demand the shot in the right place to make the next shot simpler. An attractive feature is the live narrow brooks which issue from local springs and provide attractive hazards in the form of streams or ditches. Here, as at most courses of note these days, the choice of tees makes a very big difference. Play from the back, or championship tees so called, is very much tougher than from the medal tees, 499 yards further, on the Killeen course equivalent to adding an extra par-five hole.

When we were taken round by Capt. O'Connell in his car on as fine a January day as you could ever wish for, the mountains across the steel blue lake glowed in the sun in russet and brown shades, with even a little cap of snow on Carrantuohill, the highest mountain in Ireland, and offset the vivid green of the golfing grounds.

The Killeen course starts with the old fourth, fifth and sixth of the original layout by Sir Guy Campbell in the 1940s. The first, a short par four (356 yards off the back tee and 320 off the white) can best be described as a banana hole, bending right closely hugging the lake shore. Off the back tee it looked a horribly difficult opening shot. The second, rather longer though rather more inland, also bends to the right round trees to a green tucked above by the lake, a most pretty hole this. The third too, a par three of 170 yards from the white tee, is also right along the lake with a particularly fine view. At this point I think one can say 'this is no course for slicers'.

At the fourth, another moderate length par four, a back tee has been constructed in the lake itself, which I don't think agrees very well with the belief of some of us that golf is best when fashioned by nature. After a double dog leg par five, comes the short sixth to an island green, completely surrounded by a stream; the green is a fair size but at 190/162 yards it doesn't seem so. I rate this as a splendid hole. The next one – a par five from the back and harshly a four from the medal tee – is an oddity, as the stream which menaces both flanks of the green disappears underground into pipes in the centre.

I liked hole eight with its high tee and attractive setting, but the next three on the upper levels did not set me aglow. The thirteenth (448/434 yards), however, is a beauty, driving down from a height to a narrow gap in the fairway between two truncated banks with a sudden big dip in the fairway to follow and then crossing a stream a seeking shot is needed up to a natural green. Two dog legs follow – they are very popular here – then a straightforward par five which brings us to another star hole in my view, the 366/356 yard seventeenth. Only a short pitch is needed for the second shot, but the high plateau green above you is narrow and across the line so you can easily go over and down the other side, or worse if short, fall or run into the fiendish little pot bunker under the front flank, so like the Road bunker at St Andrews. Indeed this hole is said to resemble the Road Hole. For my part I would be content to let it rest on its own merits. So home by a par-four to the eighteenth among the pines.

On the Mahoney's Point course my pleasures were engaged by the old first hole which I remember with its revetted bunkers, the par five sixteenth downhill to the lake shore and, of course, the incomparable short eighteenth across the curve of the lake to a green in a glade of pines, a picture hole if ever there was one and not easy at that, especially off the back tee at 201 yards. This must, I think, be the prize hole and the most photographed of the 36 we can so enjoyably play here.

This beautiful place now has a well deserved reputation, much created in early days by Henry Longhurst, whose friendship with the last Earl of Kenmare, who built the first course here, brought him into some involvement with the design. Golf at Killarney is a good change from the rigours of wind-blown links golf so don't miss it. Let us give the late Pat Ward Thomas, who wrote so ably and lovingly of golf, the last word here:

The pursuit of golf has taken one to many of the loveliest corners of these islands, but the beauty of the setting has few peers. All golfers should make a pilgrimage to this enchanting place and know, too, the charm of a splendid course which can be exacting for the great but never unfair to the weak.

Killarney Golf and Fishing Club, Mahoney's Point Course: Medal Card

	YARDS	PAR		YARDS	PAR
1	346	4	10	380	4
2	429	4	11	415	4
3	428	4	12	184	3
4	138	3	13	478	5
5	485	5	14	378	4
6	375	4	15	265	4
7	168	3	16	480	5
8	537	5	17	366	4
9	326	4	18	182	3
	3232	36		3128	36

Total 6360 yards: par 72

Killarney Golf and Fishing Club, Killeen Course: Medal Card

	YARDS	PAR		YARDS	PAR
1	320	4	10	179	3
2	350	4	11	495	5
3	170	3	12	423	4
4	355	4	13	434	4
5	480	5	14	357	4
6	162	3	15	386	4
7	402	4	16	495	5
8	400	4	17	356	4
9	374	4	18	411	4
	3013	35		3536	37

Total 6549 yards: par 72

Dooks

Not far from Killarney you pass through the little town of Killorglin where every August a pagan ritual known as Puck's Fair is held with a local goat exhibited on a high staging in the town square where it is well plied with food. Here all the tinkers and gypsies of Ireland gather to gossip and drink and fight and trade. The pubs in the old days stayed open for 24 hours a day; even now they don't close before 3 am and the doors are removed for easy entry and departure. After three days the scapegoat is turned loose.

Nearby, between Killorglin and Glenbeigh is the unassuming golf course called Dooks (meaning rabbit warren), a mixture of half a dozen links holes down by the edge of Dingle Bay looking over to the Dingle Peninsula, and the rest downland, simple natural golf. If, as you well may, you sometimes get satiated with great long courses, huge pro-am meetings and so-called championship back tees, enough to quell Greg Norman, and all the razzmatazz of promotions and money golf, step aside and try this simple natural golf course with its superb views of sea and mountain. I don't think you will be disappointed. There are attractive natural plateau greens and hollows for hazards, hills to drive over and down from and a few nice dune holes.

Here, beside the course on a piece of rough land, where there are patches of marsh, a pro-

		Dooks Golf Club: Medal Card				
	YARDS	PAR			YARDS	PAR
1	401	4		10	361	4
2	132	3		11	520	5
3	299	4		12	357	4
4	340	4		13	145	3
5	182	3		14	373	4
6	397	4		15	203	3
7	475	5		16	344	4
8	366	4		17	310	4
9	184	3		18	498	5
	2776	34			3111	36

Total 5887 yards: par 70

tected reptile the Natterjack Toad survives. This engaging little creature was hibernating when we called in January, but we were delighted to learn that the club regards its survival with interest and compassion and is even considering an artificial pond in front of the short fifteenth to give more breeding grounds for it. The club emblem includes the toad and it was never more proudly borne than when this comparatively minor club won the Club Championship of Kerry, from more notable competitors, in 1985.

Waterville

We end our tour of the west of Ireland at this big new links in the far west in a remote corner of County Kerry. Designed by Eddie Hackett, it is the brainchild of John Mulcahy, a rich Irish-American who also built the great splendid Waterville Lakes Hotel. The golf course lies on a promontory heading into Ballinskelligs Bay, close by where the broad estuary of the

Kenmare River becomes the open Atlantic. We have here again the ideal arrangement, a roughly triangular piece of land with water on two sides, the sea and River Inney estuary. The mountain and moorland scenery which is all around is a joyful addition to the golf.

The course is sharply divided between the inland first nine, flat under foot and relatively uninteresting to look at, and the outside homeward half, which is involved with as good a crop of sandhills and dunes, hollows, plateaux and fierce seaside rough as you could ask for. Appearances can be deceptive though, as the first nine is the harder to score on according to the former captain, Mr M. J. Courtney, who was kind enough to greet us with warm Irish hospitality and drove us all round the links in his car. Rather surprisingly, the course is laid with richer grass than is usual on linksland and so looks very green. The tees are in three widely-spread lengths to enable the tigers to be stretched from the blue markers – and indeed they are with a 7241-yard layout often aided and abetted by a stiff wind off the ocean – while the more reasonable white and yellow marks are for ordinary fallible humans. Some of the back tees looked to me to demand some pretty horrific hitting.

We set out with a flat simple par four to a generously open green, then at two we have a long par four with a huge elevated tee to suit all conditions. For some reason Christy O'Connor picks this as a hole of great distinction but I didn't grasp it; it seemed a long dog leg to the right and not one to remember. The third attracted me more, a shorter par four up to the sandhill area with a plateau green, the first of many such.

Four is a much admired short hole down to the green, as it were in a bowl among the sandhills; it looks farther than its 157 yards.

Five and six, a par five and a four, did not put stars in my notes, but seven did, a short hole back towards the clubhouse with water hazards on either hand at the entrance. If ever a hole said it – and most of them do – 'don't underclub'.

The eighth away from the club has an attractive green in a dell, a hole sweeping to the left and so leading us to the ninth back to the clubhouse, a big par four ending uphill to the green.

At this stage I think you could fairly say 'so what?' Don't be discouraged; it's fine golf all the way in.

Into the hills now at the tenth, an attractive hole with a narrow neck in front of the green which is surrounded by hills; a good short par five, followed immediately by what has been called 'the best par five in Ireland'. From a high tee in the dunes you hit down a narrow channel of fairway apparently level with the distant green, but no, the fairway dips down to a lower level still, giving you a hit up, our third or the other fellow's long second to a green on a mild hilltop. Assuredly a star hole.

The twelfth hole, the 'Mass Hole', became my favourite, 172 yards from the white tee. You play over rough ground to a green wedged into the sandhills in front of you. But in front of the green is a deep green hollow in the fairway, a pit no less, where Mass used to be celebrated away from view in the bad days far gone now, thank God, when to celebrate Mass was said to be a capital offence. When this hole was being built the men would not do work in the hollow as they said it was sacred ground and should not be defiled.

Thirteen is a par five downhill and down wind to the flat lands, a 'birdie hole', as Mr Courtney said. Fourteen takes us back to the hill country with a plateau green, Christy O'Connor's second choice, which I could see the point of. I liked fifteen very much with an attractive green down in a dell, needing say a 150-yard pitch to get home, paying attention to the little pond on the left; I give it two stars; it looked so natural.

At sixteen we are on the edge of the strand and blown sand is a problem. The green is round the corner to the left masked by some sandhills; you are meant to play up along the shore and when you get to your ball you can see the green and then pitch in a short shot to the left; in all 346 yards. The club pro, the husky Liam Higgins, just belted the ball over the humps, hollows, dales and scrub straight to the green and holed out in one, a prodigious stroke of I suppose 330/340 yards.

Seventeen, Mulcahy's favourite, has a high tee, the highest point on the course, from which

Waterville Golf Links: Championship and Medal Cards

		C	PAR	M			C	PAR	M
1	Last Easy	420	4	382	10	Bottleneck	470	4/5	476
2	Christy's Choice	468	4	425	11	Tranquillity	500	5	477
3	Innyside	424	4	383	12	The Mass Hole	206	3	172
4	The Dunes	180	3	157	13	The Twin	518	5	480
5	Tipperary	587	5	525	14	The Judge	458	4	394
6	Palm Springs	375	4	340	15	The Vale	396	4	370
7	The Island	180	3	155	16	Liam's Ace	366	4	346
8	Ponderous	437	4	417	17	Mulcahy's Peak	206	3	165
9	Prodigal	450	4	405	18	Broadway	600	5	530
	Out	3521	35	3189		In	3720	37/8	3410
						Total	7241	72	6599

the entire links is visible and a tee shot of 165/206 yards to a small isolated green sitting on its little platform in the dunes. There seems to be little choice between death or glory. Yes, a great hole all right.

At eighteen you have a long flat hole to the clubhouse with a pond on your left to guard against. From the back tee along the strand as it were it looks a very narrow shot to reach the fairway. You could say with the old Scots pro 'Dang it, it's like driving up a spout.'

So ends a splendid nine which makes you glad you came all this way. I think, too, that we can agree with what Henry Longhurst said about Irish golf courses. They are the best.

THE OPEN CHAMPIONSHIP

1860	W. Park	Prestwick		1893	W. Auchterlonie	Prestwick
1861	T. Morris	Prestwick		1894	J. H. Taylor	Sandwich
1862	T. Morris	Prestwick		1895	J. H. Taylor	St Andrews
1863	W. Park	Prestwick		1896	H. Vardon	Muirfield
1864	T. Morris	Prestwick		1897	Mr H. H. Hilton	Hoylake
1865	A. Strath	Prestwick		1898	H. Vardon	Prestwick
1866	W. Park	Prestwick		1899	H. Vardon	Sandwich
1867	T. Morris	Prestwick		1900	J. H. Taylor	St Andrews
1868	T. Morris Jnr	Prestwick		1901	James Braid	Muirfield
1869	T. Morris Jnr	Prestwick		1902	Alex Herd	Hoylake
1870	T. Morris Jnr	Prestwick		1903	H. Vardon	Prestwick
1872	T. Morris Jnr	Prestwick		1904	Jack White	Sandwich
1873	T. Kidd	St Andrews		1905	James Braid	St Andrews
1874	Mungo Park	Musselburgh		1906	James Braid	Muirfield
1875	W. Park	Prestwick		1907	Arnaud Massy	Hoylake
1876	Bob Martin	St Andrews		1908	James Braid	Prestwick
1877	J. Anderson	Musselburgh		1909	J. H. Taylor	Deal
1878	J. Anderson	Prestwick		1910	James Braid	St Andrews
1879	J. Anderson	St Andrews		1911	H. Vardon	Sandwich
1880	Bob Ferguson	Musselburgh		1912	E. Ray	Muirfield
1881	Bob Ferguson	Prestwick		1913	J. H. Taylor	Hoylake
1882	Bob Ferguson	St Andrews		1914	H. Vardon	Prestwick
1883	W. Fernie	Musselburgh		1920	G. Duncan	Deal
1884	J. Simpson	Prestwick		1921	J. Hutchison	St Andrews
1885	Bob Martin	St Andrews		1922	W. Hagen	Sandwich
1886	D. Brown	Musselburgh		1923	A. G. Havers	Troon
1887	W. Park Jnr	Prestwick		1924	W. Hagen	Hoylake
1888	Jack Burns	St Andrews		1925	Jim Barnes	Prestwick
1889	W. Park Jnr	Musselburgh		1926	Mr R. T. Jones	Lytham & St Annes
1890	Mr John Ball	Prestwick		1927	Mr R. T. Jones	St Andrews
1891	H. Kirkaldy	St Andrews		1928	W. Hagen	Sandwich
1892	Mr H. H. Hilton	Muirfield		1929	W. Hagen	Muirfield

1930	Mr R. T. Jones	Hoylake		1962	A. Palmer	Troon
1931	T. D. Armour	Carnoustie		1963	Bob Charles	Lytham & St Annes
1932	E. Sarazen	Princes		1964	Tony Lema	St Andrews
1933	D. Shute	St Andrews		1965	P. W. Thomson	Birkdale
1934	T. H. Cotton	Sandwich		1966	J. Nicklaus	Muirfield
1935	A. Perry	Muirfield		1967	R. de Vicenzo	Hoylake
1936	A. H. Padgham	Hoylake		1968	Gary Player	Carnoustie
1937	T. H. Cotton	Carnoustie		1969	A. Jacklin	Lytham & St Annes
1938	R. A. Whitcombe	Sandwich		1970	J. Nicklaus	St Andrews
1939	R. Burton	St Andrews		1971	L. Trevino	Birkdale
1946	Sam Snead	St Andrews		1972	L. Trevino	Muirfield
1947	Fred Daly	Hoylake		1973	T. Weiskopf	Troon
1948	T. H. Cotton	Muirfield		1974	Gary Player	Lytham & St Annes
1949	A. D. Locke	Sandwich		1975	T. Watson	Carnoustie
1950	A. D. Locke	Troon		1976	J. Miller	Birkdale
1951	M. Faulkner	Portrush		1977	T. Watson	Turnberry
1952	A. D. Locke	Lytham & St Annes		1978	J. Nicklaus	St Andrews
1953	Ben Hogan	Carnoustie		1979	S. Ballesteros	Lytham & St Annes
1954	P. W. Thomson	Birkdale		1980	T. Watson	Muirfield
1955	P. W. Thomson	St Andrews		1981	W. Rogers	Sandwich
1956	P. W. Thomson	Hoylake		1982	T. Watson	Troon
1957	A. D. Locke	St Andrews		1983	T. Watson	Birkdale
1958	P. W. Thomson	Lytham & St Annes		1984	S. Ballesteros	St Andrews
1959	Gary Player	Muirfield		1985	A. Lyle	Sandwich
1960	Kel Nagle	St Andrews		1986	G. Norman	Turnberry
1961	A. Palmer	Birkdale				

THE AMATEUR CHAMPIONSHIP

1885	A. F. McFie	Hoylake
1886	H. G. Hutchinson	St Andrews
1887	H. G. Hutchinson	Hoylake
1888	John Ball	Prestwick
1889	J. E. Laidlay	St Andrews
1890	John Ball	Hoylake
1891	J. E. Laidlay	St Andrews
1892	John Ball	Sandwich
1893	P. Anderson	Prestwick
1894	John Ball	Hoylake
1895	L. M. B. Melville	St Andrews
1896	F. G. Tait	Sandwich
1897	A. J. Allan	Muirfield
1898	F. G. Tait	Hoylake
1899	John Ball	Prestwick
1900	H. H. Hilton	Sandwich
1901	H. H. Hilton	St Andrews
1902	C. Hutchings	Hoylake
1903	R. Maxwell	Muirfield
1904	W. J. Travis	Sandwich
1905	A. G. Barry	Prestwick
1906	J. Robb	Hoylake
1907	John Ball	St Andrews
1908	E. A. Lassen	Sandwich
1909	R. Maxwell	Muirfield
1910	John Ball	Hoylake
1911	H. H. Hilton	Prestwick
1912	John Ball	Westward Ho!
1913	H. H. Hilton	St Andrews
1914	J. L. C. Jenkins	Sandwich
1920	C. J. H. Tolley	Muirfield
1921	W. I. Hunter	Hoylake
1922	E. W. E. Holderness	Prestwick
1923	R. H. Wethered	Deal
1924	E. W. E. Holderness	St Andrews
1925	R. Harris	Westward Ho!
1926	Jesse Sweetser	Muirfield
1927	W. Tweddell	Hoylake
1928	T. P. Perkins	Prestwick
1929	C. J. H. Tolley	Sandwich
1930	R. T. Jones	St Andrews
1931	E. Martin Smith	Westward Ho!
1932	J. de Forest	Muirfield
1933	Hon. M. Scott	Hoylake
1934	Lawson Little	Prestwick
1935	Lawson Little	Lytham & St Annes
1936	H. Thomson	St Andrews
1937	R. Sweeney	Sandwich
1938	C. R. Yates	Troon
1939	A. T. Kyle	Hoylake
1946	J. Bruen	Birkdale
1947	W. P. Turnesa	Carnoustie
1948	F. R. Stranahan	Sandwich
1949	S. M. McCready	Portmarnock
1950	F. R. Stranahan	St Andrews
1951	R. D. Chapman	Porthcawl
1952	E. H. Ward	Prestwick
1953	J. B. Carr	Hoylake
1954	D. W. Bachli	Muirfield
1955	J. W. Conrad	Lytham & St Annes
1956	J. C. Beharrel	Troon
1957	R. R. Jack	Formby
1958	J. B. Carr	St Andrews
1959	D. R. Beman	Sandwich

1960	J. B. Carr	Portrush	1974	T. Homer	Muirfield
1961	M. Bonallack	Turnberry	1975	M. M. Giles	Hoylake
1962	R. D. Davies	Hoylake	1976	R. Siderowf	St Andrews
1963	M. S. R. Lunt	St Andrews	1977	P. McEvoy	Ganton
1964	Gordon Clark	Ganton	1978	P. McEvoy	Troon
1965	M. Bonallack	Porthcawl	1979	J. Sigel	Hillside
1966	R. E. Cole	Carnoustie	1980	D. Evans	Porthcawl
1967	R. B. Dickson	Formby	1981	P. Ploujoux	St Andrews
1968	M. Bonallack	Troon	1982	M. Thompson	Deal
1969	M. Bonallack	Hoylake	1983	A. P. Parkin	Turnberry
1970	M. Bonallack	Newcastle	1984	J. M. Olazabal	Formby
1971	S. Melnyk	Carnoustie	1985	G. McGimpsey	Dornoch
1972	T. Homer	Sandwich	1986	D. Curry	Lytham & St Annes
1973	R. Siderowf	Porthcawl			

BIBLIOGRAPHY

The Golfer's Handbook 1986 (Macmillan, London)

Frank Pennink's Golfer's Companion (Cassell, London)

A Round of Golf Courses, Patric Dickinson (Evans, London)

The Links, Robert Hunter (Scribner's, New York)

A History of Golf, Robert Browning (Dent, London)

The Golf Courses of the British Isles, Bernard Darwin (Duckworth, London)

The Golf Courses of Great Britain, Bernard Darwin (Jonathan Cape, London)

Green Memories, Bernard Darwin (Hodder & Stoughton, London)

Golf Between Two Wars, Bernard Darwin (Chatto & Windus, London)

Golf, Bernard Darwin (Burke, London)

Life Is Sweet, Brother, Bernard Darwin (Collins, London)

The World That Fred Made, Bernard Darwin (Chatto & Windus, London)

Out of the Rough, Bernard Darwin (Chapman & Hall, London)

Playing the Like, Bernard Darwin (Chapman & Hall, London)

The Bobby Jones Story, O. B. Keeler and Grantland Rice (Tupper & Love, Atlanta)

Golf My Life's Work, J. H. Taylor (Jonathan Cape, London)

The Badminton Book of Golf, Horace Hutchinson (Longmans, London)

Fifty Years of Golf, Horace Hutchinson (Country Life, London)

My Game and Yours, Arnold Palmer (Hodder & Stoughton, London)

Professional Golfer, Arnold Palmer (Pelham, London)

Arnold Palmer, Mark McCormack (Cassell, London)

The Walter Hagen Story, Hagen and Margaret Heck (Heinemann, London)

The Complete Golfer, Herbert Warren Wind (Heinemann, London)

Herbert Warren Wind's Golf Book, Herbert Warren Wind (Simon & Schuster, New York)

Esquire's World of Golf, Graffis (Muller, London)

Go Golfing in Britain, L. Claughton Darbyshire (Sunday Times, London)

Golf is My Game, Robert Tyre (Bobby) Jones (Doubleday, New York)

Bobby Jones on Golf, Robert Tyre (Bobby) Jones (Doubleday, New York)

The Story of the R. and A., J. B. Salmond (Macmillan, London)

The Book of the Links, Martin H. F. Sutton (W. H. Smith, London)

Scotland's Gift – Golf, C. B. Macdonald (Scribner's, New York)

The World of Golf, Charles Price (Cassell, London)

Short History of Pine Valley, John Arthur Brown (Published by the Club)

My Golfing Album, Henry Cotton (Country Life, London)

St Andrews – Home of Golf, J. K. Robertson (Innes, Cupar)

Golf Addict Among the Scots, George Houghton (Country Life, London)

The Greatest Game of all, Jack Nicklaus with Herbert Warren Wind (Simon & Schuster, New York)

Prestwick St Nicholas Golf Club 1851 – 1951, William Galbraith (published by the club)

Dai Rees on Golf, Dai Rees (Duckworth, London)

The Royal North Devon Golf Club 1864–1964 (published by the Club)

It Was Good While It Lasted, Henry Longhurst (Dent, London)

You Never Know Till You Get There, Henry Longhurst (Dent, London)

Only on Sundays, Henry Longhurst (Cassell, London)

My Life and Soft Times, Henry Longhurst (Cassell, London)

Sheridan of Sunningdale, James Sheridan (Country Life, London)

The Best 18 Golf Holes in America, Dan Jenkins (Sports Illustrated, Delacorte Press, New York)

The Book of Golf, Louis T. Stanley (Max Parrish, London)

Golf Architecture in America, George C. Thomas Jnr (Times–Mirror Press, Los Angeles)

The Curious History of the Golf Ball, J. S. Martin (Horizon Press, New York)

The Curve of Earth's Shoulder, Peter and Consuelo Allen (Allen & Unwin, London)

Famous Fairways, Peter Allen (Stanley Paul, London)

Donald Ross of Pinehurst and Royal Dornoch, Donald Grant (Sutherland Press)

The Encyclopedia of Golf Collectibles, Olman & Olman (Books Americana)

Following Through, Herb W. Wind (Ticknor & Fields)

Golf at Prince's and Deal, Sir Guy Campbell (Newman Neame)

Five Up, P. B. Lucas (Sidgwick & Jackson)

The Sport of Prince's, P. B. Lucas (Stanley Paul)

The US Open, Flaherty (Dutton)

The Royal & Ancient, Ward Thomas (Scottish Academic)

Down the Fairway, Jones & Keeler (Mindon Balch)

Oxford & Cambridge Golfing Society, Eric Prain (Eyre & Spottiswoode)

Pine Valley Golf Club – A Chronicle, Warner Shelly

Mostly Golf – a Bernard Darwin Anthology, Peter Ryde (Watson & Viney)

Royal & Ancient, Championship Records, Ryde (Watson & Viney)

The Halford Hewitt, Ryde (Public Schools G.S.)

Thanks for the Game, T. H. Cotton (Sidgwick & Jackson)

The Shell Encyclopedia of Golf (Ebury Press)

The Best of Henry Longhurst, M. Wilson and K. Bowden (Collins)

History of St George's Hill Golf Club, George Hartley

Rye Golf Club, Denis Vidler (White Crescent Press)

The History of Royal Wimbledon Golf Club, Charles Cruikshank

The Mystery of Golf, Arnold Hautam (Ailsa)

Brochures issued by Clubs etc

Hayling Island

Reigate Heath

Walton Heath

Coombe Hill

West Sussex – Pulborough

Felixstowe Ferry

Turnberry

Royal Liverpool, Hoylake

Ashridge

Royal Porthcawl

Royal & Ancient 1985

Royal & Ancient 1986

Golf World – The World of Scottish Golf

Golf World – The Top 50 Courses in the British Isles

Golf World – Golf in Ireland

Killarney

Waterville

The Natterjack Toad – Nature Conservancy Council

PHOTOGRAPHIC
ACKNOWLEDGEMENTS

For permission to reproduce copyright photographs, the author and publishers would like to thank the following:

Colour section: Peter Dazely, Phil Sheldon, Northern Ireland Tourist Board, Irish Tourist Board, Golf International, Alan Booth, Bert Neale, Bob Thomas

Black and white section: Bert Neale, Phil Sheldon, Peter Dazeley, Alan Booth